How to Fail
at Almost
Everything
and Still
Win Big

How to Fail at Almost Everything and Still Win Big

Kind of the Story of My Life

Scott Adams

Second
Edition

How to Fail at Almost Everything and Still Win Big copyright © 2013, 2023 by Scott Adams, Inc.
Cover art: May Yin Giang and Scott Adams
Interior photos: Copyright Scott Adams, Inc.
Dilbert Comics: Copyright Scott Adams, Inc.
Editor: Joshua Lisec

Scott Adams, Inc.
Pleasanton, CA
scottadams.locals.com

Publisher's Cataloging-In-Publication Data

Names: Adams, Scott, 1957- author.
Title: How to fail at almost everything and still win big : kind of the story of my life
     / Scott Adams.
Description: Second edition. | Pleasanton, CA : Scott Adams, Inc., [2023] | Includes
     bibliographical references.
Identifiers: ISBN: 979-8-9885349-5-2 (hardcover) | 979-8-9885349-4-5 (softcover) |
     979-8-9885349-6-9 (ebook) | 979-8-9885349-7-6 (audiobook)
Subjects: LCSH: Adams, Scott, 1957- | Cartoonists--United States--Biography. |
     Vocational guidance--Humor. | Motivation (Psychology) | Success. | LCGFT:
     Autobiographies.
Classification: LCC: PN6727.A3 Z46 2023 | DDC: 741.5/6973--dc23

Table of Contents

More Content from Scott Adams

Subscribers on **scottadams.locals.com** get the new *Dilbert Reborn* daily comic strip (a spicier and unfiltered version of classic *Dilbert*), a new comic called *Robots Read News* (an irreverent analysis of the headlines), more than 200 (and counting) micro lessons on life improvement and talent stacking, frequent livestream videos available nowhere else, my novels *God's Debris* and *The Religion War*, and other special content.

On some days, subscribers help write comics and watch the drawing process in real time. There is a lot of political content too, so don't be surprised by that. The Locals community has evolved into a digital friend group, and that's the vibe.

For just the *Dilbert Reborn* comic without the other nonsense, follow and subscribe on X (formerly known as Twitter), @ScottAdamsSays.

Preface to the Second Edition

When I finished writing the first edition of this book in 2013, I had no idea how much impact it would have on the business world and on the field of personal success. If some of the content in these pages looks familiar, it's because by now you have seen my work referenced in other bestselling books and countless podcasts and video clips—particularly the ideas around talent stacks, systems over goals, micro-steps, passion, luck, and more.

Nearly every day, I hear from readers who used what they learned from this book to lose weight, find love, get fit, land a dream job, quit drinking, and generally win at everything that matters to them. That's what I hoped the book would do for people. I just didn't expect it to work so well.

When I write, I like to write for one real or imaginary reader. It's a technique for finding my right voice. When I wrote the first edition of this book, I imagined my then-young stepson someday reading it. That was my motivation for making it my side project for two years of my life. You could think of these pages as everything I thought one young man needed to know to succeed in life.

Unfortunately, Justin didn't get a chance to finish reading it before fentanyl took him. Nor did he know fate had made him an accidental agent of change for thousands of people who would someday read a book written for him.

My life went through some notable ups and downs since I authored the first edition of his book, but I find I can dig myself out of almost any hole—and eventually come out ahead—using the methods I describe here. The methods will work for you, too, if you let them.

For this new edition of the book, I decided to keep all references to my first wife, Shelly, because she was part of my my life during the initial writing. The examples that mention her are important context and still "work" all these years later.

So with gratitude and appreciation, I give you *How to Fail at Almost Everything and Still Win Big: Second Edition.*

Introduction

I f you're already as successful as you want to be, both personally and professionally, all you are likely to get from this book is a semi-entertaining tale about a guy who failed his way to success. But you might also notice some familiar patterns in my story that will give you confirmation (or confirmation bias) that your own success wasn't entirely luck. That's the sort of validation you can't get from your family and friends who see you as a hot mess.

This is the story of one person's unlikely success within the context of scores of embarrassing failures. If you're just starting your journey toward success—however you define it—or are wondering what you've been doing wrong until now, I expect you'll find some novel ideas here. Maybe the combination of what you know plus what I think I know will be enough to keep you out of the woodchipper.

Was my eventual success primarily a result of talent, luck, hard work, or an accidental just-right balance of each? All I know for sure is that I pursued a conscious strategy of managing my opportunities in a way that would make it easier for luck to find me. Did my strategy make a difference, or is luck just luck, and everything else is just rationalization? Honestly, I don't know. That's why I suggest you compare my story with the stories of other people who found success and see if you notice any patterns. That's exactly the process I have used since childhood, and it either worked for me or I simply got lucky. I'll never know which it was. If you pick up some ideas in this book and go on to great success, you won't know exactly what made the difference either. But you might think you do, and that reason will probably have something to do with your many levels of awesomeness. That's how human brains work. But hey, maybe in your case it's true. In my case, I prefer to embrace my ignorance and leave it an open question.

That said, this is not an advice book. If you've ever taken advice from a cartoonist, there's a good chance it didn't end well. For starters, it's hard to know when a cartoonist is being serious and when they are constructing an elaborate practical joke. I've crafted pranks that spanned years, sometimes when no one was in on the joke but me. Some of those pranks are still percolating. I have posed as other people online and even in person. I have written opinions I don't actually hold just to see what reaction I would get. I once wore a professional disguise and infiltrated a high-level business meeting just to get material for *Dilbert*.

On top of that, I got paid to write this book, and we all know that money distorts truth like a hippo in a thong. And let's not forget I'm a stranger to most people reading this. It's never a good idea to trust strangers.

By any objective measure, I might be one of the least credible people on earth. I'm not too proud to admit that given a choice of saying what's true versus what's funny, I'll take the path with the greatest entertainment value.

I'm also not an expert at anything, including my own job. I draw like an inebriated howler monkey, and my writing style falls somewhere between baffling and sophomoric. It's an ongoing mystery to me why I keep getting paid.

To make matters worse, there are inherent problems with the whole idea of one person giving advice to another in book form. One size doesn't fit all. I'd be surprised if there's anything in this book that makes sense for all people all the time.

So this is a good time to skip ahead and give you a preview of the failing-toward-success topics that will follow. I do this because I anticipate your curiosity. You won't learn much from my abbreviated list, but if it gooses your interest, it might give you a reason to finish the book.

Book Tease

1. Goals are for losers. Winners rely on systems.
2. Your mind isn't magic. It's a moist computer you can program.
3. The most important metric to track is your personal energy.

4. Every skill you acquire doubles your odds of success.
5. Happiness is health plus freedom.
6. Luck can be managed . . . sort of.
7. Conquer shyness by being a huge phony (in a good way).
8. Fitness is the lever that moves the world.
9. Simplicity transforms ordinary into amazing.

If I do my job well, I won't need any credibility to pull this off. In chapters in which I refer to studies, I'll show my sources. I'll be like a race car driver drafting off the credibility of people who earned it. (Good work, credible people!) But most of the time, I'll be describing my personal experiences, and I promise those are real. I love a good practical joke, but a promise is a promise. Everything you read about my life in this book is accurate as far as I know.

When I was in my twenties, I didn't know anyone who could tell me how to become a cartoonist, how to write a book, or how to be successful in general. This was a big obstacle to my success. It seemed as if other people were benefitting greatly from the wisdom of their friends and families. That's exactly the sort of inequality that pisses me off and motivates me at the same time. As a result, I've spent decades trying to figure out what works and what doesn't on the topic of success. If you want to be successful in just about any field, let me be your starting point. I'll describe over the course of this book a sort of template for success that can serve as your launching pad. I won't always have the right formula for your specific situation, but I can help narrow your choices.

Before you decide whether anything I say in this book is useful, you need a system for sorting truth from rubbish. Most people think they have perfectly good bullshit detectors. But if that were the case, trial juries would always be unanimous, and we'd all have the same religious beliefs. Realistically, most people have poor filters for sorting truth from fiction and there's no objective way to know if you're particularly good at it or not. Consider the people who routinely disagree with you. See how confident they look while being dead wrong? That's exactly how you look to them.

When it comes to any big or complicated question, humility is the only sensible point of view. Still, we mortals need to navigate our world as if we understand it. The alternative—acting randomly—would be absurd. So to minimize the feeling of absurdity in your life, I recommend using a specific system for sorting truth from fiction. The system will be useful for reading this book, and it could be even more important in your life. The system recognizes that there are at least six common ways to sort truth from fiction, and interestingly, each one is a complete train wreck.

The Six Filters for Truth

1. Personal experience (Human perceptions are iffy.)
2. Experience of people you know (Even more unreliable.)
3. Experts (They work for money, not truth.)
4. Scientific studies (Correlation is not causation.)
5. Common sense (A good way to be mistaken with complete confidence.)
6. Pattern recognition (Patterns, coincidence, and personal bias look alike.)

In our messy, flawed lives, the nearest we can get to truth is *consistency*. Consistency is the bedrock of the scientific method. Scientists creep up on the truth by performing controlled experiments and attempting to observe consistent results. In your everyday non-scientist life, you do the same thing, but it's not as impressive, nor as reliable. For example, if every time you eat popcorn, one hour later you fart so hard that it inflates your socks, you can reasonably assume popcorn makes you gassy. It's not science, but it's still an entirely useful pattern. Consistency is the best marker of truth that we have, imperfect though it may be.

When seeking truth, your best bet is to look for confirmation on at least two of the dimensions I listed. For example, if a study indicates that eating nothing but chocolate cake is an excellent way to lose weight, but your friend who tries the diet just keeps getting fatter, you have two dimensions out of agreement. (Three if you count common sense.) That's a lack of consistency.

Once you have your bullshit filter working, think about how you begin the process of tackling any new and complicated problem. There's one step you will *always do first* if it's available to you: You'll ask a smart friend how he or she tackled the same problem. A smart friend can save you loads of time and effort. Many of you have a smart friend or two already, and you are lucky to have them. But my observation is that a startling percentage of the adult population literally has no smart friends to help them in their quest for success and happiness.

I hereby deputize myself to be your smart(ish) friend in the form of this book. If you already have some smart friends, that's great. You can't have too many. What I bring to the party is a willingness to discuss a wide range of success-related topics that your in-person friends might consider awkward dinner conversation.

I'm not an expert in any of the topics I'll discuss here. But I am a professional simplifier. My main job for the past few decades has been creating the *Dilbert* comic strip. Making comics is a process by which you strip out the unnecessary noise from a situation until all that is left is the absurd-yet-true core. A cartoonist has to accomplish that feat with as few as four short sentences. I've performed that trick nearly nine thousand times, sometimes successfully.

The best example of the power of simplicity is capitalism. The central genius of capitalism is that all its complexities, all the differences across companies, and all the challenges, decisions, successes, and failures can be boiled down into one number: profits. That simplification allows capitalism to work. The underlying complexity still exists in business, but creating a clear and simple measure of progress makes capitalism possible.

No smart investor would buy stock in a company without knowing its past and projected profits. Profits tell management when they are doing something right and when they need to do something different. That one simplification—the idea of profit—sits atop the engine of capitalism and largely steers it, albeit sometimes in the wrong direction. One can debate the morality of viewing profits as the top priority in business, but you can't argue that it works. At most, you can argue that some companies take it too far. But that is the risk of any tool. A hammer is only good if you stop pounding after the nail is all the way in. Keep pounding and you break the wood.

Later in this book I will describe a simplification that can inform all the steps you take toward your own personal success. It's the human equivalent of profit. It's the one simple thing you can measure that will give clarity on all the complicated decisions in your life. But that's later.

I wish I could give you a sure-fire formula for success, but life doesn't work that way. What I *can* do is describe a model that you can compare to your current way of doing things. The right answer for you might be some combination of what you're already doing and what you read here. You're the best judge of what works for you, as long as you acquire that wisdom through pattern recognition, trial, and observation.

In summary, allow me to stipulate that if you think I'm full of crap on any particular idea or another, there's a healthy chance you're right. But being 100 percent right isn't my goal. I'm presenting some new ways to think about the process of finding happiness and success. Compare it to what you know, what you do, and what others suggest. Every person finds their own special formula.

CHAPTER 1

The Time I Was Crazy

In the spring of 2005, my doctor diagnosed me with a form of mental illness. He didn't use those exact words or anything like them, but he did refer me to the in-house psychologist at Kaiser, my health care organization. I can take a hint.

The psychologist listened to my story and came to the same conclusion: crazy. But like my doctor, she didn't use the actual word. The psychologist suggested Valium and offered her educated guess that reducing my stress level might return me to some sort of normal behavior.

I declined the Valium because I didn't *feel* crazy. I didn't even feel all that stressed, or at least I didn't feel that way until a doctor and a psychologist agreed that I was probably losing my mind. I certainly understood why both professionals leaned toward that diagnosis. By any measure, my recent behavior *appeared* crazy, even to me.

My symptom was that I had suddenly lost my ability to speak to human beings even though I could speak normally while alone or when talking to my cat. My regular doctor and Kaiser's in-house specialists had systematically eliminated each of the more likely causes for my speech problem. Allergies? Nope. Common respiratory problem? Nope. Acid reflux? Nope. Tumors or polyps in my throat? Nope. Stroke? Nope. Neurological problem? Nope. I was in seemingly perfect health, except that I had suddenly lost the ability to speak to other humans. I could speak normally to my cat. I could speak normally when alone. I could recite a poem. But on the phone, I could barely squeeze out an intelligible sentence. I had some sort of weird social laryngitis. Bottom line: crazy.

Insanity is always a reasonable diagnosis when you're dealing with writers and artists. Sometimes the only real difference between crazy people and artists is that artists write down what they imagine seeing. In the past few decades, hardly a week has gone by without a stranger on the Internet questioning my mental health. I understand that; I've read my writing, too. The rational part of my brain knows that if enough people suggest I might be crazy, I need to consider the possibility.

I also have some craziness in my genes. My mother's father spent some time in the loony bin, or whatever it was called at the time. If I recall, he was the recipient of electroshock treatments. Apparently that didn't work because my mother and grandmother later left him forever, taking nothing but the clothes on their backs, as he chased them down the road with a blunt object in his hands and, apparently, homicide on his mind. I couldn't rule out the possibility that I inherited whatever caused Grandpa to flip out.

Living as a presumptive crazy person was hard work. When I tried speaking to humans, my vocal cords clenched involuntarily on certain consonants, giving the impression of a very bad cell phone call that drops every third syllable. Asking for a Diet Coke at a restaurant turned into ". . . iet . . . oke." I usually ended up with a sympathetic look and a regular Coke. Or worse, the server would say, "I'm fine. Thanks for asking." And I would get no beverage at all.

It was a confounding, maddening problem. I could sing fluently, albeit hideously, which was entirely normal for me. And I could recite memorized pieces without much of a hitch. But I couldn't produce a normal, intelligible sentence in the context of a conversation.

Like a stutterer, I learned to avoid problem syllables that would trip me up. If I wanted gum, I knew it would come out as ". . . um," so instead I would try a workaround such as "I want the stuff you chew." That approach generally failed. People don't expect riddles in their casual conversations, and no matter how clearly I laid out the clues, all I got in return was a puzzled expression and "Huh?"

Losing your ability to speak is obviously a social nightmare. It's so surreal that you feel like a ghost in a crowded room. And I mean that literally; it feels like an actual ghost experience, or at least how one imagines that might be. The loneliness was debilitating. Research shows that loneliness damages the body in much the same way as aging.[1,2] It sure felt that way. Every day felt like losing a fight.

I learned that loneliness isn't fixed by listening to other people talk. You can only cure your loneliness by doing the talking yourself, and—most importantly—being heard. For the next three-and-a-half years, I experienced a total disconnect from normal life and a profound sense of aloneness despite the love and support of family and friends. My quality of life was dipping below the point of being worth the effort.

In the early months of my voice problems, I had a more immediate problem than loneliness. In addition to being a syndicated cartoonist for the *Dilbert* comic strip, I was a highly paid professional speaker. And I had an event scheduled in a few weeks, the first since I lost my ability to talk. I couldn't predict whether my voice would work for my canned speech in the same way I could sing or repeat a poem. Would my vocal cords slam shut on stage and stay that way? Would I stand in front of a thousand people and yammer incomprehensibly?

I informed my client of the situation by email and gave his organization a chance to cancel. They decided to forge ahead and take the risk. I agreed to take the chance, too. Luckily for me, I don't feel embarrassment the way normal people do, which I'll discuss in an upcoming chapter. The prospect of humiliation in front of a thousand strangers, many of whom would likely be video recording the disaster, wasn't as much of a showstopper as you might think. It was worth the risk to me because I needed to know what would happen with my voice in that context. I needed to find out the pattern. Would my voice work if I presented a mostly memorized routine in front of a thousand people? There was only one way to find out.

CHAPTER 2

The Day of the Talk

I'd given a hundred similar talks. On some level, every speaking event was the same: Sign the contract. Book a flight. Show up. Make small talk with the organizers. Hit the stage. Make people laugh. Sign some autographs. Pose for pictures. Rush to a waiting car service. Ride to the airport. Fly home.

This time, the small talk wasn't working. Backstage, minutes before I was introduced to a packed ballroom, the organizers tried to engage me in conversation. I did my best, but they couldn't decipher much of what I was trying to say. I whispered and gestured and used my workaround sentences, trying to assure them that things would be better onstage. But honestly, I didn't know that to be true. And I could see the panic in their eyes. The odds were high that I would walk on stage and my throat would snap shut on every third syllable.

Experts say public speaking is one of the most terrifying things a person can do. That wasn't generally the case for me. I was well-trained, experienced, a natural ham, and my audiences were generally full of friendly *Dilbert* lovers. But I had never before stood backstage waiting for an introduction while wondering if I possessed the ability to speak.

This was new.

As the host launched into my introduction, I climbed the metal steps to the side stage. The sound technicians fiddled with the mixer and prepared to go hot on my microphone. The event organizers faded into the backstage darkness. The audience was restless with anticipation. My introduction seemed to last forever.

I peeked out to see the audience, to get a feel for the room. These were my people: technical folks and office workers. I took a few deep breaths. The moderator used a joke I supplied for my introduction and the audience laughed. They were primed and ready.

I fidgeted with my shirt to get it tucked in just right. I checked the microphone cord to make sure the excess was neatly hidden under my belt. The moderator raised his voice for effect and bellowed, "***Please welcome the creator of Dilbert, Scott Adams!***" My heart pounded so hard that I could feel it in my shoes. I walked into the blinding glare of the stage lights. The audience went wild. They loved *Dilbert* and by extension were happy to see me. I crossed the stage and shook hands with the host. We made eye contact and nodded. Everything moved in slow motion. I walked toward the Elmo—a digital video device that would display my comics on the big screens. I placed my materials on the table and took two steps to the side. I put my hands in front of me, fingertips together, as speakers do, while I absorbed the applause and converted it to positive energy. The energy felt good. I was jacked-in to the audience, for better or worse.

In an instant, and right on schedule, my heartbeat dropped to a normal state, just as it had a hundred times before in front of a hundred other crowds. My training was kicking in, and with it came my confidence. In my mind, I owned the audience, and they would have it no other way. They came to surrender, in a sense. All I had to do was show them I knew it. And to do that, I needed to be able to speak.

I took two deep breaths and looked around. I smiled at the audience. I was happy to be there—genuinely happy. I was born for this. The stage always feels like home.

I waited for the applause to stop. And when it did, I waited a little longer, as I had learned. When you stand in front of an audience, your sensation of time is distorted. That's why inexperienced presenters speak too rapidly. I mentally adjusted my internal clock to match the audience's sense of timing. I also wanted them to wait in silence for a beat or two, to engage their curiosity. I knew from experience that audience members often wonder what the creator of *Dilbert* will sound like. That day, I wondered the same thing.

At this point in my story, you might have the following question: *What kind of idiot puts himself in a position to be humiliated in front of a thousand people?*

It's a fair question. The answer is a long one. It will take this entire book to answer it right. The short answer is that over the years I have cultivated a unique relationship with failure. I invite it. I survive it. I appreciate it. And then I mug the shit out of it.

Failure always brings something valuable with it. I don't let it leave until I extract that value. I have a long history of profiting from failure. My cartooning career, for example, is a direct result of failing to succeed in the corporate environment.

I was looking for a pattern with my speech that day. I needed to know why I could speak normally in some situations and not in others. Why does context matter? Is it something about my adrenaline level, or the tone of my voice, or the region of my brain that I access for memorization? If I could find the pattern, I thought it might reveal a solution to my voice problem. Would my voice be better than normal or worse than normal in front of an audience? I was about to find out.

I opened my mouth and began to speak. My voice wasn't good, but it worked in a raspy sort of way. Most people probably thought I had a cold. I spoke for forty-five minutes, showing comics that got me in trouble, and told amusing anecdotes. The audience ate it up.

When I walked off the stage, I immediately lost my ability to speak. When the context changed from my memorized speech to normal conversation, my throat locked up.

Damn, the problem was definitely in my brain.

For the next three years, I looked for patterns that would reveal a solution to my voice problems and free me from my ghostlike social existence. Over the course of this book, I'll tell you how that search went because embedded in that story is pretty much everything I know about grabbing failure by the throat and squeezing it until it coughs up a hairball of success.

CHAPTER 3

Passion is Bullshit

You often hear advice from successful people that you should "Follow your passion." That sounds perfectly reasonable the first time you hear it. Passion will presumably give you high energy, high resistance to rejection, and high determination. Passionate people are more persuasive, too. Those are all good things, right?

Here's the counterargument: When I was a commercial loan officer for a large bank in San Francisco, my boss taught us that you should never make a loan to someone who is following his passion. For example, you don't want to give money to a sports enthusiast who is starting a sports store to pursue his passion for all things sporty. That guy is a bad bet, passion and all. He's in business for the wrong reason.

My boss at the time, who had been a commercial lender for over thirty years, said the best loan customer is one who has no passion whatsoever, just a desire to work hard at something that looks good on a spreadsheet. Maybe the loan customer wants to start a dry cleaning store or invest in a fast food franchise—boring stuff. That's the person you bet on. You want the grinder, not the guy who loves his job.

So who's right? Is passion a useful tool for success, or is it just something that makes you irrational?

My hypothesis is that passionate people are more likely to take big risks in the pursuit of unlikely goals, so you would expect to see both more failures and more huge successes among the passionate. Passionate people who fail don't get a chance to offer their advice to the rest of us. But successful passionate people are writing books and answering interview questions about their secrets for success every day. Naturally those successful people want you to believe that success is a product of their awesomeness, but they also want to retain some humility. One can't be humble and say, "I succeeded because I am far smarter than the average person." But you can say your passion was a key to your success because everyone can be passionate about something or other. Passion sounds more accessible. If you're dumb, there's not much you can do about it, but passion is something we think anyone can generate in the right circumstances. Passion feels very democratic. It is the people's talent, available to all.

It's also mostly bullshit.

It's easy to be passionate about things that are working out, and that distorts our impression of the importance of passion. I've been involved in several dozen business ventures over the course of my life and each one made me excited at the start. You might even call it passion. The ones that didn't work out—and that would be most of them—slowly drained my passion as they failed. The few that worked became more exciting as they succeeded.

For example, when I invested in a restaurant with an operating partner, my passion was sky-high. And on day one, when there was a line of customers down the block, I was even more passionate. In later years, as the business got pummeled, my passion evolved into frustration and annoyance. The passion disappeared.

On the other hand, the *Dilbert* comic started out as just one of many get-rich schemes I was willing to try. When it started to look as if it might be a success, my passion for cartooning increased because I realized it could be my golden ticket. In hindsight, it looks as if the projects I was most passionate about were also the ones that worked. But objectively, my passion level moved with my success. Success caused passion more than passion caused success.

Passion can also be a simple marker for talent. We humans tend to enjoy doing things we are good at while not enjoying things we suck at. We're also fairly good at predicting what we might be good at before we try. I was passionate about tennis the first day I picked up a racket, and I've played all my life. But I also knew in an instant that it was the type of thing I could be good at, unlike basketball or football. So sometimes passion is simply a byproduct of knowing you will be good at something.

I hate selling, but I know it's because I'm bad at it. If I were a sensational salesperson or had potential to be one, I'd probably feel passionate about sales. And people who observed my success would assume my passion was causing my success as opposed to being a mere indicator of talent.

If you ask a billionaire the secret of his success, he might say it's passion because that sounds like a sexy answer that is suitably humble. But after a few drinks, he'd probably say his success was a combination of desire, luck, hard work, determination, brains, and appetite for risk.

So forget about passion when you're planning your path to success. In the coming chapters, I'll describe some methods for boosting personal energy that have worked for me. You already know that when your energy is right you perform better at everything you do, including school, work, sports, and even your personal life. Energy is good. Passion is bullshit.

CHAPTER 4

Some of My Many Failures in Summary Form

I'm delighted to admit that I've failed at more challenges than anyone I know. There's a non-zero chance that reading this book will set you on the path of your own magnificent screw-ups and cavernous disappointments. You're welcome! And if I forgot to mention it earlier, that's exactly where you want to be—steeped to your eyebrows in failure. It's a good place to be because failure is where success likes to hide in plain sight. Everything you want out of life is in that huge, bubbling vat of failure. The trick is to get the good stuff out.

If success were easy, everyone would have it. It takes effort. That fact works to your advantage because it keeps lazy people out of the game. And don't worry if you're lazy, too. Much of this book involves tricks for ramping up your energy without much effort. In fact, the process of simply reading this book might give you a little boost of optimism. I designed it to do just that. So you're already moving in the right direction.

I'm an optimist by nature or perhaps by upbringing—it's hard to know where one leaves off and the other begins—but whatever the cause, I've long seen failure as a tool, not an outcome. I believe that viewing the world in that way can be useful for you, too.

Nietzsche famously said, "What doesn't kill us makes us stronger." It sounds clever, but it's a loser philosophy. I don't want my failures to simply make me stronger,* which I interpret as making me better able to survive future challenges. Becoming stronger is obviously a good thing, but it's only *barely* optimistic. I do want my failures to make me stronger, of course, but I also want to become smarter, more talented, better networked, healthier, and more energized. If I find a cow turd on my front steps, I'm not satisfied knowing that I'll be mentally prepared to find some future cow turd. I want to shovel that turd onto my garden and hope the cow returns every week so I never have to buy fertilizer again†. Failure is a resource that can be managed.

Prior to launching the *Dilbert* comic and after, I failed at a long series of day jobs and entrepreneurial adventures. Here's a quick listing of the worst ones. I'm probably forgetting a dozen or so. I include this section because successful people generally gloss over their most aromatic failures, which leaves the impression they have some magic you don't. When you're done reading this list, you won't have that delusion about me, and that's the point. Success is entirely accessible even if you happen to be a huge screw-up 95 percent of the time.

My Favorite Failures:

Velcro™ Rosin Bag Invention: In the seventies, tennis players sometimes used rosin bags to keep their racket hands less sweaty. In college I built a prototype of a rosin bag that attached to a Velcro strip on tennis shorts so it would always be available when needed. My lawyer told me it wasn't patent-worthy because it was simply a combination of two existing products. I approached some sporting goods companies and got nothing but form letter rejections. I dropped the idea. But in the process, I learned a valuable lesson: Good ideas have no value because the world already has too many of them. The market rewards *execution*, not ideas. From that point on, I concentrated on ideas I could execute. I was already failing toward success, but I didn't yet know it.

---

*To be fair to Nietzsche, he probably meant the word "stronger" to include anything that makes you more capable. I'd ask him to clarify, but ironically he ran out of things that didn't kill him.

†I should warn you that 75 percent of my analogies involve feces, babies, or Steve Jobs. I do not apologize for that.

My First Job Interview: It was my senior year at Hartwick College, and I started interviewing for real-world jobs. One day, Hartwick hosted a career day on campus. The only company that interested me was Xerox. They were looking for two field salespeople. At the time, Xerox seemed like a good company for the long run. I just needed to get my foot in the door with an entry-level sales job and work my way up. Several of my classmates were interviewing for the same two openings. I was familiar with their academic standings, and I knew I had the best grades of the bunch. I figured my academic excellence would be the advantage I needed for a sales position. That is how ignorant I was.

As far as I knew at the time, my interview with the recruiter went well. I explained that I had no sales experience, but I loved to argue. And what is selling, I asked rhetorically, if not a form of arguing with customers until you win? Yes, I really took that approach.

That failure taught me to look for opportunities in which I had some natural advantage. When I later decided to try cartooning, it was because I knew there weren't many people in the world who could draw funny pictures and also write in a witty fashion. My failure taught me to seek opportunities in which I had an advantage.

Meditation Guide: Soon after college, a friend and I wrote a beginner's guide to meditation. I had meditated for years and found a lot of benefits in it. We advertised our meditation guide in minor publications and sold about three copies. I learned a good deal about local advertising, marketing, and product development. All of that came in handy later.

Computer Game 1: In the early eighties, I spent about half of my net worth buying a portable computer. This was before the age of laptops, when "portable" meant that an adult with good upper-body strength could lift it. I spent almost every night and every weekend for two years trying to teach myself enough about programming to create a space-themed, arcade-type game. I managed to design and build the game, and it worked quite well. But it took me so long to create it that the state of the art for computer game design had surged ahead, making my simple space game look archaic. I advertised the game in the back of computer publications and sold fewer than twenty copies. (Note: There is a successful and well-known computer game designer named Scott Adams. I'm not him.)

Computer Game 2: I decided to take another run at a space-themed game, this time with a point-of-view from the cockpit of a spaceship as you navigated through the stars and hunted satellites to blast from the sky. This was a much higher level of difficulty than the first, and it took all my free time for a year. The game worked, but I'm the only person to ever play it. The technology of the time was too primitive to build the game I imagined. Or maybe my skills were inadequate. It was probably a combination.

Psychic Practice Program: I wrote a computer program to track and graph the "psychic" ability of users. It was a simple program that involved picking the right onscreen card from a choice of four. The idea was to see if you could stay above 25 percent. I don't believe in psychic powers, and my random number generator was less random than I would have liked, but that didn't matter. It was just for fun. The fun was derived from the fact that sometimes, by pure chance, you could stay above 25 percent for a brief run. During the above-average runs, you would have the sensation of being psychic, or at least lucky. The way our brains are wired, the lucky streaks feel good even if we know they are nothing but chance.

For months I dedicated all my spare time to creating the program. It worked well, but I decided it wasn't special enough to be worth the trouble of marketing it. It just wasn't exciting.

All my computer game ideas failed, but in the process I learned enough about personal computers to look like a technical genius in those early days of computing: the eighties. That knowledge transferred to my day job at the bank and later to my cartooning career as well.

Gopher Offer: During my banking career in my late twenties, I caught the attention of a Senior Vice President at the bank. Apparently my bullshit skills in meetings were impressive. He offered me a job as his gopher/assistant with the vague assurance that I would meet important executives during the normal course of my work, and that would make it easy for him to strap a rocket to my ass—as the saying went—and launch me up the corporate ladder. On the downside, the challenge would be to survive his less-than-polite management style and do his bidding for a few years. I declined his offer because I was already managing a small group of people, so becoming a gopher seemed like a step backwards. I believe the Senior Vice President's exact characterization of my decision was "F#@*&G STUPID!!!" He hired one of my coworkers for the job instead, and in a few years that fellow became one of the youngest Vice Presidents in the bank's history.

I worked for Crocker National Bank in San Francisco for about eight years, starting at the very bottom and working my way up to lower management. That career ultimately failed when I hit the diversity ceiling, but during the course of my banking career, and in line with my strategy of learning as much as I could about the ways of business, I gained an extraordinarily good overview of banking, finance, technology, contracts, management, and a dozen other useful skills. That allowed me to jump ship to a much higher paying job at . . .

Phone Company Career: I worked at Pacific Bell for another eight years, mostly doing financial jobs—budgeting and writing business cases for projects. But I also worked as a fake (literally) engineer in a technology lab, and I had a finger in strategy, marketing, research, interface design, and several other fields. That career hit the diversity ceiling just as my banking career did, but in the process I learned a huge amount about business from every angle. And my total corporate experience formed the knowledge base upon which *Dilbert* was built.

Zippy Ship: I spent about a year writing a program in my free time to make modem-to-modem file transfers easier. This was before email could easily send large files. I turned my little condo into a technology lab. By then I was working my day job at the phone company while also producing *Dilbert*.

I'm sure the Zippy Ship name is taken, but that was my working name for it. Its coolest feature was the menu. When you fired up the program, a zipper appeared on screen and quickly unzipped with an appropriate sound effect. The rectangular menu popped out of the zipper sideways in a suggestively phallic manner that I thought would get people talking about it.

I put an enormous amount of work into getting the technology to work across all modem types, but it was a lost cause. Modems weren't standardized enough to pull it off with my meager resources and know-how. The best I could accomplish was making it work on two specific modems. That was useless. I stopped working on the product, and while I didn't gain any new technical knowledge that helped me later, I did gain a clearer understanding of how hard it would be to gnaw through a wall to make something work.

Crackpot Idea Website: I like crackpot ideas because I find them inherently interesting, and often they inspire ideas that have merit. I also like coming up with my own crackpot ideas, sometimes several per day. I figured other people might like the same thing. I created a website through my syndication company for user-submitted crackpot ideas. I hoped that perhaps it could change the world if someone were to accidentally come up with a great idea that wouldn't have found oxygen in any other way. The site was a subsidiary of the original *Dilbert* website, which had plenty of traffic, so it wasn't hard to get exposure. The problem is that the ideas people submitted were so awful they didn't even rise to the level of crackpot. It didn't take long for the site to be populated with so much well-intentioned garbage that it became worthless. We shut it down.

In the process of failing, I learned a lot about website design and new feature implementation. That knowledge has served me well on several projects.

Video on Internet: During the dotcom frenzy, I was approached by a startup that planned to allow anyone with a computer to post videos on the Internet for the collective viewing pleasure of all. They asked me to help use my *Dilbert* spotlight to get the word out. The startup didn't have much funding, so they offered me a generous chunk of stock instead. I accepted. I talked about the new service in my *Dilbert* newsletter, posted my own funny videos, and gave some interviews on the topic.

Several years later, Google bought YouTube for $1.65 billion and the shareholders made a fortune. Unfortunately, the video service in my story was not YouTube. It was a service that came before. The company I worked with was premature because Internet speeds were not quite fast enough for online video sharing to catch on. The company struggled for a few years and then shut down. YouTube got the timing right. That was about the time I started to understand that timing is often the biggest component of success. And since timing is often hard to get right unless you are psychic, it makes sense to try different things until you get the timing right by luck.

Grocery Home Delivery: An engineer friend and I decided to work together to create technology that would make home delivery of groceries more practical. The idea was to create technology that would allow a delivery van to open your garage door so the driver could place the delivery inside even when you were not home, perhaps in a cooler. Our plan was to sell the technology to grocery stores that wanted to start delivering.

I know, I know. Lots of security concerns. I'll spare the details, but we thought we could design some safeguards to bring the risks to nearly zero. We could have a long debate on whether that was possible, but it didn't matter because my friend got busy on other projects and bowed out. That didn't get far enough to generate any benefits in knowledge or talent, but I hadn't put much effort into it either.

Webvan: Some years later, in the dotcom era, a startup called Webvan promised to revolutionize grocery delivery. You could order grocery store items over the Internet, and one of their trucks would load your order at their modern distribution hub and set out to service all the customers in your area. I figured Webvan would do for groceries what Amazon did for books. It was a rare opportunity to get in on the ground floor. I bought a bunch of Webvan stock and felt good about myself. When the stock plunged, I bought some more. I repeated that process several times, each time licking my lips as I acquired ever larger blocks of the stock at prices I knew to be a steal.

When management announced they had achieved positive cash flow at one of their several hubs, I knew I was on to something. If it worked in one hub, the model was proven, and it would surely work at others. I bought more stock. Now I owned approximately, well, a boatload.

A few weeks later, Webvan went out of business. Investing in Webvan wasn't the dumbest thing I've ever done, but it's a contender. The loss wasn't enough to change my lifestyle. But boy did it sting psychologically. In my partial defense, I knew it was a gamble, not an investment per se.

What I learned from that experience is that there is no such thing as useful information that comes from a company's management. Now I diversify and let the lying get smoothed out by all the other variables in my investments.

Professional Investors: After my Webvan disaster, I figured I might need some professional investing help. *Dilbert* royalties were pouring in, and I didn't have the time to do my own research. Nor did I trust my financial skills, and for good reason.

My bank, Wells Fargo, pitched me on their investment services, and I decided to trust them with half of my investible funds. Trust is probably the wrong term because I only let them have half; I half-trusted them. I did my own investing with the other half of my money. The experts at Wells Fargo helpfully invested my money in Enron, WorldCom, and some other names that have become synonymous with losing money. Clearly my investment professionals did not have access to better information than I had. I withdrew my money from their management and have done my own thing since then, mostly in broad-market unmanaged funds. (That worked out better.)

Folderoo: In the early days of *Dilbert*, when floppy disks were still in widespread use, it was common to hand a coworker a document along with a floppy disk in case the coworker needed to make changes. The problem was that there was no elegant way to attach a floppy disk to a piece of paper. My brilliant idea was to invent a manila folder with a kangaroo-type pocket on the front to hold the disk. It wouldn't cost much more than a regular folder to produce, and it would be twice as useful. I figured the product could have a *Dilbert* tie-in because Dilbert has a shirt pocket much like I was putting on the folder. I made a prototype (which took five minutes) and pitched it to my syndicate, United Media. I hoped they could find a licensee who would produce and market the product while we collected royalties for the *Dilbert* association. This idea went nowhere because United Media was in the licensing business, not the product design business, and this idea was out of their strike zone. I assume the name Folderoo is owned by someone else at this point. Eventually some folder companies made and sold folders with pockets for disks. I don't know how well they did.

Calendar Patent: I had an idea for embedding ads in electronic calendars in a clever way that people would find useful. The idea was for a program to read your calendar entries and match your plans with vendor offers that made sense for the activities predicted by the calendar. For example, if you planned to go car shopping for a minivan next month, just put that entry on your calendar. Then vendors would populate the entry with local deals and offers. You would only see the offers if you clicked on them. The ads would be managed through a third party (in the "cloud," as we might say today), so vendors would never directly see any user's calendar information. The patent was rejected because a totally unrelated patent—meaning it had nothing to do with calendars at all—allegedly included the process I described. My reading of the existing patent was that it had nothing to do with my idea, but I consulted with my patent attorney and let it drop. Interestingly, the owner of the existing patent probably doesn't know he's sitting on a gold mine.

Keypad Patent: I filed a patent on an idea for text entry on a ten-key keypad. This was in the pre-smartphone era when people texted on their regular ten-key phones, tapping a key however many times it took to designate the character you intended. My idea involved mentally projecting a letter on the keypad and creating a two-key shortcut for each letter that was based on its shape characteristics. The patent was granted, but the evolution of phone technology quickly made it obsolete.

Dilberito: During the busiest years of *Dilbert*'s climb into popular culture, I was often too busy to eat well. I also wanted to give back, as the saying goes, to a world that was being more generous than I thought my meager talent deserved. I came up with the idea of creating a food product that was fortified with 100 percent of your daily requirements of vitamins and minerals. I worked with a food expert, my only employee, who designed a line of burritos—dubbed the "Dilberito"—and successfully sold them into almost every major grocery chain in the United States plus Seven-Eleven, Costco, and Walmart. In each case the product failed to sell and for a variety of reasons, mostly related to shelf placement. Few products on the bottom shelf sell well, and we didn't have the clout to earn better space. Also, nothing sells when your competitor sends people to "bury" you behind their own products on every store shelf—a common dirty trick that worked like a charm on us.

We also didn't do much in the way of repeat business. The mineral fortification was hard to disguise, and because of the veggie and legume content, three bites of the Dilberito made you fart so hard your intestines formed a tail.

Several years and several million dollars later, I sold off the intellectual property and exited.

Restaurant 1: After a chance encounter with an experienced restaurant manager, I agreed to partner with her to create a new restaurant in Pleasanton, California. We named the place Stacey's Café because I figured she would work harder if her name was over the door. I did the funding, mentoring, legal and financial stuff, and she did all the creative, entrepreneurial, management stuff. The restaurant opened to long lines despite less-than-stellar food and service on day one. Profits poured in. The secret to our initial success was the low number of restaurants in the area relative to population. Every restaurant in the area was busy regardless of quality or price.

What we didn't expect was that as the food quality and service improved from mediocre to among the best in the valley, everything else trended the wrong way. Operating costs rose steadily, and new restaurants started opening and nibbling at our customer base. While the first restaurant was still profitable, we decided our biggest problem was insufficient seating for the busiest nights, so . . .

Restaurant 2: We opened a second restaurant five miles down the road, with a different menu, higher-end décor, and twice the space. It was also nearly triple the rent of the first. We figured that was okay because filling a space that large would be a gold mine. What we didn't count on is that people don't choose a restaurant because it's large. We got our fair share of business, which would have been just enough for a place half the size. Meanwhile, the economy tanked and big corporations that had planned on surrounding us with major campuses pulled out of the area. Our outdoor seating turned out to be a wind tunnel with major traffic noise. And customers found the décor too upscale and expensive for families and also not as exciting as a trip to nearby San Francisco for special meals. In the worst restaurant luck I have ever seen, a strip mall of nothing but restaurants opened within walking distance. The second restaurant bled money from the start and never came close to breakeven.

Meanwhile, the original restaurant turned unprofitable, thanks mostly to two major chain restaurants setting up shop nearby and cutting deeply into our business.

Then the legal problems started. We had one lawsuit or threatened lawsuit after another, mostly for ridiculous reasons. I can't get into details because of settlement agreements, but three of the situations would make you vomit in your own mouth. None of the legal threats or lawsuits came from customers. It was the sort of stuff you've never even heard of. I had deep pockets and a big red bullseye on my back.

I sold off the assets and got out of the restaurant business. I have to say the richness of the whole restaurant experience was totally worth the money. I was in a position to afford the losses without altering my lifestyle, so I don't regret any of it. Eating dinner at a restaurant you own can be an extraordinarily good time. It sure beats cooking at home and washing the dishes. Of all my failures, I enjoyed the restaurants the most.

First Attempt at Cartooning: My first attempt at professional cartooning involved sending some single-panel comics to the two magazines that paid the most: *Playboy* and *The New Yorker*. The comics were dreadful. Both magazines wisely rejected them.

Ninja Closet: I had an idea for a website that would make it easier to know what gifts to buy for kids, especially kids that are not your own. Gift-buying can be a huge hassle if your kid is getting invited to a birthday party every two weeks. Does little Timmy already have a particular toy? Does he want one? Who else is thinking of buying him the same toy? Who wants to pitch in for a more expensive gift? The current process involves too much guesswork and too many emails and phone calls.

I decided to hire some inexpensive programmers in India to build a web-based gift registry (essentially) for kids. I called it Ninja Closet because the metaphor was that friends and family could peak into your secret closet of wishes but also see what stuff you already owned, negotiate for shared gift-buying, and more. I figured kids would love seeing what other kids owned, too. No one would be able to see a kid's closet unless a parent granted permission.

I still think it was a great idea, but managing programmers in India turned out to be impractical for me because of time differences, language issues, and my own time limitations. After too much time and expense on this side project, I let it go.

CHAPTER 5

My Absolute Favorite Spectacular Failure

M ost failures involve bad luck, ignorance, and sometimes ordinary stupidity. One day in college, I managed to combine all three into one experience. It was breathtaking.

In the winter of my senior year, I started to think I might have the right stuff to become a good accountant, perhaps someday a CPA. I figured that career path would be a good way to learn the innards of business from the numbers side. I would need that sort of experience no matter what kind of business I someday started on my own. All I needed was an entry-level position with one of the so-called Big Eight (at the time) accounting firms. I managed to line up an interview in Syracuse, New York, a two-hour drive from campus.

The day of the interview featured a typical upstate New York half-blizzard with ass-freezing temperatures. I decided I didn't need a jacket for the trip because I was only going from building to car and back. This was only one of the remarkably stupid decisions I made that day.

My second mistake was not realizing I should wear a suit and tie to an interview with an accounting firm. I figured they knew I was in college since it said so on my résumé, so why not dress like a college student? Yes, I was that ignorant. Remember, I didn't even *know* anyone who worked in a traditional white-collar environment. Nor did I own a suit or a tie.

My interviewer took one look at me and remarked that apparently I didn't know why I was there. He escorted me to the door and suggested that the next time I go to an interview perhaps I should wear a suit. I was devastated. But my evening was far from over. So far, I had only exercised my ignorance and my stupidity. The bad luck part of the day was ahead.

On the way home, I took a newly constructed highway through a sparsely populated valley in the Catskill Mountains. My engine conked out, and I managed to coast the car into a snow bank on the side of the road. There were no other cars on the road in either direction. It was after dark, and the already-frosty temperature was dropping fast. I saw no signs of civilization for miles. The temperature was about zero Fahrenheit. It wasn't a good day to leave my jacket at home. In the days before cell phones, this was the worst-case scenario.

I knew I couldn't stay in the car for long. The temperature inside started dropping the moment the engine died. I knew I couldn't run back in the direction from which I came because it had been miles since I saw a house. I wouldn't make it that far. My only hope was to run forward and hope there were homes around a bend or over a hill. And so I started running.

In less than a minute, the frozen air sucked the warmth from my body and distributed it into the atmosphere. My feet were like blocks of ice clunking on the frozen pavement. My breath formed cumulus clouds around my head. I lost most of the feeling in my hands. My ankles hardened. I figured I was about thirty minutes from falling into a frozen death sleep in the nearest snowbank. And now my legs were failing. I couldn't go much further, and when I stopped running, I knew the cold would finish me off.

As I struggled to stay upright and keep moving, I made myself a promise: If I lived, I would trade my piece of shit car for a one-way plane ticket to California and never see another f@$#!#& snow flake for the rest of my life.

Headlights appeared on the horizon. I stood in the middle of the road and signaled, like the frozen idiot I was, for the car to stop. A traveling shoe salesman in a beat-up station wagon saved my life. He drove me all the way back to campus.

A few months later, I kept my promise to myself. I bought a one-way plane ticket to the vibrant economy and easy climate of Northern California. It was the smartest decision I ever made. The experience of nearly dying in the frozen tundra of upstate New York inspired me to move to California. Thank you, failure. I no longer fear death when I go outdoors.

CHAPTER 6

Goals Versus Systems

At the age of twenty-one, college diploma in hand, I boarded an airplane for the first time in my life. Destination, California. I knew one thing about success: It wouldn't be easy to find in Windham, New York, population 2,000. A few years earlier, my older and more adventurous brother Dave had driven his Volkswagen Beetle cross-country to Los Angeles, looking for warmer weather and attractive women. He slept in his car and camped along the way. My plan was to fly to Los Angeles, sleep on his crumb-laden couch until I could find a job in banking, and make my home in the Golden State.

A few days before my flight to California, I traded my rusted-out Datsun 510 to my sister for cash so I could afford that one-way ticket to California. (More on that story later.) I proudly donned the cheap three-piece suit my parents gave me as a college graduation present—my first real suit. At the time, I assumed everyone dressed in business or formal attire to fly. I grew up in a small town and didn't know many people who had flown in a commercial aircraft. My father had taken some flights twenty-some years earlier, but he didn't volunteer much information about it or anything else for that matter. He was a man of few words. I had only a few relatives nearby, and none of them had ever flown. I was mostly guessing how the process worked, and I didn't want to take a chance of getting kicked off the flight for being poorly dressed. That's exactly the sort of mistake I make.

I also didn't know how I would go about getting my suit ironed if it got wrinkled in my luggage. I figured I would be going on job interviews as soon as I reached California and needed my one-and-only suit to look relatively less hobo-ish. It just made sense to wear it on the flight.

I was seated next to a businessman who was probably in his early sixties. I suppose I looked like an odd duck with my serious demeanor, bad haircut, and cheap suit, clearly out of my element. He asked what my story was, and I filled him in. I asked what he did for a living, and he told me he was CEO of a company that made screws. Then he offered me some career advice. He said that every time he got a new job, he started immediately looking for a better one. For him, job-seeking was not something one did when necessary. It was an ongoing process. This makes perfect sense if you do the math. Chances are, the best job for you won't become available at precisely the time you declare yourself ready. Your best bet, he explained, was to always be looking for the better deal. The better deal has its own schedule. I believe the way he explained it is that your job is not your job; your job is to find a better job.

This was my first exposure to the idea that one should have a system instead of a goal. The system was to continuously look for better options. And it worked for this businessman, as he had job-hopped from company to company, gaining experience along the way, until he became a CEO. Had he approached his career with a specific goal in mind or perhaps specific job objectives (e.g., gunning for his boss's job), that would have severely limited his options. But for him, the entire world was his next potential job. The new job simply had to be better than the last one and allow him to learn something useful for the next hop.

Did the businessman owe his current employers loyalty? Not in his view. The businessman didn't invent capitalism, and he didn't create its rules. He simply played within those rules. His employers wouldn't have hesitated to fire him at the drop of a hat for any reason that fit their business needs. He simply followed their example.

The second thing I learned on that flight—or confirmed, really—is that appearance matters. By the end of the flight, the CEO had handed me his card and almost guaranteed me a job at his company if I wanted it.

Had I boarded the flight wearing my ratty jeans, threadbare tee shirt, and worn-out sneakers, things would have gone differently.

Throughout my career, I've had my antennae up looking for examples of people who use systems versus goals. In most cases, as far as I can tell, the people who use systems do better. The systems-driven people have found a way to look at the familiar in new and more useful ways.

To put it bluntly, goals are for losers. That's literally true most of the time. For example, if your goal is to lose ten pounds, you will spend every moment until you reach the goal—if you reach it at all—feeling as if you are short of your goal. In other words, goal-oriented people exist in a state of nearly continuous failure that they hope will be temporary. That feeling wears on you. In time, it becomes heavy and uncomfortable. It might even drive you out of the game.

If you achieve your goal, you celebrate and feel terrific, but only until you realize you just lost the thing that gave you purpose and direction. Your options are to feel empty and useless, perhaps enjoying the spoils of your success until they bore you, or set new goals and reenter the cycle of permanent pre-success failure.

The systems-versus-goals point of view is burdened by semantics, of course. You might say every system has a goal, however vague. And that would be true to some extent. And you could say that everyone who pursues a goal has some sort of system to get there, whether it is expressed or not. You could word-glue goals and systems together if you choose. All I'm suggesting is that thinking of goals and systems as very different concepts has power. Goal-oriented people exist in a state of continuous pre-success failure at best and permanent failure at worst, if things never work out. Systems people succeed every time they apply their systems in the sense that they did what they intended to do. The "goals" people are fighting the feeling of discouragement at each turn. The systems people feel good every time they apply their system. That's a big difference in terms of maintaining your personal energy in the right direction.

The system-versus-goals model can be applied to most human endeavors. In the world of dieting, losing twenty pounds is a goal, but eating right is a system. In the exercise realm, running a marathon in under four hours is a goal, but exercising daily is a system. In business, making a million dollars is a goal, but being a serial entrepreneur is a system.

For our purposes, let's say a *goal* is a specific objective that you either achieve or don't sometime in the future. A *system* is something you do on a regular basis that increases your odds of happiness in the long run. If you do something every day, it's a system. If you're waiting to achieve it someday in the future, it's a goal.

Language is messy, and I know some of you are thinking that exercising every day sounds like a goal. The common definition of goals would certainly allow that interpretation. For our purposes, let's agree that goals are a reach-it-and-be-done situation, whereas a system is something you do on a regular basis with a reasonable expectation that doing so will get you to a better place in your life. Systems have no deadlines, and on any given day, you probably can't tell if it's moving you in the right direction.

My proposition is that if you study people who succeed, you will see that most of them follow systems, not goals. When goal-oriented people succeed in big ways, it makes the news. At the very least, it makes an interesting story. This gives you a distorted view of how often goal-driven people succeed. When you apply your own truth filter to the idea that systems are better than goals, consider only the people you know personally. If you know some extra-successful people, ask some probing questions about how they got where they did. I think you'll find a system at the bottom of it all and usually some extraordinary luck as well. (Later in this book, I'll tell you how to improve your odds of getting lucky.)

Consider Olympic athletes. When one Olympian wins a gold medal or multiple gold medals, it's a headline story. But for every medalist there are thousands who had the goal of being on that podium and failed.

Those people had goals and not systems. I don't consider daily practices and professional coaching a system because everyone knows in advance that the odds of any specific individual winning a medal through those activities are miniscule. The minimum requirement of a system is that a reasonable person expects it to work more often than not. Buying lottery tickets is not a system no matter how regularly you do it.

On the system side, consider Mark Zuckerberg, founder of Facebook. It's apparent that his system for success involved studying hard, getting extraordinary grades, going to a top college—in his case Harvard—and developing a skill set with technology that virtually guaranteed riches in today's world. As it turns out, his riches came quickly through the explosive growth of Facebook. But had that not worked out, he would likely be a millionaire through some other startup or just by being a highly paid technical genius for an existing corporation. Zuckerberg's system (or what I infer was his system) was almost guaranteed to work, but no one could have imagined at the time how well.

Warren Buffett's system for investing involves buying undervalued companies and holding them forever, or at least until something major changes. That system (which I have grossly oversimplified) has been a winner for decades. Compare that to individual investors who buy a stock because they expect it to go up 20 percent in the coming year; that's a goal, not a system. And not surprisingly, individual investors generally experience worse returns than the market average.

I have a friend who is a gifted salesman. He could have sold anything, from houses to toasters. The field he chose (which I won't reveal because he wouldn't appreciate the sudden flood of competition) allows him to sell a service that almost always auto-renews. In other words, he can sell his service once and enjoy ongoing commissions until the customer dies or goes out of business. His biggest problem in life is that he keeps trading his boat for a larger one, and that's a lot of work. Observers call him lucky. What I see is a man who accurately identified his skill set and chose a system that vastly increased his odds of getting "lucky." In fact, his system is so solid that it could withstand quite a bit of bad luck without buckling. How much passion does this fellow have for his chosen field? Answer: zero. What he has is a spectacular system, and that beats passion every time.

CHAPTER 7

My System

When I was six years old, I got hooked on the comic strip *Peanuts*. The drawings fascinated me. They were so simple and yet so perfect in an indescribable way. As soon as I learned to read, I devoured every *Peanuts* book I could get my hands on. I declared to my parents that one day I would be a famous cartoonist like Charles Schulz. That was my goal, clear as can be. I spent countless hours with crayons, pencils, markers, and paper. I practiced and practiced. But I never became good. I wasn't even the best artist in my class of forty kids. I didn't give up though.

At the age of eleven, I applied to the Famous Artists School for Young People. It was a correspondence course. This was perfect for me because I wouldn't need to leave home, which would have been problematic. I filled out the application, drew the assignments they requested, and answered the multiple-choice questions about design. Sadly, I was rejected by the Famous Artists School for Young People because their cutoff age was twelve. I was too young. I was crushed.

My mother, in the style of the times, told me I could do anything I set my sights on. She said I could be the president, an astronaut, or the next Charles Schulz. I believed her because at that point in my life, I hadn't yet noticed the pattern of her deceptions. Her lies included Santa Claus, the Tooth Fairy, the Easter Bunny, and something about cheaters never prospering.

In time, I started to understand something called "the odds." Some things were, by their very nature, likely, and some were not. I learned by observation that people who pursued extraordinarily unlikely goals were overly optimistic at best, delusional at worst, and just plain stupid most of the time. The smart people in my little Republican-dominated town made practical plans and stuck to them. Some joined the Marines to get experience and education. Some went into the family business. Some married and became homemakers and moms. A few superstars studied hard and pursued jobs in medicine and the law. At the time, if you had asked me to name twenty different types of jobs an adult could have, I would have tapped out after fifteen. The jobs I had heard of were the ones I saw around me in my little town plus whatever I saw on television. And by television, I mean the one channel we received via rabbit ears that had both a picture and sound.

My father worked at the local post office and painted houses at night when the weather allowed. His advice to my brother and me was to pursue a career in the postal profession. The United States Postal Service was steady work, it was mostly indoors, and it had excellent benefits. Sometimes when my mother was busy, my siblings and I would hang out at the Post Office with my dad. We were fascinated by the loaded handgun that was always within easy reach. Apparently, the government expected its employees to resist armed robberies by reaching for their pieces and blazing away. Those were different times.

My mother decided to try her hand at selling real estate once her three kids were old enough to stay alive on their own. She became an agent and did well enough to build up some savings that would go toward our college educations. My mother told us from the time we could understand language that all three of us were college-bound, like it or not. In my family, only an aunt had ever attended college. My mother decided to change that. Later, when the real estate market got saturated with brokers and agents, she took a job for minimum wage on an assembly line, winding copper wires around speaker magnets for eight hours a day. That money, too, went toward our education. It wasn't nearly enough, but it was a step in the right direction.

My mother decided that I should become a lawyer. She spent a good deal of energy convincing me that it was a good plan. The two lawyers in our town were doing well, and my grades seemed strong enough to make a legitimate run at the legal profession. I didn't know much about the job of lawyering, but I did like the idea of making good money and someday escaping my little town. I signed on to my mother's plan and set my sights on a career in law. All I needed to do was figure out how to pay for college.

One day in eleventh grade health class, our gym teacher/health teacher mentioned that our small school (there were about forty kids in my class) had never produced a student who earned an academic scholarship to college. He explained that one unusually tall and athletic student had managed to get a basketball scholarship before blowing out his knee in his freshman year, but no one had earned a college scholarship based on academics alone. The teacher speculated with confidence that this was about to change. He announced that one student in our grade was likely to get an academic scholarship. This news surprised me. I looked around my small classroom and couldn't figure out who he meant. Curiosity got the best of me, and I raised my hand. "Who are you talking about?" He stared at me in a gym coach way, either annoyed or surprised by the question. Then he answered in a confident voice, "You."

I didn't believe him. He was just one guy with an opinion. But my mother told me I was going to college one way or another, so I set about the task of figuring out how that happens. This was well before the days of highly involved parents. I was pretty much on my own. Our guidance counselor pointed to a wall-length shelf that was full of college pamphlets and books and gave me this valuable career guidance: *Pick a few colleges that look good and fill out some applications.* This was not the precise sort of career advice that one would hope for. I skimmed a few college books and felt lost. How could I possibly know the best choice for me?

Luckily, a new kid had joined my class a year earlier. New students were rare. I attended kindergarten with about thirty-five of the forty kids I graduated with, and most of those classes were in the same building. This new kid, Peter, came from some exotic city, or maybe it was a suburb, where people knew how the world worked. I followed his lead and did what he did. I decided to major in economics because Peter told me that would be a good pre-law degree. Then I followed him around in the guidance counselor's tiny library of college information and learned that the process for applying to each college was described in those books.

Eventually, I picked two colleges that looked good on paper. And by that I mean the schools were located within driving distance, they offered degrees in economics, and the photographs of the campus were pleasing.

My first choice, Cornell, had two factors working against it. The first was a tragic men-to-women ratio that guaranteed I would graduate a virgin. The other problem is that I applied too late and missed their deadline. Cornell informed me that I was on their wait list. My only chance of getting into that school was if some sort of fast-moving plague killed all the people who knew there was a deadline for applying.

The only other college I applied to was Hartwick College in Oneonta, New York. Hartwick had several things going for it. It was a one-hour drive from home, so travel would be affordable. They had a well-respected nursing major so there were more women than men. And they accepted me. It was my only option. This is when I learned that one should not seek life-altering advice from a kid named Peter whose primary credentials were that he once lived in a suburb or maybe a city. Either way, it was a bad idea to apply to only two colleges and a worse idea to choose those two colleges based on the quality of the photographs in the brochures. (Full disclosure: Attending a college with a favorable male-female ratio turned out to be genius.)

My next problem was that my parents couldn't afford to send me to Hartwick, which is a pricey private college. So I applied for an academic scholarship. To my surprise, but not the surprise of my gym teacher/health teacher, Hartwick granted me a partial academic scholarship. I also received some small scholarships from the state of New York. With my parents' savings plus my own savings from mowing lawns and shoveling snow for years, I had almost enough. I figured I could work a few jobs at school and close the gap. And so my college career began. I would study economics and aim for law school later. I escaped from Windham, New York, but just barely. Things would not get easier.

Soon into my first semester at Hartwick, I discovered several interesting pastimes that might fit under the heading of adult fun. The drinking age was eighteen in those days, and I was fresh off the leash. Soon, thanks to many delightful distractions, my grades dipped below the level that Hartwick expected from an academic scholarship recipient. The dean sent a letter putting me on notice. The scholarship would be rescinded unless I got my grades up. At about that same time, I came down with a world-class case of mononucleosis. The college nurses were impressed; they had never seen a case so severe. My glands were so swollen that my throat almost closed entirely. I couldn't even swallow. The college physician advised me that I would be too drained and sleepy to study, and my best bet was to pack up my stuff and drop out. He suggested that maybe I could come back to college someday and start over. It was my choice, he explained, but his medical advice was to regroup, recover at home, and try college another time. I had only been in college for one semester, and I was on the verge of complete failure.

This was one of those times when the difference between wishing and deciding mattered. I didn't *wish* to stay in school; I *decided*. For the next two weeks, I stayed in a bed in the college infirmary, struggling to stay awake long enough to read my textbooks and keep up to where I assumed the class would be. Upon release, I discovered I was actually a month ahead in some of my classes. My grades climbed back where they needed to be, and I marched on.

I had ignored my father's advice to work for the Postal Service. That turned out to be a good idea. I got into college without much help from my guidance counselor, and I stayed in school against my doctor's advice. This was about the time that my opinion of experts and authority figures in general began a steady descent that continues to this day.

As I learned more about the legal profession, I realized it wasn't a good fit for my personality. I'm not the sort of person who feels comfortable winning when it means the other side loses something of equal or greater value. I'd feel even worse if I were to win a victory for my client that was ill-deserved and accomplished only through my weaseltastic skills. I had been raised to decline offers of candy from family friends under the theory that I had done nothing to deserve it. I was the kind of person who needed a job that made other people happy, ideally with a side benefit of making me rich and famous, too. And for that I needed a system.

I decided that my talents would be best suited for creating and running some sort of company. To acquire the necessary skills, I would complete my economics degree and get an entry-level job at a big bank. I would take as many company-paid training classes as I could and learn all there was to know about business from a banking perspective. I also hoped to complete my MBA at night on the company's dime. I was agnostic about what specific sort of business I would someday run. All I knew for sure is that I needed to be ready when the time was right.

This brings me to my system. I still have the diary I wrote when I graduated from Hartwick in which I outlined my entrepreneurial plan. The idea was to create something that had value and—this next part is the key part—I wanted the product to be something that was *easy to reproduce in unlimited quantities*. I didn't want to sell my time, at least not directly, because that model has an upward limit. And I didn't want to build my own automobile factory, for example, because cars are not easy to reproduce. I didn't want to do any sort of custom work such as building homes because each one requires the same amount of work. I wanted to create, invent, write, or otherwise concoct something widely desired that would be easy to reproduce.

My plan wasn't the one and only practical path to success. Another perfectly good plan might involve becoming a salesperson who works on commission in an industry that handles extraordinarily expensive items such as rare art, airplanes, or office buildings. It might take years to get into one of those positions, but no one said success would be fast or easy. I don't have the salesperson gene, so selling expensive items wasn't a good plan for me. I figured my competitive edge was creativity. I would try one thing after another until something creative struck a chord with the public. Then I would reproduce it like crazy. In the near term, that would mean one failure after another. In the long term, I was creating a situation that would allow luck to find me.

It helps a great deal to have at least a general strategy and some degree of focus. The world offers so many alternatives that you need a quick filter to eliminate some options and pay attention to others. Whatever your plan, focus is always important.

My system of creating something the public wants and reproducing it in large quantities nearly guaranteed a string of failures. By design, all my efforts were long-shots. Had I been goal-oriented instead of system-oriented, I imagine I would have given up after the first several failures.

It would have felt like banging my head against a brick wall. But being systems-oriented, I felt myself growing more capable every day, no matter the fate of the project I happened to be working on. And every day during those years I woke up with the same thought, literally, as I rubbed the sleep from my eyes and slapped the alarm clock off.

Today's the day.

CHAPTER 8

My Corporate Career Fizzled

In the spring of 1979, adorned in the same cheap suit I wore on the flight to California, I walked into a San Francisco branch of Crocker National Bank and asked for a job as a teller. The manager hired me, the fresh Hartwick grad, on the spot. I needed a job right away because all I owned was my ill-fitting clothes, a plastic alarm clock, a watch that worked occasionally, a toiletry bag, and $2,000 that my parents scraped together as a college graduation present. My plan was to start at the bottom and claw my way to the top.

My degree in economics made me somewhat overqualified for the teller job, and yet I still managed to be dreadful at it. My people skills were good enough, but I somehow found a different way to misplace money or transpose numbers nearly every shift. I'm not good at any sort of task that must be done right the first time. I'm more of a do-it-wrong-then-fix-it personality.

My supervisor liked me, but my sloppiness at keeping track of people's transactions—which in those days involved writing down numbers with a pen and paper—made me unfit for the job. My supervisor warned me that unless I improved quickly, she would be forced to let me go. I knew I wasn't likely to get better at handling details. I was a failure at my first job.

I figured I had two ways to leave my job. I could get fired or—and here's the optimist emerging—I could get promoted. I wrote a letter to the Senior Vice President for the branch system, who was probably seven or eight layers of management above me, and described all my naïve suggestions for improving the bank. My ideas had one thing in common: They were impractical for reasons a twenty-one-year-old wouldn't yet appreciate. I closed my letter by asking for a rare and coveted spot on the management training program, a fast track to upper management. It was a long shot for a guy who had on his permanent work record some version of "Too incompetent to write numbers on a piece of paper."

I included in my letter a list of my qualifications that contained a witty reference to getting robbed twice at gunpoint in the course of my work, which was true. As luck would have it, the Senior Vice President was a 6'10" red-headed, bearded elf of a man who had a great sense of humor. He read my letter and invited me to his office for an interview.

The Senior Vice President told me that my suggestions for improving the bank were underwhelming, but he liked my sense of humor, and because of that had a hunch about my potential. A month later, I started the management training program. Somehow I'd failed my way to a much better job.

In my eight years at the bank, I was incompetent at one job after another. At various times I was a branch banking trainee, a project manager, computer programmer, product manager, lending officer, budget supervisor, and a few other jobs I've forgotten. I never stayed in one job long enough to develop any legitimate competence, and I'm not entirely sure additional experience would have helped in my case. It seemed as if my only valuable skill was interviewing for the next job. I got hired for almost every job I pursued in the bank, and each was a promotion and a raise. It was starting to seem as if I might be able to interview my way to some sort of senior executive position in which no one would notice I was totally skill-free. That was my hope.

My banking career ended when my boss called me into her office and informed me that the order had come down to stop promoting white males. The press had noticed that senior management was comprised almost entirely of white males, and the company needed to work harder to achieve something called "diversity." No one knew how many years that might take, so I put my résumé together and sent it to some of the other big companies in the area. I had officially failed at my banking career and, against all odds, my incompetence wasn't the cause.

The local phone company, Pacific Bell, unwisely offered me a job, and I accepted. Once again I got a big raise, thanks to my interviewing skills and to the fact that I had nearly completed my MBA at Berkeley, attending classes at night. I looked great on paper. Little did they realize that looking good on paper was my best skill.

A few weeks after leaving my job at Crocker, an acquiring bank fired everyone in the department I left behind. My failure as a banker allowed me to escape to a new job before the firing. This was one of many examples in which the universe makes sure there isn't much of a link between job performance in the corporate world and outcomes.

Pacific Bell put me on their version of the fast-track, which they referred to as being "in the binder." Higher levels of management kept printed lists of the up-and-comers in three-ring binders so they could mentor us and, one presumes, so they could hedge their bets in case one of us passed them on the management ladder. It's a bad idea to be a jerk to someone who might be your boss in five years.

About 60 percent of my job at Pacific Bell involved trying to look busy. I was in charge of budgeting, and the actual work was far from challenging, even for me. Most of my budget spreadsheets had formula errors, but that didn't matter because all the inputs from the various departments were complete lies and bullshit. If anything, my errors probably smoothed out some of the bullshit and brought it closer to truth. It was a truly absurd existence.

My biggest complaint was that smoking was allowed in offices in those days, and a chain smoker was in the cubicle next to me. I sat in a cloud of her tobacco stench all day. I tried asking her not to smoke, but all that did was turn her into an unfriendly smoker, and that wasn't an upgrade. I asked my boss to relocate my cubicle, but there were so many smokers that the new location had just as much of a tobacco fog.

As luck would have it, the company had a robust workplace safety program, and one day they passed around a document listing common workplace hazards and asked us to sign it. One of the listed hazards was secondhand smoke. The company encouraged employees to be proactive about safety, so I did just that. I declared my workplace a safety hazard and informed my boss that I would need to stay home until it was remediated. I don't think he took me seriously.

The next day I stayed home and called in to see if the hazard had been eliminated. My boss said it had not, so I cheerily thanked him for the update and said I would keep checking back. I was happy to do my part to make the workplace safer. Telecommuting wasn't yet practical because the Internet was still a zygote, so I didn't even need to work from home. So far, I had a paid day off and nothing but fresh air to breathe. My plan was working.

By day two, my boss's boss called and asked what the problem was. I explained the situation, and he listened. He was an engineer by training and couldn't find a flaw in my reasoning. I was applying the company policy exactly as it was intended. He wasn't a smoker, so I think he saw the point. I thanked him for listening and said I would check back periodically to see if the workplace was safe for me to return. I was professional and upbeat about it in part because I thought it was funnier that way.

I expected to get fired. And I expected to call the local newspaper afterwards and see if they wanted an interesting story. This was the first time I realized how attracted I am to controversy.

By day three, if I recall, my boss's boss called to say he discussed the issue with a few levels of management above and they agreed to make everything but their own private offices smoke-free. And they agreed to close their doors when they smoked. I returned to work, happy in the knowledge that my cubicle was relatively smoke free and, as a bonus, the smokers in senior management were closing their doors and turning their offices into extra-effective carcinogenic hot-boxes. It's hard to imagine a better result.

I thought my career at Pacific Bell was going well. I finished my MBA classes at Berkeley's evening program and probably moved ahead of a few people in "the binder." One day a District Manager position opened, and I was a contender, or so I thought. My boss's boss's boss called me into his office and explained that the order had come down to stop promoting white males. Pacific Bell had a diversity problem, and it might take years to fix it, if ever. My bid for upper management at Pacific Bell was officially a failure.

On the plus side, I no longer felt the need to give my employer my best efforts or even to work long hours for no extra pay. It was an unwanted freedom but freedom nonetheless. I took some time to work on my tennis game, and I started thinking seriously about a new direction, ideally one that didn't require me to have a boss.

I decided to revive a long-lost passion and try my hand at cartooning. But it was an unlikely dream given my complete lack of artistic talent and the rarity of success stories in that business. So I decided to try affirmations, which I will describe in more detail later in the book. I bought some art supplies, practiced drawing every morning before work, and wrote my affirmation fifteen times a day: "I, Scott Adams, will be a famous cartoonist."

CHAPTER 9

Deciding Versus Wanting

O ne of the best pieces of advice I've ever heard goes something like this: *If you want success, figure out the price and then pay it.* It sounds trivial and obvious, but if you unpack the idea, it has extraordinary power.

I know a lot of people who wish they were rich or famous or otherwise fabulous. They wish they had yachts and servants and castles, and they wish they could travel the world in their own private jets. But these are mere wishes. Few of these wishful people have *decided* to have any of the things they wish for. It's a key difference, for once you decide, you take action. Wishing starts in the mind and generally stays there.

When you *decide* to be successful in a big way, you acknowledge the price, and you're willing to pay it. That price might mean sacrificing your personal life to get good grades in school, pursuing a college major that is deadly boring but lucrative, putting off having kids, missing time with your family, or taking business risks that put you in jeopardy for embarrassment, divorce, or bankruptcy. Successful people don't wish for success; they decide to pursue it. And to pursue it effectively, they need a system. Success always has a price, but the reality is that the price is negotiable. If you pick the right system, the price will be a lot nearer what you're willing to pay.

I can't change the fact that success requires a lot of work. But if you learn to appreciate the power of systems over goals, you might lower the price of success just enough to make it worth a go.

CHAPTER 10

The Selfishness Illusion

During your journey to success, you will find yourself continually trying to balance your own needs with the needs of others. You will always wonder if you are being too selfish or not selfish enough. I'm glad I could be here to help you sort it all out.

For starters, when it comes to the topic of generosity, there are three kinds of people in the world:

1. Selfish
2. Stupid
3. Burden on others

That's the entire list. Your best option is to be selfish because being stupid or a burden on society won't help anyone. Society hopes you will handle your selfishness with some grace and compassion. If you do selfishness right, you automatically become a net benefit to society. Successful people generally don't burden the world. Corporate raiders, overpaid CEOs, and tyrannical dictators are the exceptions. Most successful people give more than they personally consume in the form of taxes, charity work, job creation, and so on. My best estimate is that I will personally consume about 10 percent of the total wealth I create over my career. The rest goes to taxes, future generations, startup investments, charity, and stimulation of the economy.

As a future or current rich person, you might pay far more than your share of taxes because of your selfish pursuit of income. Selfish successful people don't cause worry and stress for those who care about them. As a selfish successful person, you can be a role model for others. Selfish successful people can be fun company if they've squirreled away all they need and have no complaints to voice.

By selfishness, I don't mean the kind where you grab the last donut so your coworker doesn't get it. That wouldn't be enlightened selfishness because that sort of pettiness can bite you in the ass later. And it might rob you of some energy if you feel guilty about it or get caught.

The most important form of selfishness involves investing time on your fitness, eating right, pursuing your career, and still spending quality time with your family and friends. If you neglect your health or your career, you slip into the second category—stupid—which is a short slide to becoming a burden on society.

I blame society for the sad state of adult fitness in the Western world. We're raised to believe that giving of ourselves is noble and good. If you're religious, you might have twice as much pressure to be unselfish. All our lives, we are told it's better to give than to receive. We're programmed for unselfish behavior by society, our parents, and even our genes to some extent. The problem is that our obsession with generosity causes people to think short term. We skip exercise to spend an extra hour helping at home. We buy fast food to save time to help a coworker with a problem. At every turn, we cheat our own future to appear generous today.

So how can you make the right long-term choices for yourself, thus being a benefit to others in the long run and without looking like a selfish turd in your daily choices? There's no instant cure, but a step in the right direction involves the power of permission. I'm giving you permission to take care of yourself first so you can do a better job of being generous in the long run.

What?

You might be wondering how a cartoonist's permission to be selfish can help in any way. The surprising answer is that it can, in my opinion. If you've read this far, we have a relationship of sorts. It's an author-reader relationship, but that's good enough. We humans are wired to be easily influenced by the people who are in relationships with us, no matter what those relationships are. Sometimes we call that influence "peer pressure."

Sometimes it's called modeling or imitating. Sometimes it's learning by example. And most of the time it's just something we do automatically, without thinking.

Luckily, most of us have filters that prevent us from being influenced in the most obviously damaging ways. If I were to encourage you to buy a rifle with a high-powered scope and wait on a bridge for further instructions, you probably wouldn't do that. Influence works best when the person being influenced has no objection to the suggested change. Often all one needs is some form of *permission* to initiate a change, and it doesn't always matter what form the permission is in or if it even makes sense. I'm sure you already want to be fit and successful and happy. You already want to skip some of your chores at home or at work to take care of your own needs. I'm simply your cartoonist friend telling you that generous people take care of their own needs first. In fact, doing so is a moral necessity. The world needs you at your best.

I should pause here for my more literal readers and explain that being selfish doesn't mean you should let a runaway baby carriage roll into traffic if you think stopping it will make you ten seconds late for work. Humans are so emotionally and societally connected with each other that often the best thing we can do for ourselves is to help others. I'll trust you to recognize those situations. Being selfish doesn't mean being a sociopath. It just means you take the long view of things.

One of the more interesting surprises for me when I started making more money than I would ever spend is that it automatically changed my priorities. I could afford any car I wanted, but suddenly I didn't care so much about my possessions beyond the utility they provided. Once all my personal needs were met, my thoughts automatically turned to how I could make the world a better place. I didn't plan the transformation. It wasn't something I thought about and decided to do. It just happened on its own. Apparently, humans are wired to take care of their own needs first, then family, tribe, country, and the world, roughly in that order.

I'm sure there are plenty of selfish turds who make billions and spend it all on helicopters and mansions with never a thought given to the wellbeing of others. I meet a lot of super-successful people in my line of work, especially living in the San Francisco Bay Area, and my observation is that it's rare to find a selfish successful person. I assume some or even most successful people started out selfishly, but success changes you. It's not a coincidence that Brad Pitt helped rebuild homes after the Hurricane Katrina disaster or that Bill Gates is one of the most important philanthropists of all time. Success does that.

The healthiest way to look at selfishness is that it's a necessary strategy when you're struggling. In hard times or even pre-success times, society and at least one cartoonist want you to take care of yourself first. If you pursue your selfish objectives and do that well, someday your focus will turn outward. It's an extraordinary feeling. I hope you can experience it.

CHAPTER 11

The Energy Metric

We humans want many things: good health, financial freedom, accomplishment, a great social life, love, sex, recreation, travel, family, career, and more. The problem with all this wanting is that the time you spend chasing one of those desires is time you can't spend chasing any of the others. So how do you organize your limited supply of time to get the best result?

The way I approach the problem of multiple priorities is by focusing on just one main metric: my energy. I make choices that maximize my personal energy because that makes it easier to manage all the other priorities.

Maximizing my personal energy means eating right, exercising, avoiding unnecessary stress, getting enough sleep, and taking all other obvious steps. It also means having something in my life that makes me excited to wake up. When I get my personal energy right, the quality of my work is better, and I can complete it faster. That keeps my career on track. And when all of that is working, and I feel relaxed and energetic, my personal life is better, too.

You might be familiar with a television show that was called *The Dog Whisperer*. On the show, Cesar Millan, a dog training expert, helped people get their seemingly insane dogs under control. Cesar's main trick involves training the humans to control their own emotional states because dogs can pick up crazy vibes from the owners. When the owners learn to control themselves, the dogs calm down, too. I think this same method applies to humans interacting with other humans. You've seen for yourself that when a sad person enters a room, the mood in the room drops. And when you talk to a cheerful person who is full of energy, you automatically feel a boost. I'm suggesting that by becoming a person with good energy, you lift the people around you. That positive change will improve your social life, your love life, your family life, and your career.

When I talk about increasing your personal energy, I don't mean the frenetic, caffeine-fueled, bounce-off-the-walls type of energy. I'm talking about a calm, focused energy. To others, it will simply appear that you are in a good mood. And you will be.

Before I became a cartoonist, I worked in a number of awful corporate jobs. But I still enjoyed going to work partly because I exercised most evenings and usually woke up feeling good—and partly because I always had one or two side projects going on that had the potential to set me free. Cartooning was just one of a dozen entrepreneurial ideas I tried out during my corporate days. For years, the prospect of starting "my own thing" and leaving my cubicle behind gave me an enormous amount of energy.

This book is another example of something that gets my energy up. I like to think that someone might read this collection of ideas and find a few thoughts that help. That possibility is tremendously motivating for me. So while writing takes me away from my friends and family for a bit, it makes me a better person when I'm with them. I'm happier and more satisfied with my life. The energy metric helps make my choices easier.

Energy is a simple word that captures a mind-boggling array of complicated happenings. For our purposes, I'll define your personal energy as anything that gives you a positive lift, either mentally or physically. Like art, you know it when you see it. Examples will help.

For me, shopping is an energy killer. The moment I walk into a busy store, I feel the energy drain from my body. The exhaustion starts as a mental thing, but within minutes I feel as if my body has been through a marathon. Shopping is simply exhausting for me.

Your situation might be different. For some people, shopping is a high. It boosts energy. So using my example, a person like me should seek to minimize shopping (and I do) while a person who gets a buzz from it should indulge, so long as it doesn't take too much away from other priorities in life.

Managing your personal energy is like managing budgets in a company. In business, every financial decision in one department is connected to others. If the research and development group cuts spending today, eventually that will ripple through the organization and reduce profits in some future year. Similarly, when you manage your personal energy, it's not enough to maximize it in the short run or in one defined area. Ideally, you want to manage your personal energy for the long term and the big picture. Having one more cocktail at midnight might be an energy boost at the time, but you pay for it double the next day.

At this point in the book, allow me pause to acknowledge your entirely appropriate skepticism about my notion that organizing your life around the concept of personal energy is useful. I applaud your healthy skepticism. But I'll ask you to hold off on judging the usefulness of personal energy as an organizing principle until you see how it's woven into the following chapters.

By analogy, imagine explaining the idea of capitalism to someone who had never heard of it. You'd be greeted with severe skepticism and legitimate questions:

> Wouldn't it cause you to cut expenses now and underinvest?
>
> Wouldn't it cause you to become sort of a jerk to your employees?
>
> Wouldn't it cause you to cheat your customers whenever you can?

The honest answer to all those concerns is yes, they are entirely valid. Capitalism is rotten at every level, and yet it sums up to something extraordinarily useful for society over time. The paradox of capitalism is that adding a bunch of bad-sounding ideas together creates something incredible that is far more good than bad. Capitalism inspires people to work hard, to take reasonable risks, and to create value for customers. On the whole, capitalism channels selfishness in a direction that benefits civilization, not counting a few fat cats who have figured out how to game the system for a short while.

You have the same paradox with personal energy. If you look at any individual action that boosts your personal energy, it might look like selfishness. *Why are you going skiing when you should be working at the homeless shelter, you selfish bastard?!*

My proposition is that organizing your life to optimize your personal energy will sum up to something incredible that is more good than bad.

As I write this paragraph, my family and a few good friends are wondering why I'm selfishly lagging behind and not meeting them for an afternoon of sitting in the sun. I'll get there soon. And when I do, I'll feel energized, satisfied, and far more fun to be around. No one will think worse of me in the long run for being thirty minutes behind for a full day of fun that they have already started. But everyone will appreciate that I'm in a better mood when I show up. That's the tradeoff. Like capitalism, some forms of selfishness are enlightened.

Matching Mental State to Activity

One of the most important tricks for maximizing your productivity involves matching your mental state to the task. For example, when I first wake up, my brain is relaxed and creative. The thought of writing a comic is fun, and it's relatively easy because my brain is in exactly the right mode for that task. I know from experience that trying to be creative in the midafternoon is a waste of time. By 2:00 PM, all I can do is regurgitate the ideas I've seen elsewhere. At 6:00 AM, I'm a creator, and by 2:00 PM I'm a copier.

Everyone is different, but you'll discover that most writers work either early in the morning or past midnight. That's when the creative writing juices flow most easily.

When lunchtime rolls around, I like to grab a quick snack and go to the gym or play tennis. At that time of day, I have plenty of energy, so exercise seems like a good idea. I know that if I wait until after dinner I won't have the sort of physical energy I need to talk myself into exercising. In my twenties, I could exercise at midnight with no problem, so keep in mind that you might want to make adjustments to your daily patterns over time.

My comic-creating process is divided into two stages to maximize my natural energy cycles. In the late afternoon and early evening, my hand is steady. I'm relaxed from exercising and ready to do some simple, mindless, mechanical tasks such as drawing the final art for *Dilbert* or paying bills online. It's the perfect match—my lower energy level to a mindless task. Without the exercise, I wouldn't have the attention span to handle boring tasks. I would be bouncing around from one thing to another and accomplishing nothing.

Most people aren't lucky enough to have a flexible schedule. I didn't have one either for the first sixteen years of my corporate life. So I did the next best thing by going to bed early and getting up at 4:00 AM to do my creative side-projects. One of those projects became the sketches for *Dilbert*.

You might not think you're an early morning person. I didn't think I was either. But once you get used to it, you might never want to go back. You can accomplish more by the time other people wake up than most people accomplish all day.

Simplifiers Versus Optimizers

Some people are what I call simplifiers, and some are optimizers. A simplifier will prefer the easy way to accomplish a task while knowing that some amount of extra effort might have produced a better outcome. An optimizer looks for the very best solution even if it means that the extra complexity increases the odds of unexpected problems. Allow me to compare and contrast the two approaches.

My wife, Shelly, is a world-class optimizer. I, on the other hand, cling to simplicity like a monkey on a coconut. As I write this chapter, we have plans tonight for a simple dinner thirty minutes from home followed by a movie that is near the restaurant. We'll stop to pick up friends who conveniently live on the shortest path to our destination. Once we get to the restaurant, we don't even need to move the car. Parking will be easy, the drive will avoid all rush hour traffic, and the timing allows for a leisurely evening with no worries. I, the simplifier, made these plans.

In about an hour, the optimizer in the family will return home from whatever she is optimizing and potentially introduce several changes to my plan. If the changes work, our evening will be even better than I imagined or perhaps more productive. That's great! But the changes will also introduce new opportunities for things to go wrong. This balance works well for Shelly because she has nerves of steel. I'm more like a squirrel that wandered into a Monster Truck rally. I don't have the constitution to optimize.

Tonight, Shelly might try to complete several urgent tasks before we leave, which might make us get a late start, but not too late. No big deal. Then perhaps Shelly will recommend that we drive her car, which has no gas, so we can refuel it on the way. She needs it in the morning and won't have much time then. But before we leave the house, Shelly might produce a shopping bag with an item that needs to be returned to the store that is "right on the way." Perhaps the receipt will be misplaced, which means there might be some negotiating in the store. All of this would make us fifteen minutes late for our dinner reservation and put us at risk of losing our table. That thought would spike my blood pressure until my head begins to look like the bottom of a thermometer, all red and bulbous. I would need to remind myself that Shelly makes her optimized plans work about 90 percent of the time. *Relax, Scott. Just relax.*

Allow me to predict the rest of the story as if narrating in real time. I might be exaggerating a little just to paint the picture.

As we leave the house, Shelly suggests we take a shortcut that I am not familiar with. I'm driving, and Shelly tells me that all I need to do is listen to her directions. No problem. At least I think it's no problem until her cell phone rings just when I need to know which way to go. Now Shelly is talking on the phone and solving some thorny issue like missile defense or climate change while occasionally saying things that sound as if they might be meant for me. Does "Right" mean I should turn right, or is she just agreeing with whoever she's talking to on the phone?

Soon I am lost, and I look to Shelly for help. She waives me off because she's deep into solving whatever problem is happening on the phone. I pull over and look at my watch. I get the brilliant idea of using GPS to find the store, but I'm not entirely sure which store it is. The shopping bag is in the trunk. So now I'm opening the trunk, finding the bag, and hoping to find the store's address on my smartphone. But my phone has no Internet connection on this stretch of highway. So I drive while holding my phone like a signal meter, waiting for a data icon to appear and hoping the police are not watching.

I find a signal, pull over, and try to find the store's address, but it takes forever on my phone. Finally, I got it! Now I enter the address into GPS, but I forget to change the route preferences from freeway to shortest route. Shelly sees me heading for an on ramp during rush hour traffic and starts gesturing in a way that means I should go in a different direction or possibly it means something about chopping wood or taxiing a plane. I can't interpret the gestures. I pull over and wait for the call to end.

By now we are so late that our plan will only work if the restaurant allows us to be thirty minutes late *and* if there is a different movie all four of us want to watch that starts later. This seems unlikely to me.

But like I said, 90 percent of the times we try to optimize, we get several errands completed, get a perfectly good table, have a nice meal, and see a movie that might even be better than the one we first picked. Optimizing works often enough to reinforce the habit.

The cost of optimizing is that it's exhausting and stress-inducing, at least for people like me. Sometimes I think I'm literally going to have a heart attack from all the optimizing. It also requires full concentration. I prefer simple, foolproof plans that allow my heart to beat normally and my mind to wander toward blissful thoughts of puppies and rose petals. (Update: Our dinner and movie followed my simple plan and worked flawlessly. Shelly took the night off from optimizing. My prediction of optimized mayhem did not come to pass. Imagining what might have gone wrong makes me look like more of a jerk than usual, which is funny, so I decided to leave this chapter intact.)

I have a bias for simplification, but surely there are situations in which optimizing is the better play. So how do you know which approach works better in a given situation?

If the situation involves communication with others, simplification is almost always the right answer. If the task is something you can do all by yourself or with a partner who is on your wavelength, optimizing might be a better path if you can control most variables in the situation. And realistically, sometimes you simply must get three hours of tasks completed in two hours, so we don't always have the luxury of being able to choose simple paths.

I prefer simplicity whenever I'm choosing a *system* to use. People can follow simple systems better than complicated ones. I'll give you some examples of that in later chapters about fitness and diet. The most optimized diet or fitness plan will also be the most complicated. But few people have enough willpower in reserve to follow complicated plans.

If you can't tell whether a simple plan or a complicated one will be the best, choose the simple one. If it's a coin toss, you might as well do whatever is easier.

If the cost of failure is high, simple tasks are better because they are easier to manage and control. Missing a dinner reservation isn't the end of the world, so doing some optimizing in that case is defensible. But if you are driving to an important business meeting, you don't want to don't want to pile on some errands that are "on the way" because that introduces unwanted stress and uncertainty.

In my career, I've always felt that my knack for simplicity was a sort of superpower. For example, when I draw *Dilbert*, I include little or no background art in most panels, and when I do, it's usually simple. That's a gigantic time-saver. I assume that other cartoonists retire early at least in part because they were optimizers, and that level of energy can be hard to sustain in the long run.

No one reads *Dilbert* comics for the artwork. I have the luxury of being able to do simple drawings directly on the computer using a Wacom Cintiq™ device (a computer screen on which you can draw). I type the dialog using a special font I created based on my own handwriting. Over the years, I have streamlined this system to the point I can bang out a comic in about an hour if I need to, although I usually take longer. *Dilbert* was designed from the start to be simple to create, and I continue to streamline the process. That simplicity has paid off big-time because it frees me to post and livestream every day, write books, do interesting side projects, and still enjoy life. **Update:** these days I have an art director who does the final art from my rough drafts.

Optimizing is often the strategy of people who have specific goals and feel the need to do everything in their power to achieve them. Simplifying is generally the strategy for people who view the world in terms of systems. The best systems are simple, and for good reason. Complicated systems have more opportunities for failure. Human nature is such that we're good at following simple systems and not so good at following complicated ones.

Simple systems are probably the best way to achieve success. Once you have success, optimizing begins to have more value. Successful people and successful businesses have the luxury of being able to optimize toward perfection over time. Startups often do better by slapping together something that is 80 percent good and seeing how the public responds. There's time to improve things later if the market cares about the product.

Another big advantage of simplification is that it frees up time, and time is one of your most valuable resources in the world. If you give an ant infinite time, it can move a mountain all by itself. In my case, I can run the equivalent of three separate careers (cartoonist, author, entrepreneur) in the same forty-hour week that would normally accommodate one job.

Simplification frees up energy, making everything else you do just a little bit easier. That's a huge deal. You don't want your job interview to go poorly because you completed four complicated errands on the way to the interview that turned you into a ball of stress. When you are trying to decide on optimizing or simplifying, think of your entire day, not the handful of tasks in question. In other words, maximize your personal energy, not the number of tasks.

As I mentioned earlier, we don't always have an option of choosing simplicity, especially if we have a thousand things to complete in a day, as Shelly often does. But it's a good idea to have an overarching plan to move toward simple systems as opportunities allow. You can chip away at the complexity of your life over time. Simplicity is a worthy long-term goal. That's how you will free your personal energy so you can concentrate it where you need it.

Sitting Position

Your brain takes some of its cues from what your body is doing. My experience is that when I sit in a position I associate with relaxation such as slumping on the couch, my brain will start the lazy relaxation subroutine. But if I sit with good posture, both feet on the floor, it seems that my body signals to my brain that it's time to concentrate on work.

Consistency might be more important than the specific position you choose. If you train yourself to do deep concentration when sitting on the couch with your laptop, that position might become a good place for you to work. Just don't make the mistake of using the same sitting position for work that you use for relaxation. If the couch is where you like to nap or watch television, it will probably be a poor place for doing serious work.

Sleep experts will tell you that the worst place to watch TV is in bed. If you do it often enough, you won't be able to fall asleep without watching something first. Watching a thought-provoking or emotion-grabbing show is a bad way to relax into your evening snooze. A better approach is to use your bed for sex, sleep, and nothing else.[7,8]

Likewise, it's a good idea to dedicate certain sitting positions and workspaces to work, and other spaces to relaxation or play. That makes your physical environment a sort of user interface for your brain, and it becomes a way to manipulate your energy levels and concentration. To change how you feel and how you think, you can simply change where you are sitting.

This is the sort of idea you're likely to dismiss as unimportant unless you try it yourself for an extended time. In my experience, the way I sit makes a huge difference to my productivity.

Tidiness

Tidiness is a personal preference, but it also has an impact on your energy. Every second you look at a messy room and think about fixing it is a distraction from your more important thoughts.

I realize that clutter and messiness don't affect everyone the same way. Some people need to have things just right, and others don't seem to mind living in chaos. My experience is that after straightening up my office and working through the piles of miscellaneous tasks, I feel more clear-headed and energetic. I don't assume my experience is universal, but the cause-and-effect in my case is so strong that I do recommend you experiment with it. All you need to do is pay attention to how you feel after you have tidied up your workspace compared to how you felt when it was a mess.

Cleaning and organizing your space is boring work, and you might never see it as a priority. One trick I've learned is that I automatically generate enthusiasm about tidying up if I know someone is stopping by. That's why it's a good idea to invite people over on a regular basis. It will inspire you to keep your space straightened up, and that might in turn cause your mind to have a bit more energy.

Knowledge and the Lack Thereof

One of the biggest obstacles to success—and a real energy-killer—is the fear that you don't know how to do the stuff that your ideal career plans would require. For example, you might have a terrific idea for a small business, but you don't know how to get a fictitious name, how to do your accounting, how to build a website, how to delegate work, and so on. When you don't know anything about a particular topic, it's easy to assume it would be too hard to learn it quickly. I run into that all the time, and I've developed a few tricks and workarounds you might find helpful.

When my first editor of comics called to offer me a contract for newspaper syndication, I quickly said yes, but I secretly worried that I didn't know how to do the coloring for the Sunday comics. I was in awe of the established cartoonists who seemed to color within the lines so perfectly. And what tools did they use? Were they using special marker pens or watercolors? Why was the color in the newspaper so perfect? I panicked—I didn't know the basic tools of my own chosen profession.

And I didn't think I could learn in a reasonable time. I wondered if this was all taught in some sort of art school.

I decided to confess to my editor my lack of knowledge in the comic coloring arts. She simply said, "The printer does that." All I needed to do was indicate which colors I wanted where. End of story. (Today, I use Photoshop and point the paint bucket icon at the area I want to color. It's probably the easiest work-related thing I do all week.)

And so it has been with about 90 percent of the topics that have intimidated me throughout my career. When you start asking questions, you often discover that there's a simple solution, a website that handles it, or a professional who takes care of it for a reasonable fee. Keep in mind that every time you wonder how to do something, a few hundred million people have probably wondered the same thing. And that usually means the information has already been packaged and simplified and in some cases sold. But it's usually free for the asking.

I'm a big fan of flash research, the type you do in less than a minute using Google. You might think a topic is too complicated to master for your use, but you might learn otherwise in less than a minute if you bother to check. I do that process several times per week; I wonder how complicated something is, and I check it out. I'm routinely surprised that someone else had the same question and left a simple breadcrumb trail for me to follow.

My business mistakes, of which there have been plenty, were rarely caused by not being able to find the information I knew I needed. Most of my problems were caused by my own bad decisions, lack of skill, and bad luck. I can't think of a single instance in which I was stopped because there was information I needed but couldn't find. I think most entrepreneurs would tell you the same thing. And more to the point of this chapter . . . when you know how to do something, you feel more energized to take it on.

Don't Be an Asshole

One of the best ways to pollute the energy in a group situation is by being a total asshole. You might succeed in getting people fully energized, but it won't be in a productive way. If you think of your bad behavior as a lifestyle choice, as in "being yourself" or "just being honest," you might be ignoring the cost to your personal energy. When you piss off the people around you, there is bound to be some blowback and wasted efforts cleaning up the mess you made. It can all be quite distracting and draining.

I've noticed that an alarming number of people have adopted the asshole lifestyle and decided it works well enough to stay on that path. While the word asshole usually makes you think of males, in this context it's gender-inclusive.

There's no single, agreed definition of what it means to be an asshole. It might include selfishness, arrogance, mean-spiritedness, or any number of character flaws. You know asshole behavior when you see it. And if you're normal, you've probably been one for at least a few minutes of your life.

I would define an asshole as anyone who chooses to make the lives of others less pleasant for reasons that don't appear productive or necessary. Asshole behaviors:

1. Changing the subject to themselves.
2. Dominating conversation.
3. Bragging.
4. Cheating or lying.
5. Disagreeing with any suggestion no matter how trivial.
6. Using honesty as a justification for cruelty.
7. Withholding simple favors out of some warped sense of social justice.
8. Abandoning the unspoken rules of civil behavior such as saying hello or making eye contact.

I assume asshole behavior exists because it feels good when you do it. In that sense, it's like an addiction. The long-term cost of being an asshole can't be good for the person immersed in the lifestyle, but it must feel good in the short term.

That's a bad tradeoff. Your self-interest is best served by being a reasonable person whenever you can muster it.

Priorities

It's useful to think of your priorities in terms of concentric circles, like an archery target. In the center is your highest priority: you. If you ruin yourself, you won't be able to work on any other priorities. So taking care of your own health is job one.

The next ring—and your second-biggest priority—is economics. That includes your job, investments, and even your house. You might wince at the fact that I put economics ahead of your family, friends, and the rest of the world, but there's a reason. If you don't get your personal financial engine working right, you place burdens on everyone else, from your family to the entire country.

Once you are both healthy and financially sound, it's time for the third ring: family, friends, and lovers. Good health and sufficient money are necessary for a base level of happiness, but you need to be right with your family, friends, and romantic partners to enjoy life to the fullest.

The next rings are your local community, country, and the world, in that order. Don't even bother trying to fix the world until you get the inner circles of your priorities under control.

The problem, of course, with my neat little model of priorities is that life is never that simple. You can't tell your boss that your assignment will be late because you want to go for a long, healthy walk. All your priorities overlap and conflict. What you need is a simple rule for keeping your priorities on track while handling the inevitable exceptions. One simple way to keep your priorities straight is by judging how each of your options will influence your personal energy. It's not a foolproof gauge, but if you know a particular path will make you feel more stressed, unhealthy, and drained, it's probably the wrong choice. Right choices can be challenging, but they usually charge you up. When you're on the right path, it *feels* right, literally.

For example, if your boss asks you to work the weekend to finish something worthwhile and challenging, you might be willing to give up a little of your personal life and health. Meaningful work can be energizing. And if things work out, perhaps you will be promoted because of your efforts. That's a tradeoff that might charge you up both in the short and long run.

On the other hand, if your boss routinely asks you to work overtime for no good reason other than to claw through piles of brain-deadening administrative work, you probably need to look for a new job.

In both examples, your boss is asking for extra work at the cost of your higher priorities, but only one of those situations increases your personal energy.

The risk with using energy as your guide is that there are plenty of bad choices that also get you energized in the short run. But realistically, we all know, for example, that shoving cocaine up our noses isn't a good long-term strategy. The dumb choices are generally obvious.

When I speak of priorities, I don't mean that in terms of what you love the most. You can love your family more than you love your job and still spend all day working so they have food and opportunities. Priorities are the things you need to get right so the things you love can thrive.

CHAPTER 12

Managing Your Attitude

Your brain is wired to continuously analyze your environment, your thoughts, and your health, then to use that information to generate a sensation you call your attitude. You know from experience that you do better work and enjoy life more when your attitude is good. If you could control your attitude directly as opposed to letting the environment dictate how you feel on any given day, it would be like a minor superpower. It turns out you *do* have that superpower. You can control your attitude by manipulating your thoughts, your body, and even your environment.

Your attitude affects everything you do in your quest for success and happiness. The best way to manage your attitude is by understanding your basic nature as a moist robot that can be programmed for happiness—if you understand the user interface. For starters, pay attention to the attitudes of people who have recently exercised. You'll discover they are almost always happy and upbeat. Now also look at the attitudes of people who have recently eaten versus people who are hungry. You'll see a big difference. Tired people are grumpy; rested people are less so. Exercise, food, and sleep should be your first buttons to push if you're trying to elevate your attitude and raise your energy. But what if you're doing everything right on the physical health front yet are still not enjoying life as much as you think you should?

A simple trick you might try involves increasing your ratio of happy thoughts to disturbing thoughts. If your life doesn't provide you with plenty of happy thoughts to draw upon, try daydreaming of wonderful things in your future. Don't worry that your daydreams are unlikely to come true. The power of daydreaming is like the power of well-made movies that can make you laugh or cry. Your body and your mind will respond automatically to whatever images it spends the most time pondering. If you imagine winning a Nobel Prize, buying your own private island, or playing in the NBA, don't worry that those things are unlikely. Putting yourself in that imagination-fueled frame of mind will pep you up. Imagination is the interface to your attitude. You can literally imagine yourself to higher levels of energy.

This is the same reason why you should avoid exposure to too much news of the depressing type—and why it's a good idea to avoid music, books, and movies that are downers. Show me someone who you think is always in a good mood, and I'll show you a person who (probably) avoids overexposure to sad forms of entertainment. The easiest way to manage your attitude is to consume as much feel-good entertainment as you can.

Realistically, the last advice you want to hear when you are in a terrible mood is "Think of something happy." If you're experiencing genuine misfortune, you probably just need time and distance to recover. The daydreaming strategy is more of an everyday practice. It won't get you out of a deep slump. For the truly bad moods, exercise, nutrition, sleep, and time are the smart buttons to push. Once you get back to your baseline level of happiness, you'll be in a better position to get the benefits of daydreaming.

A powerful variation on the daydreaming method involves working on projects that have a real chance of changing the world, helping humanity, or making a billion dollars (or all three). I try to have one or more change-the-world projects going at all times.

As I write this, I'm shopping for money partners to launch an idea that has the potential to be transformative to the entire economy of the world, assuming it works as planned. Will it succeed? Probably not. But the idea of it excites me and raises my energy today. That's my system.

By the time you read this book, a lot will have transpired with those efforts. Any new business is risky. But for the past several months, my attitude and energy have been sky-high because of the potential my project has for making the world a better place. My imagined future acts as a cue to keep my mood elevated today.

You might be thinking this is all well and good for famous authors and cartoonists, but ordinary people don't have many chances to change the world. I disagree. Ideas change the world routinely, and most of those ideas originate from ordinary people. You might have a patent idea, a product idea, or a process idea that could change the world. Before my cartoon career, I had plenty of big ideas that didn't work out. When one idea failed, I usually had two more to take its place. And every one of my ideas had real-world potential even if the odds were bad.

Don't worry if your idea is a long shot. That's not what matters right now. Today, you want to daydream of your idea being a huge success so you can enjoy the feeling. Let your ideas for the future fuel your energy today. No matter what you want to do in life, higher energy will help you get there.

Another benefit of having a big, world-changing project is that you almost always end up learning something valuable in the process of failing. And fail you will most of the time, so long as you are dreaming big. But remember, goals are for losers anyway. It's smarter to see your big idea projects as part of a system to improve your energy, contacts, and skills. From that viewpoint, if you have a big, interesting project in the works, you're a winner every time you wake up.

When I consider taking on a new, big project, I first ask myself who I know that would be helpful and who might want to partner, invest, or just give advice. In my universe of contacts, which is fairly huge at this point in my career, I would say I met half of those folks in the process of failing at one thing or another. And if I ask myself what skills and knowledge I need for my next big idea, invariably that means drawing on knowledge I gained while circling the drain in some doomed project of yore.

Let's say you wake up tomorrow full of energy for your exciting new project. Over the course of the day, you learn a few things in the process of doing your research, and you meet some new people along the way. If you accomplish that and nothing more, you're succeeding—no matter what happens with your project.

The Power of Smiling

Smiling makes you feel better, even if your smile is fake. This is the clearest example of how your brain has a user interface. When you're in a bad mood, the physical act of forcing a smile may trigger the feel-good chemistry in your brain that is associated with happiness. [1,2]

The smiling-makes-you-happy quirk is part of the larger and highly useful phenomenon of faking-it-until-you-make-it. You'll see this two-way causation in a wide variety of human activities. Later, I'll tell you that putting on exercise clothes will make you feel like working out. I've also discovered that *acting* confident makes you *feel* more confident. Feeling energetic makes you want to play a sport, but playing a sport will also make you feel energetic. Loving someone makes you want to have sex, but having sex also releases the bonding chemicals that make you feel love. High testosterone can help you win a competition, but winning a competition can also sometimes raise your testosterone. [3-7] Being tired makes you want to lie down, but lying down when you are rested can put you in the mood for a nap. Feeling hungry can make you want to eat simple carbs, but eating simple carbs can make you feel hungry.

Understanding this two-way causation is highly useful for boosting your personal energy. To take advantage of it, I find it useful to imagine my mind as a conversation between two individuals. It feels that way because I think in sentences, as if talking to another entity that is also me. One of me tends to be rational and reasonable while the other me is a bit more emotional and instinctual. When the rational me wants to perk up the emotional me—the part of me that controls my energy—the rational me has to act as a programmer and push the right buttons.

The next time you're in a gloomy mood, try smiling at a stranger you pass on the street. You'll be surprised how many people reflexively return the smile, and if you smile often enough, eventually that cue will boot up the happiness subroutine in your brain and release the feel-good chemicals you desire.

As a bonus, smiling makes you more attractive to others. [8-10] When you're more attractive, people respond to you with more respect and consideration, more smiles, and sometimes even lust. That's exactly the sort of thing that can cheer you up.

If you're not comfortable faking a smile, try hanging around friends who are naturally funny. Equally important, avoid friends who are full-time downers. You want friends with whom you can share both the good and the bad, but you aren't a therapist. Walk away from the soul-suckers. You have a right to pursue happiness and an equal right to run as fast as you can from the people who would deny it.

Success Premium

I've come to believe that success at anything has a spillover effect into other areas. You can take advantage of that effect by becoming good at things that require nothing but practice. Once you become good at a few unimportant things such as hobbies or sports, the habit of success stays with you on more important quests. When you've tasted success, you want more. And the wanting gives you the sort of energy that is critical to even greater success.

In my case, I was extra-talented at several trivial games:

◆ Scrabble
◆ Pool
◆ Tennis
◆ Ping-Pong

In each of those activities, my so-called "talent" was little more than the result of insane hours of practice. I grew up in a small town where there weren't many ways to stay entertained. We had the world's cheapest and worst pool table in our converted cellar/bomb shelter. It was so cheap that it didn't have a slate bed, and it became warped soon after we got it. A soft shot meant your ball would roll to one side and stay there. On two ends of the table there wasn't enough room between the table and the wall, so I needed to raise the cue stick toward the corner of the ceiling and shoot down on the cue ball. It wasn't pretty. But I spent so many hours by myself practicing shot after shot that I became quite good. At this point in my life, the only people who can regularly beat me at pool are the ones who wasted an even greater proportion of their youth practicing.

The same was true for Scrabble, Ping-Pong, and tennis. I'm better than 99 percent of the world* in each of those games because I put in more practice time than 99 percent of the world. There's no magic to it.

Thanks to my experience with these exceedingly minor successes, I have a realistic understanding of how many hours it takes to be good at something. That keeps me from bailing out of things too soon. But more importantly, I know what winning feels like (great!), and it energizes me to seek more of it. In that sense, I'm like any trained animal seeking a treat.

A great strategy for success in life is to become good at something, anything, and let that feeling propel you to new and better victories. Success can be habit-forming.

Pick the Delusion That Works

When my dog, Snickers, wants to play fetch in the backyard, she follows me around and stares into my eyes with freakish intensity, as if using her Jedi doggy powers on me. More often than not, it works. I know what she wants, and I take a break from work to accommodate her. The interesting thing is that I'm not sure she understands that it's my choice whether I go play with her or not. Her mental control of me works so reliably that I'm certain she thinks all that matters is how hard she stares at me and how vividly she imagines† herself chasing a tennis ball.

To me, the fascinating thing about Snickers' flawed view of the world is that it works perfectly. She has a system for getting what she wants, and it *seems* to work, albeit for different reasons than she imagines. The deeper reality is that I've learned that her stares mean it's time for some tennis ball fun. My experience with Snickers begs bigger questions: Are humans so different from dogs? Do we have totally flawed assumptions

---

*I'm including in my estimate babies, coma patients, and people who have never heard of those games.

†I'm assuming there is such a thing as a dog-brained version of imagination. If not, don't let the analogy derail the point.

about reality? Do our flawed assumptions work for reasons we don't understand?

Athletes are known to stop shaving for the duration of a tournament or to wear socks they deem lucky. These superstitions probably help in some small way to bolster their confidence, which, in turn, can influence success. It's irrelevant that lucky socks aren't a real thing. The socks can still improve an athlete's performance even if the wearer has a flawed idea of why.

Our brains have a limited capacity to know the true nature of reality. Most times, our misconceptions about reality are benign, sometimes even helpful. Other times, not so much.

Physicists tell us that reality seems to depend on the observer. If you and I were to move through an empty and infinitely large universe at the same speed and in the same direction, we would feel as if we weren't moving at all. And arguably that would be the case since movement only makes sense in relation to other objects. If you and I strap identical rockets to our backs in this otherwise empty universe, face the same direction, and fire them up, it would be a matter of debate whether we were moving at all. You'd feel the rocket press into your back, but you wouldn't know if that was the beginning of forward momentum or just a pressure on your back that relaxed after some time. (Okay, okay, a pressure on your body in space will always cause movement, and you're smart enough to know that. But let's assume for this example that you didn't pay attention in science class.)

Reality outside the quantum world of particles and waves might be fixed and objective, at least according to most scientists. But how we think of our reality is clearly subject to regular changes. We've all had the experience of meeting someone for the first time and having a wildly inaccurate first impression, which in turn drove the way we acted toward them. Later, once you know more about the person, you start behaving differently. The external reality doesn't change, but your point of view does. In many cases, it's your point of view that influences your behavior, not the universe. And you can control your point of view even when you can't change the underlying reality.

For over a decade, I've been semi-famous for creating *Dilbert*, but I'm still generally unrecognized in public. When I meet people for the first time without the benefit of a full introduction, I'm treated like any other stranger. But if the topic of my job comes up, people immediately become friendlier, as if we had been friends forever. The underlying reality doesn't change, but the way people think of me does, and that changes how they act.

My main point about perceptions is that you shouldn't hesitate to modify your perceptions to whatever makes you happy because you're probably wrong about the underlying nature of reality anyway. If I had to bet my life, I'd say humans are more like my dog trying to use psychic powers on me to play fetch than we are like enlightened creatures who understand their environment at a deep level. Every generation before us believed, like Snickers, that they had things figured out. We now know that every generation before us was wrong about a lot of it. Is it likely that you were born at the tipping point of history in which humans know enough about reality to say we understand it? This is another case where humility is your friend. When you can release your ego long enough to view your perceptions as incomplete or misleading, you set yourself free to imagine new and potentially more useful ways of looking at the world.

In practical terms, the reason my dog happily plays fetch three times a day is that she chose an illusion that works. I believe she imagines she can make me play fetch just by visualizing it. You, too, can sometimes get what you want by adopting a practical illusion. Reality is overrated and impossible to understand with any degree of certainty. What you do know for sure is that some ways of looking at the world work better than others. Pick the way that works even if you don't know why.

The process of writing this book is a good example of what I'm talking about. Writing a book is hard work—far harder than most people imagine, and you probably imagine it to be plenty hard. The way I motivate myself to take on a task this large is by imagining that I have fascinating and useful things to say that will help people. The reality might be quite different. I can't see the future, so I have the option of imagining it in whatever way gives me the greatest utility. I choose to imagine that the book will do well because that illusion is highly motivating. It increases my energy.

The worst-case scenario is that I will spend a lot of time writing a book no one will find useful or entertaining. It wouldn't be the first time. But because of my imaginary future in which the book is enjoyed by millions, I'm able to find great satisfaction in writing it. No matter what reality delivers in the future, my imagined version of the future has great usefulness today.

Free yourself from the shackles of an oppressive reality. What's real to you is what you imagine and what you feel. If you manage your illusions wisely, you might get what you want, but you won't necessarily understand why it worked.

CHAPTER 13

It's Already Working

You already passed the first filter for success. By reading this book, you've established yourself as a seeker of knowledge. Seekers obviously find more stuff than the people who sit and wait. Your decision to read this book is confirmation that you are a person of action who has a desire to be more effective. I'm reinforcing that thought to help lock it in.

You also get some automatic benefits by reading this book and in a sense joining a new group. Specifically, you're on your way to being one of the people who have read this book. When you define yourself as a member of any group, you start to automatically identify with the other members and take on some of the characteristics of the group.[1,2] The group of people who read books on how to succeed is an excellent group to be in. You're the people most likely to succeed because you're putting real thought and research into the mechanics of success.

You might fairly ask if this is a trivial point. I suppose everyone who reads this book will be influenced in a different way, and there's no way to accurately measure this sort of thing. But I think you've seen examples in your life in which a person changes dramatically upon becoming a member of a group, getting a promotion, or doing anything that redefines them as a person.

The most striking example of this effect happened to me. My cartooning skills improved dramatically within a week of United Media offering to syndicate *Dilbert*. The simple knowledge that I had become an official professional cartoonist had a profound effect on unlocking whatever additional talent I had.

In my corporate career, I often marveled at how people changed as soon as they got promoted from worker bee to management. I saw one of my coworkers transform from a hesitant and unimpressive personality to confident and powerful within two months of his promotion. Obviously there was some acting involved, but we are designed to become in reality however we act. We fake it until the fake becomes real. Our core personality doesn't change, but we quickly adopt the mannerisms and skills associated with our new status and position.

So congratulations on being a person who studies the mechanics of success. It's a bigger deal than you might realize.

CHAPTER 14

My Pinky Goes Nuts

By the early nineties, *Dilbert* was a modest success, but it was nowhere near the point where I was tempted to quit my day job at the phone company, Pacific Bell. I would wake at 4:00 AM to draw before my commute, then work all day in my cubicle prison and come home to draw all night. My time windows for drawing were always compressed, which put a lot of pressure on my drawing hand. The overuse took its toll, and my pinky finger started to spasm whenever I touched pen to paper, making it nearly impossible to draw.

I went to see my doctor in the Kaiser healthcare system, and he said he might know another doctor in the system who was an expert in this very problem. By wonderful coincidence, one of the world's most knowledgeable doctors in this specific condition worked for Kaiser, and his office was just down the road from my home.

Pause for a moment to reflect on that. There were over six billion people in the world at the time, and one of the most published experts in the field worked within walking distance of my home. Never assume you understand the odds of things.

I met with the doctor, and he diagnosed me in minutes. I had something called a focal dystonia, common to people who do repetitive tasks with their hands, primarily musicians, draftsmen, and the like. It wasn't carpal tunnel. This was different.

"What's the cure?" I asked.

"Change jobs," he said. "There's no known treatment."

I walked out of the doctor's office with my life demolished. My dream of being a cartoonist for the rest of my life was over—unless I found a way to be the first person in the world to beat a focal dystonia.

What were the odds of that?

It took a few days for my baseline optimism to return. My optimism is like an old cat that likes to disappear for days but I always expect to return. And frankly, the cumulative events in my life up to that point gave me a sensation of being exempt from the normal laws of chance, and that's probably the source of my optimism. If you need a more scientific-sounding explanation, perhaps I'm just bad at estimating the odds of things. Or perhaps I have selective memory and forget the things that don't work out. No matter how you explain the perception, I like to leave room for hope, and hope has practical value. I don't need to know why my long shots seem to work out more often than my faulty brain expects; I just need to perceive—accurately or not—that it happens.

Realistically, what were my odds of being the first person on Earth to beat a focal dystonia? One-in-a-million? One-in-ten-million? I didn't care. That one person was going to be me. Thanks to my odd life experiences and odder genes, I'm wired to think things will work out well for me no matter how unlikely it might seem.

In a follow-up visit, the doctor asked if I would be willing to try a few experimental treatments, joining with some other human guinea pigs he was working with. I agreed. For weeks, I tried various hand exercises, went to a physical therapist, and tried meditation, galvanic skin response feedback, self-hypnosis, and anything else that seemed like it made a grain of sense. Nothing worked, not even a little.

Meanwhile, I tried to draw *Dilbert* left-handed, which I could do with a lot of effort. I'm mildly ambidextrous, but drawing with the non-dominant hand is highly difficult. I could tell that drawing lefty wouldn't be a long-term solution. My drawings were extra terrible for a few months during that period.

I tried strapping down my pinky, but that had the odd effect of making the rest of my hand dysfunctional. And it hurt like crazy.

I also lost the ability to write simple notes using pen on paper, which was obviously inconvenient at my day job. Oddly, the pinky spasms only happened during the specific motions involved in writing or drawing. Otherwise, my hand was 100 percent normal. Weirder still, when I drew with my left hand, the pinky on my *right* hand would spasm, so obviously the wiring in my brain was the problem, not the architecture of my hand. My experience was consistent with the doctor's research. None of the people who have focal dystonias seem to have anything abnormal in the structure of their hands. It seems to be some sort of short-circuit in the brain.

At my day job, as I sat through endless boring meetings, I started practicing my drawing motion by touching my pen to paper and then pulling up before the spasm started. I tapped the page hundreds of times per meeting under the table on the notepad on my lap. My idea was to rewire my brain gradually, to relearn that I can touch pen to paper and not spasm. I was literally trying to hack my brain. My hypnosis training (more on that later) suggested this might be possible.

Over the next several weeks, I noticed I could hold my pen to paper for a full second before feeling the onset of a pinky spasm. Eventually, it was two seconds, then five. One day, after I trained myself to hold pen to paper for several seconds without a spasm, my brain suddenly and unexpectedly rewired itself and removed the dystonia altogether. Apparently, I broke the spasm cycle and reinforced the non-spasm association.

And so I was the first person in the world to cure a focal dystonia, at least as far as I know. It's entirely possible that I'm wrong about that since I can't know what everyone else is doing or what worked for them. Still, it was an unlikely result.

I went back to drawing right-handed, paced myself, and didn't have a problem again for years. My hand doctor said I'm part of the literature on this topic now, although my name is not mentioned.

In 2004, after once again doing too much drawing in a compressed time, the dystonia returned. This time, I tried a smarter workaround. I made an educated guess that somewhere in the world a company was probably making a computer tablet or screen on which I could draw my comic. My hypothesis was that drawing on a computer would feel different enough from pen on paper that the dystonia wouldn't trigger, even though I would be drawing with a stylus just as I would with a pen.

I did some Google searches and discovered that Wacom was making a special computer monitor for artists. I ordered it the same day. In a week, it was up and running. As I hoped, drawing on the computer was different enough that the dystonia didn't reoccur. And by not reinforcing the trigger and the spasm, I allowed the dystonia to simply fade away. I'm sure it would come back if I tried drawing or writing on paper for a long time, but since that will never happen, it's a non-issue in my life.

By the way, drawing on the Wacom product cut my total workday in half. The focal dystonia was a case of extraordinary bad luck for a cartoonist. But when I got done beating the dystonia problem to death and rifling through its pockets, I came out the other end a far more efficient cartoonist. The quality of my drawing improved dramatically on the Wacom because it's so easy to make small adjustments. On balance, I came out way ahead.

CHAPTER 15

My Speaking Career

Here's an example of how useful it is to have a smart friend. When I was a few years into my cartooning career, a Canadian woman called and asked if I would give a speech to an organization of petroleum engineers in Calgary. I said I didn't do that sort of work, but she persisted, saying the organization had asked for me, specifically, and that there would be a healthy payment involved. I continued to balk because I had very little flexibility in my schedule. At that point, I was still working my full-time job at Pacific Bell and creating *Dilbert* before and after work, plus on weekends. Traveling to Canada just wasn't a practical option.

The Canadian woman suggested I give her a price for my services that would make it worthwhile for me. If my price was too high, at least she could take it back to her organization and say she tried. She made it sound as if I would be doing her a favor to come up with a price for something I didn't want to do.

But how does one come up with a price for giving a speech? I had no idea where to start. So I did what anyone in that situation would do: I sought out a friend who might have a template for this sort of thing.

At the time, *Dilbert* was syndicated by an organization within United Media, a large licensing and syndication business headquartered in New York City. I figured correctly that someone in that hierarchy would have experience with professional speaking. I called a Senior Vice President who had once been a bestselling author and had decades of experience that made him far more qualified than I was for this sort of topic.

I put the question to him: "What should I say is my price for speaking?" I told him that I would be perfectly happy to price myself out of the job. He said, "Ask for five thousand dollars. If they say no, you avoid a trip to Canada." I laughed at his suggestion, knowing that I wasn't worth that kind of money. But I had my plan. I practiced saying "five thousand dollars" until I thought I could say it without laughing. I called back my Canadian contact. That conversation went like this:

Canadian: "Did you come up with a price?"

Me: "Yes . . . five thousand dollars."

Canadian: "Okay, and we'll also pay for your first-class travel and hotel."

I flew to Canada and gave a speech.

As time went by and *Dilbert* became more well-known, more speaking requests flowed in, often several per day. I raised my price to $10,000. The requests kept coming. I tried $15,000. The requests accelerated. By the time I got to $25,000, the speakers bureaus started to see me as a source of bigger commissions and advised me to raise my price to $35,000, then $45,000. The largest offer I ever turned down because of a scheduling conflict was $100,000 to speak for an hour on any topic I wanted.

All of this was possible because I had access to a smart friend who told me how to find the simple entry point into the speaking circuit. All I needed to do was overprice myself and see what happened. As simple as that sounds in retrospect, I doubt I would have taken that path on my own. I think I would have politely declined the invitation.

It's a cliché that who you know is helpful for success. What is less obvious is that you don't need to know CEOs and billionaires. Sometimes you just need a friend who knows different things than you do. And you can always find one of those.

CHAPTER 16

My Voice Problem Gets a Name

Six months after losing my voice back in 2005, I still didn't know what the source of the problem was. It was immensely frustrating. I don't mind a fair fight, but this invisible, nameless problem was kicking my ass, and I didn't even know which direction to punch back. I needed a name for my condition. I figured if I knew its name, that would lead me down the trail for a cure.

But how could I find the name for a condition that was unfamiliar to two ear-nose-throat doctors, two voice specialists, a psychologist, a neurologist, and my general practitioner? There was only one creature smarter than all those doctors put together: the Internet. (Yes, it's a creature, okay?)

I opened a Google search box and tried a variety of voice-related keywords. I found nothing useful. My searches were too broad. Then something interesting happened. It's a phenomenon that people in creative jobs experience often, but it might sound unfamiliar to everyone else. Suddenly, out of nowhere, two totally unrelated thoughts—separated by topic, time, and distance—came together in my head. For some reason, I had a spontaneous memory of the problem with my drawing hand that I had experienced several years earlier. In that case, I lost control of my pinky. Now I was losing control of my voice. Could the two problems be related?

I entered the search string "voice dystonia" because my hand problem was called a focal dystonia. Bingo. The search popped up a video of a patient who had something called spasmodic dysphonia, a condition in which the vocal cords clench involuntarily when making certain sounds. I played the video and recognized my exact voice pattern—broken words and clipped syllables—coming out of the patient in the video. Now I had its name: spasmodic dysphonia, which I discovered is often associated with other forms of dystonia. As I learned with further research, it's common for someone who has one type of dystonia to get another. (Luckily, it doesn't tend to progress beyond that.)

My secret assassin had a name, and now I knew it. It felt like a turning point.

I printed out a description of spasmodic dysphonia and took it to my doctor. He referred me back to one of my ear-nose-throat doctors, who in turn referred me to a doctor I hadn't yet seen in the Kaiser healthcare system. She turned out to be an expert in that exact condition. Within ten seconds of opening my mouth in her office, the doctor confirmed the diagnosis. I had a classic case.

"What's the cure?" I whispered.

"There is none," she replied.

But that isn't what I heard. The optimist in me translated the gloomy news as "Scott, you will be the first person in the world to be cured of spasmodic dysphonia." And I decided that after I cured myself, somehow, someway, I would spread the word to others. I wouldn't be satisfied simply escaping from my prison of silence; I was planning to escape, free the other inmates, shoot the warden, and burn down the prison.

Sometimes I get that way.

It's a surprisingly useful frame of mind.

CHAPTER 17

The Voice Solution That Didn't Work

The standard treatment for spasmodic dysphonia involves a doctor pushing a needle filled with Botulinum toxin (better known by its trade name Botox) through the front of the patient's neck and hoping it finds the vocal cord region on the back side of the throat. Doctors who give the shot use a mixture of experience, guesswork, and electronics to find the right dose and the right place to put it. If all goes well, a patient's voice can normalize after a few weeks and stay functional for several weeks until the Botox wears off. Then you repeat. It's a creepy process because the needle is so thick you need an initial shot of local anesthetics just to keep you from going through the roof when the second needle goes in. It's not a fun day.

I tried the Botox treatments for a few months. It worked well enough to say, "I do" when I got married to Shelly, which was great, but it wore off in a few weeks. Subsequent shots were not nearly as effective. The problem is that no two shots were ever the same, in part because you never knew how much Botox was still in your system, and partly because the shot never hits exactly the same place twice. And the dose is always either ramping up or wearing off. It only hits the right dose level by accident for a week or so on the way up or down.

The bigger issue for me was that the Botox masked the impact of any other type of treatment I might want to experiment with. I made the decision to stop the Botox and give myself a chance to find a lasting fix.

With the Botox, I knew I could find a way to talk almost normally some of the time. Without it, I was pretty much shut off from the world of the living. I was taking a big swing at a ball I couldn't even see.

CHAPTER 18

Recognizing Your Talents and Knowing When to Quit

I f you have world-class talent—for anything—you probably know it. In fact, your parents probably dragged you from place to place when you were young to develop your skill. But world-class talent is such an exception that I prefer ignoring it for this book. I'm going to focus on ordinary talents and combinations of ordinary talents that sum up to something extraordinary. In the case of ordinary talent, how do you know which of your various skills can be added together to get something useful? It's a vital question because you want to put your focus where it makes a real difference.

One helpful rule of thumb for knowing where you might have a little extra talent is to consider what you were obsessively doing before you were ten years old. There's a strong connection between what interests you and what you're good at. People are naturally drawn to the things they feel comfortable doing, and comfort is a marker for talent.

In my case, I was doodling and drawing obsessively from the time I could pick up a crayon. I never became a talented artist, but my high level of interest in drawing foreshadowed my career decades later. Granted, most kids enjoy art, and some enjoy it a lot more than others. But I was off the chart. I doodled all through my classes in school. I drew in the dirt with sticks. I drew in the snow. For me, drawing was more of a compulsion than a choice. Childhood compulsions aren't a guarantee of future talent.

But my unscientific observation is that people are born wired for certain preferences. Those preferences drive behavior, and that's what can make a person willing to practice a skill. A study that got a lot of attention in the past few years involved the discovery that becoming an "expert" at just about anything requires 10,000 hours of disciplined practice.[1] Author Malcolm Gladwell wrote about it in his book *Outliers*. Few people will put in that kind of practice for one skill. But early obsessions can predict which skills a kid might someday be good at.

Another clue to talent involves tolerance for risk. When I was in grade school, I often drew humorously inappropriate comics involving my teachers and fellow students. I would show them to classmates, and I enjoyed making them laugh, all the while knowing that getting caught by an authority figure meant a serious penalty. I was willing to take a significant personal risk for my so-called art, and this was in sharp contrast to my otherwise risk-averse lifestyle. People generally only accept outsized risk when they expect big payoffs. Drawing inappropriate comics made me happy. To me, it was worth the risk.

I owned a very used, very old motorcycle when I was a teen. I paid $150 from my earnings as an entrepreneurial mower of lawns, shoveler of show, and a farmer's incompetent assistant. The motorcycle was dangerous, of course, especially in the hands of a teen. I laid it down a few times on the local back roads. On a number of occasions, I barely missed deer, angry dogs, and other motorists. One day I was barreling across a field and drove the front wheel into a woodchuck hole, thus taking flight and miraculously landing on nothing hard in a field littered with large rocks. I enjoyed having a motorcycle, but it wasn't an obsession for me. And eventually I concluded that it wasn't worth the risk. Clearly I was not destined to be a motorcycle daredevil or motocross star. I wasn't willing to accept a high risk in return for the joy of riding. But when it came to comics, I eagerly accepted the risk of expulsion and great bodily harm that comes with insulting larger kids. My risk profile predicted my future.

When you hear stories about famous actors as kids, one of the patterns you notice is that before they were stars, they were staging plays in their living rooms and backyards. That's gutsy for a kid. A child who eagerly accepts the risk of embarrassment in front of a crowd—even a friendly crowd—probably has some talent for entertaining.

Consider the biographies of Bill Gates and Steve Jobs. As young men, both took legal risks in the field of technology. Bill Gates famously found ways to hone his technical skills by stealing time on a mainframe.[2]. Jobs' and Wozniak's first product involved selling technology that allowed people to steal long distance phone calls. Where there is a tolerance for risk, there is often talent.

Childhood obsessions and tolerance for risk are only rough guides to talent at best. As you grow and acquire more talents, your potential paths for success multiply quickly. That makes it extra hard to know which possibility among many would put you in a position of competitive advantage. Should you pursue a career that uses your knowledge of photography and software, or something that uses your public speaking skills and your gift for writing? There's no way to be completely sure which path will be most fruitful.

The smartest system for discerning your best path to success involves trying lots of different things—sampling, if you will. For entrepreneurial ventures, it might mean quickly bailing out if things don't come together quickly.

That approach might conflict with the advice you've heard all your life—that sticking with something, no matter the obstacles, is important to success. Indeed, most successful people had to chew through a wall at some point. Overcoming obstacles is normally an unavoidable part of the process. But you also need to know when to quit. Persistence is useful, but there's no point being an idiot about it.

My guideline for deciding when to quit is informed by a lifetime of trying dozens of business ideas, most of them failures. I've also carefully observed others struggling with the stay-or-quit decision. There have been times I stuck with bad ideas for far too long out of a misguided sense that persistence is a virtue. The pattern I noticed was this: Things that will someday work out well *start out* well. Things that will never work start out bad and stay that way. What you rarely see is a stillborn failure that transmogrifies into a stellar success. Small successes can grow into big ones, but failures rarely grow into successes.

To illustrate my point, consider the history of cell phones. Early cell phones had bad reception all the time. They dropped calls. They had few features. They were expensive. They didn't fit in your pocket. Yet cell phones were successful, at least in terms of demand, on day one. Despite the many flaws with cell phones—flaws that lasted decades—demand started brisk and stayed strong. The poor quality of the product made no difference. Cell phones started as a small success and grew.

Fax machines followed a similar path. The early fax machines were slow and spectacularly unreliable. They would eat your original and only sometimes deliver a legible copy to the other machine. Still, fax machines had demand from the beginning and grew until the age of computers rendered them less necessary.

The first personal computers were slow, expensive, non-intuitive, and crash-prone. And still the demand was explosive. In each of the examples, the quality of the early products was a poor predictor of success. The predictor is that customers were clamoring for the *bad* versions of the product before the good versions were even invented. It's as if a future success leaves bread crumbs that are visible in the present.

When FOX launched *The Simpsons* in 1989, it was a national phenomenon from day one. Everywhere I went, the topic of the Simpsons came up: "Did you see it?" Interestingly, as much as *The Simpsons* is rebroadcast in syndication, you won't often see that first season repeated. The reason, I assume, based on clips I've seen, is that by today's standards it would be judged to be embarrassingly bad. The original art looked amateurish, and the writing was violent, sophomoric slapstick. Compared to today, the first Simpsons season was an awful product. Again, the quality didn't predict success. The better predictor is that *The Simpsons* was an immediate hit despite its surface quality. It had the X-factor. In time, it grew to be one of the most important, creative, and best shows of all time.

My experience with *Dilbert* followed the same pattern. I submitted my original samples of *Dilbert* to several comic syndication companies in 1988. United Media offered me a contract and successfully sold it into a few dozen newspapers at its launch in 1989. A year later, sales to newspapers stalled, and United Media turned its attention to other comic properties. Over the next five years, I found a way to generate more interest in *Dilbert* by writing books and exploiting the Internet. The turning point for *Dilbert* came in 1993 after I started printing my email address in the margins of the strip. It was the first time I could see unfiltered opinions about my work. Until then, I'd relied on the opinions of friends and business associates, which had limited value because that group of folks rarely offered criticism. But WOW, the general public doesn't hold back. They were savage about my art skills—no surprise— and that was just the tip of the hateberg. But I noticed a consistent theme that held for both the fans and the haters: They all preferred the comics in which Dilbert was in the office. So I changed the focus of the strip to the workplace, and that turned out to be the spark in the gasoline.

But the thing that predicted *Dilbert*'s success in year one is that it quickly gained a small but enthusiastic following. My best estimate, based on shaky anecdotal evidence, is that 98 percent of newspaper readers initially disliked *Dilbert*, but 2 percent thought it was one of the best comics in the paper despite all objective evidence to the contrary. In other words, it had the X-factor on day one. And this brings me to a lesson I learned in Hollywood, or at least near Hollywood.

In the late nineties, I spent some time in the Los Angeles area trying to get a *Dilbert* TV pilot off the ground. The first attempt, which failed miserably, involved live actors portraying the *Dilbert* characters. During that process, I got to observe a test audience watch the pilot and register their opinions in real time. Moving graphs appeared on monitors so we could see the ebb and flow of the audience's enjoyment at each point in the show. I was chatting with the television executive in charge of the project and asked what the cut-off was for an acceptable test audience response. The executive explained that for television shows, the best predictor is not the average response. Averages don't mean much for entertainment products. What you're looking for is an unusually strong reaction from a subset of the public, even if the majority hates it. The *Dilbert* pilot got an okay response from the test audience, but no one seemed enthusiastic. The project went no further. But during the process, I learned enough about making a television show that the next attempt went far better. The animated *Dilbert* show ran for two half-seasons on the now-defunct UPN and got decent ratings for that tiny network. When that show got cancelled for reasons I describe later in this book, I emerged with just enough new skills, knowledge, and contacts that my odds of someday getting a *Dilbert* movie made are far higher. I've been trying and failing to get a *Dilbert* movie made for about twenty-five years. Every failure so far has been because of some freakish intersection of bad luck. But bad luck doesn't have the option of being that consistent forever. I'll get it done unless I die first.

Back to my point, the Enthusiasm Model, if I may call it that, is a bit like the X-factor. It's the elusive and hard-to-predict quality of a thing that makes some percentage of the public nuts about it. When the X-factor is present, the public—or some subset of it—picks up on it right away. For the excited few, the normal notions of what constitutes quality don't apply. In time, the products that inspire excitement typically evolve to have quality, too. Quality is one of the luxuries you can afford when the marketplace is spraying money in your direction and you have time to tinker.

Consider the first iPhone. The first version was a mess, yet it was greeted with an almost feverish enthusiasm. That enthusiasm and the enormous sales that followed funded improvements until the product became superb.

One of the best ways to detect the X-factor is to watch what customers *do* about your idea or product, not what they *say*. People tend to say what they think you want to hear, or what they think will cause the least pain. What people *do* is far more honest. For example, with comics, a good test of potential is whether people stick the comic to the refrigerator, post it, email it to friends, put it on a blog page, or do anything else active.

You might be tempted to think that sometimes an idea with no X-factor and no enthusiastic fans can gain those qualities over time. I'm sure it's happened, but I can't think of an example in my life. It's generally true that if no one is excited about your art/product/idea in the beginning, they never will be.

If the first commercial version of your work excites no one to action, it's time to move on to something different. Don't be fooled by the opinions of friends and family. They're all liars.

If your work inspires some excitement and some action from customers, get ready to chew through some walls. You might have something worth fighting for.

CHAPTER 19

Is Practice Your Thing?

One day, a friend's three-year-old was playing around on our tennis court* along with a bunch of teenagers. Some kids were shooting baskets at the hoop on one end. A few kids were firing tennis balls at each other, and others were slapping volleyballs around. But the three-year-old was intensely practicing the art of hitting a tennis ball. He would bounce it once, lock his eyes on it, and swing the racket. He hit the ball a lot more often than you'd expect for a three-year-old, but that wasn't the interesting part. I watched for several minutes as he worked alone, ignoring older kids around him. He's an otherwise social kid, but this simple task of hitting a tennis ball captured his focus. He hit it again and again and again.

Then it got stranger. I decided to give him an impromptu lesson on the proper way to swing a racket. Remember, he's three. He barely had language skills. I asked for the racket, saying I wanted to show him how to swing, and amazingly—for a three-year-old—he handed it over. He looked at me and absorbed every word I said. I demonstrated how to hold the racket and how to swing. He tried it and with some coaching duplicated my swing, more or less. He was fully coachable at the age of three. Some adults—maybe most—never have that capability. As I walked away, he went back to his solitary practice amid a foaming sea of teenagers. Again. Again. Again.

---

*Yes, I do realize that mentioning the tennis court at my house makes me sound like a gigantic douchebag, but I couldn't figure out how to tell the story in a less douchey way.

I know this kid well, and tennis is the fourth or fifth sport he's picked up the same way. He watches how it's done, on television or in person, then he imitates and practices endlessly. I've never seen him get bored while practicing.

There's no denying the importance of practice. The hard part is figuring out *what* to practice.

When I was a kid, I spent countless bored hours in my bedroom on winter nights trying to spin a basketball on one finger. Eventually I mastered that skill only to later learn that it has no economic value. In a similar vein, none of my past bosses have ever been impressed with my ability to juggle up to three objects for as long as fifteen seconds, or to play Ping-Pong left-handed. I can also flip a pen in the air with one hand while swiping my other hand under it just as it takes off—which looks cooler than it sounds—then I catch it cleanly after a full rotation. These and other skills have not served me well. It matters what you practice.

My observation is that some people are born with a natural impulse to practice things while others find mindless repetition without immediate reward to be a form of torture. Whichever camp you're in, it probably won't change. It's naïve to expect the average person to embrace endless practice in pursuit of long-term success. It makes more sense to craft a life plan for yourself that embraces your natural inclinations, assuming you're not a cannibal. Most natural inclinations have some sort of economic value if you channel them right.

A good start for deciding where to spend your time is an honest assessment of your ability to practice. If you're not a natural "practicer," don't waste time pursuing a strategy that requires it. You know you won't be a concert pianist or a point guard in the NBA. That's not necessarily a bad thing. You're not doomed to mediocrity. You simply need to pick a life strategy that rewards novelty-seeking more than mindless repetition. For example, you might want to be an architect, designer, home builder, computer programmer, entrepreneur, website designer, or even doctor.

Those professions all require disciplined study, but every class will be different. And later in your career, all your projects are likely to be unique. Your skills will increase with experience, which is the more fun cousin of practice. Practice involves putting your consciousness in suspended animation. Practicing is not living. But when you build your skills through an ever-changing sequence of experiences, you're alive.

CHAPTER 20

Managing Your Odds for Success

The primary purpose of schools is to prepare kids for success in adulthood. That's why it seems odd to me that schools don't have required courses on the systems and practices of successful people. Success isn't magic; it's generally the product of picking a good system and following it until luck finds you. Unfortunately, schools barely have the resources to teach basic coursework. Students are on their own to figure out the best systems for success.

If we can't count on schools to teach kids the systems of success, how else will people learn those important skills? The children of successful people probably learn by observation and parental coaching. But most people are not born to highly successful parents. The average kid spends almost no time around highly successful people, and certainly not during the workday when those successful people are applying their methods. The young are intentionally insulated from the adult world of work. At best, kids see the television and movie versions of how to succeed, and that isn't much help.

Books about success can be somewhat useful. But for marketing reasons, a typical book is focused on a single topic to make it easier to sell—and packed with filler to get the page count up. No one has time to sort through that much filler.

When I speak to young people on the topic of success, as I often do, I tell them there's a formula for it. You can manipulate your odds of success by how you choose to fill out the variables in the formula. The formula, roughly speaking, is that every skill you acquire doubles your odds of success.

The Success Formula: Every skill you acquire doubles your odds of success.

Notice I didn't say anything about the level of proficiency you need to achieve for each skill. I didn't mention anything about excellence or being world-class. The idea is that you can raise your market value by being *merely* **good**—not extraordinary—at more than one skill.

In California, for example, having one common occupational skill plus fluency in Spanish puts you at the head of the line for many types of jobs. If you're also a skilled public speaker (good but not great) and you know your way around a PowerPoint presentation, you have a good chance of running your organization. To put the Success Formula into its simplest form:

Good + Good > Excellent

Success-wise, you're better off being good at two complementary skills than to be excellent at one. I'm ignoring the outlier possibility that you might be one of the best performers in the world at some skill or another. That can obviously be valuable, too. But realistically, you wouldn't be reading this book if you could throw a baseball a hundred miles per hour or compose hit songs in your head.

When I say each skill you acquire will double your odds of success, that's a useful simplification. Obviously, some skills are more valuable than others, and the twelfth skill you acquire might have less value than each of the first eleven. But if you think of each skill in terms of doubling your chances of success, it will steer your actions more effectively than if you assume the benefit of learning a new skill will get lost in the rounding. Logically, you might think it would make more sense to either have an accurate formula for success or none at all. But that's not how our brains are wired. Sometimes, an entirely inaccurate formula is a handy way to move you in the right direction—if it offers the benefit of simplicity. I realize that's not an obvious point, so allow me to give you an example.

A handy trick you'll learn from résumé writing experts is to ask yourself if there are any words in your first draft that you would be willing to remove for $100 each. Here's the simple formula:

Deleting Each Unnecessary Word = $100

When you apply the formula to your résumé, you surprise yourself by how well the formula helps you prune your writing to its most essential form. It doesn't matter that the $100 figure is arbitrary and that some words you remove are more valuable than others. What matters is that the formula steers your behavior in the right direction. As is often the case, simplicity trumps accuracy. The $100 in this case is not only inaccurate, it's entirely imaginary. And it still works.

Likewise, I think it's important to think of each new skill you acquire as doubling your odds of success. In a literal sense, it's no more accurate than the imaginary $100 per deleted word on your résumé, but it still helps guide your behavior in a productive direction. If I told you that taking a class in website design during your evenings might double your odds of career success, the thought would increase the odds that you will act. If instead I only offer you a vague opinion that acquiring new skills is beneficial, you won't feel particularly motivated. When you *accept without necessarily believing* that each new skill doubles your odds of success, you effectively hack (trick) your brain to be more proactive in your pursuit of success. Looking at the familiar in new ways can change your behavior even when the new point of view focuses on the imaginary.

I'm a perfect example of the power of leveraging multiple mediocre skills. I'm a rich and famous cartoonist who doesn't draw well. At social gatherings, I'm usually not the funniest person in the room. My writing skills are good, not great. But what I have that most artists and cartoonists do not have is years of corporate business experience plus an MBA from Berkeley's Haas School of Business. In the early years of *Dilbert*, my business experience served as immediate fodder for the comic. Eventually I discovered that my business skills were essential in navigating *Dilbert* from a cult hit to a household name. My combined mediocre skills are worth far more than the sum of the parts. If you think extraordinary talent and a maniacal pursuit of excellence are necessary for success, I say that's just one approach and probably the hardest. When it comes to skills, quantity often beats quality.

This would be a good time to tell you what kind of student I was in Berkeley's MBA program. In my first semester, I often had the lowest grades in the class. I worked hard and rose to scholastic mediocrity through brute force. In the end, all that mattered is that I learned skills that complemented my other meager talents.

When I combined my meager business skills with my bad art skills and my fairly ordinary writing talent, the mixture was powerful. With each new skill, my odds of success increased substantially. But there was still one more skill I acquired in my day job at Pacific Bell that ended up mattering a lot: I knew how to use the Internet before most people had even heard of it.

My day job at Pacific Bell involved demonstrating a new thing called the World Wide Web, later known as the Internet, to potential customers. I saw the possibilities early, and when *Dilbert* stalled in newspaper sales, I suggested moving it to the Internet to generate more exposure, as sort of a back-door marketing plan. I wanted people to read *Dilbert* online, then request it in their local newspapers. And that's what happened. *Dilbert* was the first syndicated comic to run for free on the Internet, although in the beginning it ran a week behind newspapers. Today it's hard to imagine that it ever seemed a huge risk to put *Dilbert* on the Internet for free. There were concerns that piracy would go through the roof (it did) and that newspapers would see the Internet as competition and cancel (none did). In the days when more exposure was a good thing, the piracy helped far more than it hurt.

My early comfort with technology helped me in another big way, too. I was the first syndicated cartoonist to include my email address in every strip. Email was still a geeky novelty in the early nineties, and some of my business associates worried that client newspapers would consider my email address a form of advertisement. But my business training told me I needed to open a direct channel to my customers and modify my product based on their feedback. That's exactly what I did,* making it a workplace-focused strip as readers requested. From there, *Dilbert* took off.

Recapping my skill set: I have poor art skills, mediocre business skills, good but not great writing talent, and an early knowledge of the Internet. And I have a good but not great sense of humor. I'm like one big mediocre soup. None of my skills are world-class, but when my mediocre skills are combined, they become a powerful market force.

My sixteen years in corporate America added half-a-dozen other useful skills to the mix as well. I managed people, did contract negotiations, made commercial loans, wrote business plans, designed software, managed projects, developed systems to track performance, contributed to technology strategies, and more. I took company-paid classes in public speaking, time management, managing difficult people, listening, business writing, and lots of other useful topics. During my corporate career, I finished my MBA classes in the evening while working full time. I was a learning machine. If I thought something might someday be useful, I tried to grasp at least the basics. In my cartooning career, I've used almost every skill I learned in the business world.

Another huge advantage of learning as much as you can in different fields is that the more concepts you understand, the easier it is to learn new ones. Imagine explaining to an extraterrestrial visitor the concept of a horse. It would take some time. If the next thing you tried to explain was the concept of a zebra, the conversation would be shorter. You would simply point out that a zebra is a lot like a horse but with black and white stripes. Everything you learn becomes a shortcut for understanding something else.

---

*Changing art to satisfy customers probably makes real artists ill just thinking about it. I considered myself an entrepreneur, not an artist, so I had no trouble being flexible with my so-called art.

One of my lifelong practices involves reading about world events every day, sometimes several times a day. Years ago, that meant reading a newspaper before work. Now it usually involves checking X whenever I have a minute or two of downtime. The great thing about reading diverse perspectives from the fields of business, health, science, technology, politics, and more is that you automatically see patterns in the world and develop mental hooks upon which you can hang future knowledge. The formula for knowledge looks something like this:

The Knowledge Formula: The More You Know, the More You *Can* Know.

If your experience of reading the news is that it's always boring, you're doing it wrong. The simple entry point for developing a news-reading habit is that you only read the topics that interest you, no matter how trivial they might be. That effectively trains you to enjoy the time you spend reading the news—even if the only thing you look at involves celebrity scandals and sports. In time, your happy experience reading the news will make you want to enjoy it longer. You'll start sampling topics that wouldn't have interested you before. At first, perhaps you'll do little more than skim the headlines. But in time, you'll find yourself drawn in. It will feel easy and natural—the sign of a good system. If I had suggested starting every morning by reading the hard news in *The Wall Street Journal*, it would feel daunting for many people, and it's unlikely you would follow through. A smarter approach is to think of learning as a system in which you continuously expose yourself to new topics, primarily the ones you find interesting.

My one caution about reading the news every day is that it can be a huge downer if you pick the wrong topics. Personally, I try to avoid stories involving tragic events and concentrate on the more hopeful topics in science, technology, and business. I don't ignore bad news, but I don't dwell on it. The more time you spend exposing yourself to bad news, the more it will weigh on you and sap your energy. I prefer stories about breakthroughs in green technology, even knowing that 99 percent of those stories are pure bullshit. I don't read the news to find truth, as that would be a foolish waste of time. I read the news to broaden my exposure to new topics and patterns that make my brain more efficient in general and to enjoy myself because learning interesting things increases my energy and makes me feel optimistic. Don't think of the news as information. Think of it as a source of energy.

CHAPTER 21

The Math of Success

You can't directly control luck, but you can move from a game with low odds of success to a game with better odds. That seems like an obvious strategy, and you probably think you already do it. The hard part is figuring out the odds of any given game, and that's harder than it looks.

Several years ago, I gave a talk to a fifth-grade class. I started by asking them to finish my sentence. The sentence was "If you play a slot machine long enough, eventually you will . . ." The class yelled out in unison "WIN!" As most adults know, that is exactly the wrong answer. Slot machines are engineered to make everyone but the casino a loser in the long run. But kids don't know that. I presume they confused the benefits of persistence, which is drilled into them as kids, with the actual odds of succeeding.

If you're reading this book, you're probably an adult or soon to become one, and you understand the odds of slot machines. If you play them, you probably think of it as recreation and not an investment. But are you equally clear about the odds that rule over other areas of your life?

I'll give you another example about odds using my favorite topic: tennis. For a period of about seven years, I played tennis once a week with the same friend. He beat me 100 percent of the time. In the early years, his wins made sense because his game was stronger in every way. Eventually, my shot-making improved to the point where I felt I should have been winning, but I never did. I could get close, but I lost every match during those years. I didn't feel as if I was choking from the psychological pressure because I typically perform better in stressful situations. My natural optimism always tells me I'm going to pull a rabbit out of the hat and win against all odds no matter how far behind I am. That feeling is so strong in me that the only reason it isn't classified as mental illness is that it works more often than you'd expect.

So I wasn't getting psyched out by my losing record, and my strokes were good enough. Why did I lose every match against this particular opponent? I would routinely win against players who seemed about the same level as him. My losing streak was a mystery that dogged me for years. Apparently, I had some sort of blind spot about . . . what? How could I learn to see the thing I couldn't see? And if I saw it, would it help me win?

My tennis partner and I were good friends off the court, and we chatted a lot about our matches. I was always on the lookout for him to inadvertently spill his tennis secrets. I got little hints here and there as we talked about what was working and what wasn't on any given day. Our tennis conversations swirled around in my brain for years until one day the pattern revealed itself.

Some of the most powerful patterns in life are subtle. This tennis pattern was extraordinarily so. The quick explanation is that while I was playing tennis, my opponent was doing math. He was a card counter with a tennis racket. Over the course of several decades of tennis, he had learned the odds associated with just about everything that can happen on a tennis court.

Learning the odds with tennis is harder than it looks because so much of it is counter-intuitive. For example, when your opponent hits a forehand-to-forehand shot that takes you wide, leaving half of his court unguarded, most amateurs would try for a blistering forehand winner up the line into the open court. That shot was almost always my choice, and I missed it about 80 percent of the time. It turns out that hitting down the line when you're moving at a right angle to your target is exceptionally challenging for a weekend player. The down-the-line shot works best when you have time to set up and step toward it. Hitting down the line while on the run only *feels* like it would be easy. The illusion is surprisingly strong. Every time I missed a down-the-line shot I was surprised, no matter how many times in a row I missed the same way. I assumed I would be able to lock in that shot if I just tried it a few more times. It turns out I was wrong about that—for years.

I could give a dozen more tennis examples where the odds are exactly opposite of how they feel when you're on the court. And I could give you a dozen examples of how my opponent always played the high-percentage shots while cleverly goading me into one low-percentage shot after another. The point is that while we all think we know the odds in life, there's a good chance you have some blind spots. Finding those blind spots is a big deal.

In time, I learned to avoid the low-percentage tennis shots more often, and I won our matches about half the time, exactly as our shot-making skills would predict. I mentioned earlier in the book that seeing tennis as a game of stealing time from your opponent allows you to move to a higher level. That's true, but managing time only helps if you're also taking the high-percentage shots.

So how does any of this help you?

The idea I'm promoting here is to see the world as math, not magic. It would've been easy for me to assume my tennis losing streak was due to my lacking the will to win. Or perhaps I might have thought my losses were lessons from the Creator of the Universe, who realized I needed help maintaining a socially appropriate level of humility. But no, it was just math.

If you find yourself in a state of continuous failure in your personal life or career, you might be blaming it on fate or karma or animal spirits or some other form of magic—when the real reason is simple math. There's usually a pattern, but it might be subtle. Don't stop looking just because you don't see the pattern in the first seven years.

The future is thoroughly unpredictable when it comes to your profession and your personal life. So the best way to increase your odds of success—in a way that might look like luck to others—is to systematically become good but not amazing at the types of skills that work well together and are highly useful for just about any job. This is another example in which viewing the world as math (adding skills together) and not magic allows you to move from a strategy with low odds of success to something better. I call this building a Talent Stack. (Note: The Talent Stack strategy has become standard advice in the success field. This book is where it started.)

I made a list of the skills in which I think every adult should gain a working knowledge. I wouldn't expect you to become a master of any, but mastery isn't even necessary. Luck has a good chance of finding you if you become merely good in most of these areas. I'll make a case for each one, but here's the preview list.

Public speaking
Psychology
Business writing
Accounting
Design (the basics)
Conversation skills
Overcoming shyness
Second language
Golf
Proper grammar
Persuasion
Technology (hobby level)
Proper voice technique

I'll defend the economic value of each of these skills in the rest of this chapter.

Public Speaking

I took one public speaking class in college. It helped a little. I took two more classes in public speaking during my corporate career. The company paid for both. Those classes helped a little, too. Then one day my employer—the local phone company—announced they would pick up the tab for any employee who took the Dale Carnegie class on their own time. Anyone who wanted to learn more could attend a presentation in the big lecture room. I was curious and had heard good things about Dale Carnegie courses, so I decided to go and see what it was all about.

The Regional Director for Dale Carnegie, whose name I inexplicably remember twenty years later—Tony Snow—gave the shortest and most persuasive sales pitch I have ever seen. I'll condense it further here, but the essence was this: "Instead of describing the Dale Carnegie course myself, I've asked two of your fellow employees who took the course to tell you what they think." He introduced the first guy and walked off. Tony Snow was done selling.

My fellow employee bounded onto the stage like he had just won the lottery. His energy and enthusiasm were infectious. He had no notes. He prowled the stage and owned it. We, the audience, locked onto him like a tail and let him wag us. He was funny, expressive, engaging, and spontaneous. It was the best speech by a non-professional I had ever seen. I could tell he loved every second on stage, and yet he had the discipline to keep things brief.

When he was done, Tony Snow thanked him and introduced the second speaker. The second guy was completely different in style from the first speaker but every bit as good. He was enjoying himself. He projected. He was clear and concise. He owned us.

When he was done, Tony Snow thanked the audience and told us how we could get more information about the course. Tony Snow: magnificent bastard.

I signed up that day.

There are several flavors of Dale Carnegie courses. I don't remember what my particular course was called, and it has probably changed names by now. The focus was on public speaking, but for reasons that took a long time for me to understand, Dale Carnegie didn't classify it as a speaking course. It had a broader agenda.

On day one, our instructor explained the Dale Carnegie method he would be employing. Rule one was that no one would ever be criticized or corrected. Only positive reinforcement would be allowed, from the instructor and from the other students. I was immediately skeptical. How was I supposed to learn if I didn't know what I was doing wrong?

The next rule was that every person would speak to the rest of the class during each session, but we had to volunteer to go next. This rule is more important than you might first think because most of the people in the class were deathly afraid of public speaking. The instructor acknowledged that sometimes the class would need to sit quietly for long periods waiting for the next volunteer. And wait we did.

That first day of the course, we all sat there motionless like frightened squirrels, hoping someone else would go first. For some reason, going first seemed extra bad even though we all knew we would go eventually. The instructor stood in front of the frozen class and waited patiently, not judging, clearly having gone through this before.

Eventually someone volunteered, then another. Our speaking assignment was something simple. I think we simply had to say something about ourselves. For most people, including me, this was a relatively easy task. But for many in the class, it was nearly impossible. One young lady who had been forced by her employer to take the class was so frightened that she literally couldn't form words. In the cool, air-conditioned room, beads of sweat ran from her forehead down to her chin and dropped onto the carpet. The audience watched in shared pain as she battled her own demons and tried to form words. A few words came out, just barely, and she returned to her seat defeated, humiliated, broken.

Then an interesting thing happened. I rank it as one of the most fascinating things I have ever witnessed. The instructor went to the front and looked at the broken student. The room was dead silent. I'll always remember his words. He said, "Wow. That was brave."

My brain spun in my head. Twenty-some students had been thinking this woman just crashed and burned in the most dramatically humiliating way. She clearly thought the same thing. In four words, the instructor completely reinterpreted the situation. Every one of us knew the instructor was right. We had just witnessed an extraordinary act of personal bravery, the likes of which one rarely sees. That was the takeaway. Period.

I looked at the student's face as she reacted to the instructor's comment. She had been alone in her misery, fighting a losing fight. But somehow the instructor understood what was happening inside her, and he respected it. I swear I saw a light come on in her eyes. She looked up from the floor. She had a reprieve. She was still in the fight.

The next week, she volunteered to speak again. (See how powerful this volunteering thing is? She owned the choice.) She didn't do well, but she got through it without perspiring or locking up, and the instructor praised her for her progress.

By the end of the course some weeks later, every member of the class could have sold Tony Snow's product. Every time we spoke, we got compliments from the instructor and sometimes other students. We got applause. It felt great. Today when I see a stage and a thousand people waiting to hear me speak, a little recording goes off in my head that says, *Today is a good day. I'm the happiest person in the room. The audience only gets to listen, but I get to speak, to feel, to be fully alive. I will absorb their energy and turn it into something good. And when I'm done, there's a one hundred percent chance people will say good things about me.*

There are several takeaways from that story. The most important is the transformative power of praise versus the corrosive impact of criticism. I've had a number of occasions since then to test the powers of praise, and I find it an amazing force, especially for adults. Children are accustomed to a continuous stream of criticisms and praise, but adults can go weeks without a compliment while enduring criticism both at work and at home. Adults are starved for a kind word. When you understand the power of honest praise (as opposed to bullshitting, flattering, and sucking up), you realize that withholding it borders on immoral. If you see something that impresses you, a decent respect for humanity insists you voice your praise.

"Wow. That was brave," is the best and cleanest example I've heard in which looking at something in a different way changed everything. When the instructor switched our focus from the student's poor speaking performance to her bravery, reality itself shifted. Positivity is far more than a mental preference. It changes your brain, literally, and it changes the people around you. It's the nearest thing we have to magic.

Another lesson I learned from my Dale Carnegie experience is that we don't always have an accurate view of our own potential. I think most people who are frightened of public speaking can't imagine they might feel different as a result of training. Don't assume you know how much potential you have. Sometimes the only way to know what you can do is to test yourself.

Psychology

It's hard to imagine any business or social activity that doesn't require a basic understanding of how the human brain perceives the world. Almost any decision you make is in the context of managing what other people will think of you. We're all in the business of selling some version of ourselves. Psychology is embedded in everything we do.

For example, a real estate salesperson might show you the worst house first, knowing it will make you appreciate the better home you see later—which might make you reach deeper in your pockets. A car salesman knows that a high sticker price will make the eventual negotiated price look better than it would have otherwise. Salespeople know they can manipulate buyers by controlling what they compare.

A building contractor knows that when customers see the house during the framing phase, the rooms will look too small. Later, when the rooms are finished and furnished, they look larger. A smart builder warns the customers in advance that everything will look smaller in the framing phase. That way the customer doesn't flip out. That's psychology.

Even an engineer who deals mostly with the material world needs to understand how his boss feels, how customers think, and how users will perceive the product. You can't get away from the need to make decisions based on psychology.

The examples I gave are the common ones that most people figure out on their own. But given that the field of psychology is miles deep, most people only know the stuff that qualifies as common knowledge. How much more effective would you be if you had a greater understanding of psychology? Answer: a lot.

Psychology was a huge factor in my eventual success with *Dilbert*. By the time United Media offered me a syndication contract for *Dilbert*, my confidence had taken some direct hits. The other syndication companies had turned me down flat. One editor suggested that perhaps I could find an actual artist to do the drawing for me. Ouch. So when Sarah Gillespie, editor at United Media, called and offered a contract, I apologized for my poor drawing skills and suggested that perhaps she could pair me with someone who could do the artwork. Sarah, who evidently understood a lot about psychology, told me my drawing skill was fine; no improvement necessary. That triggered a highly unexpected change in my actual level of talent: It went up. Overnight, my drawing skill went from about a three on a scale of one-to-ten to about a six. That's still not good, but apparently it was good enough. The sudden improvement was entirely due to Sarah's compliment of my artistic ability. I became a more confident artist—and a better one—because she changed what I thought of my own talent. It was a Wizard of Oz moment.

When I look at the list of my personal failures and successes, one of the things that stand out is psychology. When I got the psychology right, either by accident or cleverness, things worked out better. When I was blind to the psychology, things went badly.

For example, after *Dilbert* became a hit, I briefly considered launching a second comic. I posted on the original *Dilbert* website some early samples of what I hoped would be a comic about a young Elbonian boy who didn't fit in. His name was Plop, and he was the only unbearded Elbonian in the world, and that included the women and babies. On day one, the Plop comic was a lot better than the first *Dilbert* comics, but not nearly as good as *Dilbert* had become by that time. What I didn't count on—my blind spot—was that my new comic would be compared to *Dilbert*, not to other new comics. Compared to *Dilbert*, it was flat and lacked an edge. Compared to all the new comics that launched that same year from unknown cartoonists, it was fairly competitive. Most of my feedback by email was of the "Keep your day job" variety along with "It's no Dilbert." I wouldn't have guessed that being a successful cartoonist would be a barrier to launching a new comic, but in my case it was. I could have saved a lot of time if I understood that in advance.

Dilbert was the first syndicated comic that focused primarily on the workplace. At the time, there was nothing to compare it to. That allowed me to get away with bad artwork and immature writing until I could improve my skills to the not-so-embarrassing level. Since the launch of *Dilbert* in 1989, dozens of cartoonists have tried to enter the workplace-comic space and got clobbered by unfavorable comparisons to a mature *Dilbert*. If I were to disguise my identity and launch a new workplace comic tomorrow, with all new characters, readers would compare it to *Dilbert*, and it wouldn't stand a chance.

For the past twenty years or so, I have been in a few dozen meetings on the topic of turning *Dilbert* into a feature film. I always get the question of how we could make a *Dilbert* movie different enough from the TV show *The Office* or the cult movie *Office Space*. The implication is that the quality of a *Dilbert* movie might be less important to its success than whatever the public reflexively compares it to. Quality is not an independent force in the universe; it depends on what you choose as your frame of reference.

When my restaurant partner and I built our second restaurant, we decided to make it more upscale than the first so it wouldn't cannibalize business, given that the two restaurants were only five miles away. The upscale décor strategy seemed like a perfectly good idea until I observed women walk in for lunch, look at the upscale décor, look at their own casual clothes, and proclaim to the hostess that they were underdressed. The self-assessed underdressed customer would turn and leave. I saw that scenario repeat itself over and over. None of the women who rejected themselves from the restaurant looked underdressed to me. The restaurant wasn't *that* upscale. It was still a neighborhood restaurant in a suburban strip mall. But compared to other restaurants in the area, it was a step up in design. It made people feel uncomfortable. To make matters worse, our food quality wasn't up to the level people expected for a place with that type of décor. The restaurant's appearance caused us to be compared to the very best of fine dining restaurants. Our business model assumed people would prefer eating upscale comfort food in an unusually attractive setting. It was a bad idea. Customers were confused. Was the restaurant supposed to be casual or upscale? People compared our décor to casual restaurants and decided it was too fancy to be a casual eating experience. They compared our food to the top restaurants in San Francisco and decided it wasn't sufficiently special. We failed to predict how customers would stack us up against alternatives.

This book itself presents an especially challenging comparison problem. If I add too much humor to this book, reviewers and readers will compare it to other humor books, and it will come up short because many of the chapters don't lend themselves to jokes. If I leave out all humor, the book will be compared to self-help books, which would be misleading in its own way, but I'd probably come out better in that sort of comparison. In other words, to increase your perceived enjoyment of the book, I might leave out some humor that you would otherwise enjoy.

When I talk of the comparison problem, I don't mean a simple comparison of one thing to its competition. If the competition is simply better than you, your problem is more than customer perception. I'm talking about comparisons that common sense tells you should be irrelevant, such as comparing *Dilbert* the TV show to *The Simpsons*. They weren't competitors in any real way. They didn't run during the same slot or exhaust the limited supply of the public's discretionary time in any meaningful way. And yet the comparison to *The Simpsons* was a big obstacle to the show's success because it contrasted a seasoned, big-budget show against a poorly-funded upstart that was still trying to find its rhythm. Animated shows take longer to "tune" than live action because the writers for animation can't know what worked in a particular show until it is fully animated and too late to change. Success in anything usually means doing more of what works and less of what doesn't. For animated TV shows, that means you don't hit your pace until about the third season. We got cancelled after the second half-season. I believe that if *The Simpsons* had never existed as the gold standard of animated primetime TV shows, the *Dilbert* show would have had time to reach the next level.

I've spent a lot of time describing just one psychological phenomenon: the tendency to make irrational comparisons. But how many psychological tips and tricks does a person really need to understand to be successful in life?

My best guess is that there are a few hundred rules in psychology you should have a passing familiarity with. I've been absorbing information in this field for decades, and I don't feel as if I'm getting anywhere near the end of it. And just about everything I learn about human psychology ends up being helpful.

I went to Wikipedia to get a quick list of the psychological and cognitive traps that humans often fall into. Psychology is an immense field and well beyond the scope of this book. My point is to impress upon you how many useful nuggets of information are at your disposal, and most of them are free. Every psychological trap on this list can be used to manipulate you. If there's something on this list that you're not familiar with, you're vulnerable to deception. In some cases, you're missing opportunities to make your product and yourself more attractive to others.

It's a good idea to make psychology your lifelong study. Most of what you need to know as a regular citizen can be gleaned from the Internet.

Below is Wikipedia's list of cognitive biases.[1] It looks like a lot to know, but you have your entire life to acquire the knowledge. Think of it as a system in which you learn a bit every year. That will be easier if you understand how important psychology is to everything you want to accomplish in life. On a scale of one to ten, the importance of understanding psychology is a solid ten.

Ambiguity effect   Anchoring

    Availability heuristic   Availability cascade

Backfire effect   Bandwagon effect

Barnum effect   Base rate neglect or Base rate fallacy

    Belief bias   Bias blind spot

Choice-supportive bias   Clustering illusion

    Confirmation bias   Congruence bias

Conjunction fallacy   Conservatism or Regressive Bias

    Conservatism (Bayesian)   Contrast effect

Curse of knowledge   Decoy effect

Denomination effect   Distinction bias

    Duration neglect   Empathy gap

Endowment effect   Essentialism

Exaggerated expectation   Experimenter's or Expectation bias

    False-consensus effect   Functional fixedness

Focalism   Focusing effect   Forer effect

Framing effect   Frequency illusion   Gambler's

fallacy   Hard-easy effect   Hindsight bias

Hostile media effect   Hyperbolic discounting

    Illusion of control   Illusion of validity

Illusory correlation   Impact bias

Information bias

Insensitivity to sample size

Irrational escalation

Just-world hypothesis

Less-is-better effect

Loss aversion

Ludic fallacy

Mere exposure effect

Money illusion

Moral credential effect

Negativity bias

Neglect of probability

Normalcy bias

Observer-expectancy effect

Omission bias

Optimism bias

Ostrich effect

Outcome bias

Overconfidence effect

Pareidolia

Pessimism bias

Planning fallacy

Post-purchase rationalization

Pro-innovation bias

Pseudocertainty effect

Reactance

Reactive devaluation

Recency bias

Recency illusion

Restraint bias

Rhyme as reason effect

Selective perception

Semmelweis reflex

Selection bias

Social comparison bias

Social desirability bias

Status quo bias

Stereotyping

Subadditivity effect

Subjective validation

Survivorship bias

Texas sharpshooter fallacy

Time-saving bias

Unit bias

Well travelled road effect

Zero-risk bias

Zero-sum heuristic

Social biases

Actor-observer bias

Defensive attribution hypothesis

Dunning–Kruger effect

Egocentric bias

Extrinsic incentives bias

Forer effect (aka Barnum effect)

False consensus effect

Halo effect

Illusion of asymmetric insight

Illusion of external agency

Illusion of transparency

Illusory superiority

Ingroup bias

Just-world phenomenon

Moral luck

Naive cynicism

Outgroup homogeneity bias

Projection bias

Self-serving bias

System justification

Trait ascription bias

Ultimate attribution error

Worse-than-average effect

Memory errors and biases

Bizarreness effect:

Choice-supportive bias

Change bias

Childhood amnesia

Conservatism or Regressive Bias

Consistency bias

Context effect

Cross-race effect

Cryptomnesia

Egocentric bias

Fading

affect bias

False memory

Generation effect (Self-generation effect)   Google effect

Hindsight bias   Humor effect

Illusion-of-truth effect   Illusory correlation

Lag effect   Leveling and Sharpening

Levels-of-processing effect: List-length effect

Misinformation effect   Misattribution

Modality effect   Mood congruent memory bias:

Next-in-line effect   Osborn effect

Part-list cueing effect   Peak-end rule

Persistence   Picture superiority effect

Placement bias   Positivity effect

Primacy effect, Recency effect & Serial position effects

Processing difficulty effect   Reminiscence bump

Rosy retrospection   Self-relevance effect

Self-serving bias   Source Confusion

Spacing effect   Stereotypical bias

Suffix effect   Suggestibility   Subadditivity effect

Telescoping effect   Testing effect

Tip of the tongue   Verbatim effect

Von Restorff effect   Zeigarnik effect

Some entries on the list are common sense, and you might already know them by other names. I include the comprehensive list just to give you a feel for how deep the field is. And I would go so far as to say that anything on the list you don't understand might cost you money in the future.

You've heard the old saying that knowledge is power. But knowledge of psychology is the purest form of that power. No matter what you're doing, or how well you're doing it, you can benefit from a deeper understanding of how the mind interprets its world using only the clues that somehow find a way into your brain through the holes in your skull.

When I was in my twenties, I took a certification course in hypnosis. I thought it would be fascinating and maybe useful. I even considered making some money on the side as a hypnotist. I decided against it because I didn't want to be in the business of selling my time. But the skills and insights I gleaned from studying hypnosis have improved my performance in just about everything I've done since then, from business to my personal life. It was time well spent.

In hypnosis, you don't spend much time asking why one technique works and why another does not. Hypnosis is largely a trial-and-error process that uses your own experience plus that of hypnotists who have gone before to reduce the number of wrong moves. In that sense, hypnosis treats people as if they are machines that can be programmed. If you provide the right inputs, you get the outputs you want.

Hypnosis is an inexact process because every brain has a different mix of chemistry. For example, if I ask you to relax and imagine a forest in the summer, you might find that a pleasing image. Unless you are afraid of bears or are scared of getting lost in the wilderness, then you might get agitated by the thought of a forest. A hypnotist learns to detect slight changes in breathing, posture, movement, and skin tone to know if the images presented are working as planned. Adjustments are made accordingly. In the simplest terms, a hypnotist tries to do more of whatever works and less of what doesn't.

My experience with hypnosis completely changed the way I view people and how I interpret the choices they make. I no longer see *reason* as the driver of behavior. I see simple cause and effect, similar to the way machines operate. If you believe people use reason for important decisions, you will go through life feeling confused and frustrated that others seem to have bad reasoning skills. The reality is that reason is just one of the drivers of our decisions, often the smallest one.

Recently, my wife and I went shopping for a new vehicle. We looked at a lot of models online and in person, and none were irresistible. Then we came upon a vehicle that was so "us" that I laughed when I saw it. I could almost feel my brain make up its mind before we had done one iota of reasoning, data gathering, or negotiating. I could tell that my wife had the same experience. This car was so obviously going to belong to us that seeing it was like peering into the future.

Predictably, everything we learned about the car after that point seemed either good or good enough. We convinced ourselves that the price was reasonable. We convinced ourselves that the features were just what we wanted. And eventually, we convinced ourselves we had negotiated a good deal.

The normal way people would look at our car-buying experience is that we saw a model that looked good enough to interest us, then we did our homework, applied our reasoning abilities, and came to a rational decision. The reality is quite different. The amateur hypnotist in me knows that our visceral reaction to the car was the beginning and end of the "thinking" that went into the purchase. We did some due diligence to make sure it met our basic requirements, yes, but we already "knew" it would. The purchase was an irrational decision that tried and failed to sell itself to me as the product of reason.

It is tremendously useful to know when people are using reason and when they are rationalizing the irrational. You're wasting your time if you try to make someone see reason when reason is not influencing the decision. If you've ever had a frustrating political debate with a friend who refuses to see the logic in your argument, you know what I mean. But keep in mind that the friend sees you exactly the same way.

When politicians lie, they know the press will call them out. They also know it doesn't matter. Politicians understand that reason will never have much of an effect on voting decisions. A lie that makes a voter feel good is more effective than a hundred rational arguments. That's even true when the voter knows the lie is a lie. If you're perplexed at how society can tolerate politicians who lie so blatantly, you're thinking of people as rational beings. That worldview is frustrating and limiting. People who study hypnosis start to view humans as moist machines that are simply responding to inputs with programmed outputs. No reasoning is involved beyond eliminating the most absurd options. Your reasoning can prevent you from voting for a *total* imbecile, but it won't stop you from supporting a halfwit with a great haircut.

If your view of the world is that people use reason for their important decisions, you are setting yourself up for a life of frustration and confusion. You'll find yourself continuously debating people and never winning except in your own mind. Few things are as destructive and limiting as a worldview that assumes people are mostly rational.

On an episode of *The Bachelorette*, a show on ABC, one of the contending single men played a practical joke on the young woman he hoped to marry. The joke involved taking her to his parents' home and convincing her that he still lived there, which he didn't. The joke was well-executed, complete with a fake bedroom that was a disgusting mess. What the suitor failed to understand is that the bachelorette would still *feel* the scenario in the joke long after the truth was revealed. In the bachelorette's mind—the irrational part we all have—the memory of this fellow being a live-at-home loser was like a stain that couldn't be removed. I think the bachelorette genuinely appreciated the joke and had a good laugh. But my wife and I turned to each other and said, "He's toast." He was eliminated soon after. We can't know how much impact the joke had on the bachelorette's decision, but my training with hypnosis tells me it was probably huge.

Apple owes much of its success to Steve Jobs' understanding that the way a product makes users feel trumps most other considerations, including price. If Steve Jobs saw people as rational beings, he might have followed a path similar to Dell, selling highly capable machines at the lowest possible price. Dell succeeded, too, of course, but if buyers were rational, there would have been only one computer manufacturer left after about a year; consumers would always buy the best computer for the money and drive out the bad players overnight. Luckily for Dell and several other Windows computer manufacturers, there are enough irrational people with poor information to keep several companies afloat so long as their products are confusingly similar. Jobs' worldview led him to a business model with high margins, whereas Windows computers have become commodities.

If you feel I'm overstating the case that people are irrational, allow me to put some boundaries around that idea. People certainly make small decisions based on rational considerations. You probably invest your money in ways that are prudent—or so you think. But keep in mind that the financial meltdown of 2009 happened because even the best investors were irrationally optimistic about financial instruments they couldn't hope to understand.

Rational behavior is especially useless in any situation that is too complex for a human to grasp. Cellphone companies exploit that fact by offering pricing plans too complicated to compare to the competition. (I coined the word "confusopoly" to describe that strategy.) The intent is to prevent consumers from using whatever small reasoning power they possess to compare prices and features. Instead, consumers make largely uninformed decisions and convince themselves they did well. I speak from experience, having recently moved from one wireless carrier to another while planning a third move soon. I tell myself that each of the moves was based on price, coverage, and features. But reason didn't help me the first two times I chose a wireless carrier, and it probably won't help the next time because the pricing plans are intentionally hard to compare.

I don't think you need to become a hypnotist to understand human psychology, although it helps. But I do think a working knowledge of psychology is essential to your success—both personally and professionally. Consider it a lifelong learning process. You'll be glad you undertook it. Over time, knowing the psychology basics starts to feel like a superpower that allows you to understand what confuses and confounds those around you.

Business Writing

I never took a writing class in high school or in college. I learned the basics in English classes, and those seemed good enough. I could write sentences that people understood. What else did I need?

I did notice that some people in the business world wrote with an impressive level of clarity and persuasiveness. But I figured that was just because those people were extra smart. It never occurred to me that there was some technique involved and that we unwashed citizens could easily learn it.

One day during my corporate career, I signed up for a company-sponsored class in business writing. This was part of my larger strategy of learning as much as I could about whatever might someday be useful while my employer was willing to foot the bill. I didn't have high hopes that the class would change my life. I was just looking for some tips and tricks for better writing.

I was very wrong about how useful the class would be. If I recall, the class was only two afternoons long. And it was life-altering.

As it turns out, business writing is all about getting to the point and leaving out all the noise. You think you already do that in your writing, but you probably don't.

Consider the previous sentence. I intentionally embedded some noise. Did you catch it? The sentence that starts with "You think you already do that . . ." includes the unnecessary word "already." Remove it, and you get the same meaning: "You think you do that . . ." The "already" part is assumed and unnecessary. That sort of realization is the foundation of business writing.

Business writing also teaches that brains are wired to better understand concepts that are presented in a certain order. For example, your brain processes "The boy hit the ball" more easily than "The ball was hit by the boy." In editor's jargon, the first sentence is direct writing and the second is passive. It's a tiny difference, but over the course of an entire document, passive writing adds up and causes reader fatigue.

Eventually, I learned that the so-called persuasive writers were doing little more than using ordinary business writing methods. Clean writing makes a writer seem smarter and makes their arguments more persuasive.

Business writing is also the foundation for humor writing. Unnecessary words and passive writing kill the timing of humor the same way they kill the persuasiveness of your point. If you want people to see you as smart, persuasive, and funny, consider taking a two-day class in business writing. There aren't many skills you can learn in two days that will serve you this well.

Accounting

I found accounting nearly impossible to learn because of the bubbling moat of boredom that surrounds the entire field. But a basic understanding of accounting is necessary to be a fully effective adult in a modern society, even if you never do any actual accounting on your own.

Accounting is part of the vocabulary of business, and if you don't understand it on a concept level, the world will be a confusing place. In particular, it's helpful to be able to create your own cash flow projection on a spreadsheet and feel some confidence that you understand the tax impact and the so-called time value of money.* Accounting overlaps with the fields of economics and business, and in each of those fields, you need to understand accounting practices.

In my town there's a tiny restaurant that has changed hands several times, always with a new concept and menu. The one thing that all the concepts have in common is that they can't work because there aren't enough tables in the place to cover their expenses. (I have a good idea what their expenses are because I once owned two restaurants in the area.) My guess is that the new operator has plenty of culinary expertise but no accounting knowhow. No one with accounting skill would get involved with a business model that can't work on paper.

---

*Simply put, a dollar today is worth more than a dollar tomorrow because the dollar you have today can be invested. The math of it is more complicated.

You can pay others to do your accounting and cash flow projections, but that only works if you can check their work in a meaningful way. The smarter play is to learn enough about accounting and spreadsheets that you understand the basics.

Design

In today's world, we're all designers whether we like it or not. You might be designing PowerPoint presentations, a website for your startup, or flyers for your kid's school event. You're also furnishing your home, buying clothes you hope look nice to others, and so on. Design used to be the exclusive domain of artists and other experts. Now we're all expected to have a working understanding of design.

If you're like me, you were born with no design skills whatsoever. I was amazed to learn, well into my adult years, that design is rules-based. One need not have an "eye" for design; knowing the rules is good enough for civilians.

For example, landscape designers will tell you that it's better to put three of the same kind of bush in your yard, not two and not four. Odd numbers just look better in that context. You don't need an eye for design to count to three, and you get the same result as the expert, at least in that limited example.

I also learned that art composition for anything from a magazine cover to an oil painting to a PowerPoint slide should conform to a few basic templates. The most common is the *L*-shaped layout. You imagine a giant letter *L* on the page and fill in the dense stuff along its shape, leaving less clutter in one of the four open quadrants. Artists call the uncluttered part negative space. In the case of an oil painting, you might have a tree going up one side, some landscape on the bottom, and the open sky in the top left. You can change it up by rotating the *L* and leaving a different quadrant less busy than the rest, but it's still the L concept.

When you take a photograph, you can use the same concept. Instead of centering the person in the pictures, adjust your field until the person is one side of the *L* and the ground is the bottom. The less busy quadrant might be some landscape or the sunset.

When you design a PowerPoint slide or a web page, it's the same idea. You leave one quadrant less busy than the rest. Skim through any well-designed magazine and you'll see the *L* design in 80 percent of the art and photography. The other 20 percent will be some special cases that I won't go into here. I'm only trying to convince you of the importance of design and the ease with which you can pick up the main idea. Learn just a few design tricks, and people will think you're smarter without knowing exactly why.

Conversation Skills

Few people are skilled conversationalists. Most people are just talking, which is not the same thing. The difference is that skilled conversationalists have learned techniques that are surprisingly non-obvious to a lot of people. I was among the clueless about conversation skills for the first half of my life. When I was a teen, I thought conversation was a complete waste of time and something to be avoided. I was aware that there were several alleged reasons for conversation, but I didn't see much value in them. I was a bore.

There are probably a dozen or more reasons to have a conversation, depending on how you slice it. You might start a conversation to . . .

Exchange information
Plan
Complain
Entertain
Feel connected
Befriend
Seduce
Persuade
Be polite
Avoid awkward silence
Brag

A bad conversationalist will focus on the impoverished part of the list, doing a lot of bragging, complaining, and exchanging information. It's fair to say that such a person doesn't understand what conversation is and how to do it. I fell into that category for the first few decades of my life.

My first inkling that conversation was a learnable skill and that the benefits of conversation were larger than I imagined happened while I was taking the Dale Carnegie course I mentioned earlier. The focus of the class was on public speaking, but we also learned techniques for making conversation with strangers, such as one might in a party or business situation. The technique is laughably simple and 100 percent effective. All you do is introduce yourself and ask questions until you find a point of mutual interest.

I'll paraphrase the Dale Carnegie question stack as best I remember it. It goes something like this:

1. What's your name?
2. Where do you live?
3. Do you have a family?
4. What do you do for a living?
5. Do you have any hobbies/sports?
6. Do you have any travel plans?

If you're like me, the questions seem a bit too awkward and personal for someone you just met. Prior to experiencing the Dale Carnegie course, I would meet someone new and immediately go into joking mode because I didn't know what else to talk about. I discovered that perhaps only 5 percent of the general population wants to get into joking mode with a stranger. And of that 5 percent, maybe only half of them will appreciate whatever you think is funny. Everyone else will want you to go away. While most people enjoy humor, the typical person doesn't go directly there before getting to know someone.

The secret to making the list of five questions work without seeming awkward is in understanding that the person you meet will feel every bit as awkward as you. That person wants to talk about something interesting and sound knowledgeable. Your job is to make that easy. Nothing is easier than talking about oneself. I would go so far as to say that 99 percent of the general public LOVE talking about themselves. When you ask a stranger a personal question, you make that person happy. Your question relieves the stress of awkward silence and gets the conversation moving. Best of all, it signals that you have interest in the stranger, which most people interpret as friendliness and social confidence, even if you're faking it. And faking social confidence leads to the real thing over time.

Your job as a conversationalist is to keep asking questions and keep looking for something you have in common with the stranger or something that interests you enough to wade into the topic. In my entire life, I have never met a stranger who didn't have some fascinating life experiences that spill out—if you ask the right questions. *Everyone* is interesting if you make the situation feel safe. Here's a summary of good conversation technique:

1. Ask questions.
2. Don't complain (much).
3. Don't talk about boring experiences (TV show, meal, dream, etc.).
4. Don't dominate the conversation. Let others talk.
5. Don't get stuck on a topic. Keep moving.
6. Planning is useful, but it isn't conversation.
7. Keep the sad stories SHORT, especially medical stories.

The point of conversation is to make the other person feel good. If you do that one simple thing correctly, the other benefits come along with the deal. For example, a person who likes you is more likely to be persuaded, to recommend you for good opportunities, to share information, and to want a relationship with you. And if you must complain because it's just too hard to keep it in, you're better off complaining to someone who already likes you; that way, you'll get the empathy you want.

So how do you get a stranger to like you? It's simple. It starts by smiling and keeping your body language open. After that, just ask questions and listen as if you care, all the while looking for common interests. Everyone likes to talk about their own life, and everyone appreciates a sympathetic listener. Eventually, if you discover some common interests, you'll feel a connection without any effort.

If you're physically attractive, it probably isn't a good idea to talk too much. People are predisposed to liking attractive people. Talking can only make it worse. If you're attractive, be sure you've created a solid connection before discussing your hobby of collecting baby animal skulls or whatever-the-hell you're into. The less you say, the better, at least in the early stages of getting to know someone.

If you're unattractive—and this is my area of expertise—your conversation skills will be especially important. Those might be all you have to sell yourself unless you're accomplished in some world-class way. So you'll need to take your conversation skills up a notch. And that means becoming the master of short but interesting stories.

As a writer, I reflexively translate whatever I observe into a story form with a setup, a twist if there is one, and some sort of punch line or thought that ties it in a bow. You can do the same thing. Try to get in the habit of asking yourself how you can turn your interesting experiences into story form. I find it helps to imagine telling the story to someone in particular, such as a spouse, friend, or relative. Try a few versions in your head, telling the story and feeling how it goes. Was it brief? Did you save the surprise for just the right moment? Did you have a way to end the story with a punch line or interesting observation?

It's a good idea to always have a backlog of stories you can pull out at a moment's notice. And you'll want to continually update your internal story database with new material. For example, if I know I'll be seeing friends in a few days, I make a special note to myself to turn my recent experiences into story form because I know I'll have a reason to bust one out. The most popular type of stories are . . . *funny stories*.

I think everyone should learn how to tell a funny story. I don't think people realize that storytelling is a learnable skill and not a genetic gift. Once you know the parts that comprise any good story, you have all you need to sculpt your own out of your everyday experiences.

The most important key to good storytelling is preparation. You don't want to figure out your story as you tell it. If something story-worthy happens to you, spend some time developing the story structure in your head—a structure I will explain in a minute—and practice telling the story in your head until you have it down.

The basic parts of a good party story are:

Setup

There's only one important rule for a story setup: Keep it BRIEF. And I mean really brief, as in "So, I took my car in for a brake job . . ." That's it. Don't tell us the problem with the brakes. Don't tell us what made you think you had a brake problem, unless for some reason it is relevant. Try to keep your setup to one sentence, two at most.

Pattern

Establish a pattern that your story will violate. For example, you could say, "Whenever I take my car for any kind of service, I'm always amazed how expensive it is." That establishes the pattern. Now we know that what follows will be a violation of the pattern. And we call that hint of things to come . . .

Foreshadowing

Foreshadowing means you leave some clues where the story is going. The foreshadowing can happen as early as the setup, as in, "My in-laws in Arkansas have something they call the 'fraidy hole' that everyone climbs into in case of tornadoes. It's meant to hold no more than four people." That's the setup with the foreshadowing built in.

The Characters

Every story involves characters, and you might be one of them. For people who know all your foibles, defects, and preferences, no elaboration is required. But if you are talking to strangers or talking about unfamiliar others, fill in the story with some character traits that will be relevant.

For example, "Our friend Bob has been borrowing our power tools for years because he's too cheap to buy his own." That sort of brief caricature profile is essential to any story that involves people. All good stories are about personalities.

Relatability

There is one topic that people care more about than any other—themselves. Pick story topics that your listeners will relate to. If your story is about dealing with a stubborn bureaucrat, most adults can relate to it no matter the bureaucracy involved. But if your story is about the inner working of competitive quilting, you'd better make it short and extra witty. People drift off when you stop talking about stuff that isn't, well, them.

The Twist

Your story isn't a story unless something unexpected or unusual happens. That's the plot twist. If you don't have a twist, it's not a story. It's just a regurgitation of your day. That's fine for catching up with a spouse, but it won't make you the life of a party.

Topics to Avoid

It's important to tell stories about interesting events. It's even more important to avoid telling stories about deadly boring or downer situations. Here are a few topics you should avoid:

Food: People don't care how good your meal was unless they plan to eat at the same place soon. I will agree that some extreme foodies can get pleasure from hearing about food. But even in that case, you want to keep it short.

Television Show Plots: Talking about TV shows that you and your conversation partner both enjoy can be fun and entertaining. But no one wants to hear the entire plot of a television show that you watched and they didn't.

Dreams: No one cares about the details of your dream. If you must discuss your dreams, keep it to one sentence, as in, "I dreamed that a chipmunk with a face that looked like Winston Churchill was swimming in my cereal bowl."

Medical Stories: If you are normal or anywhere near it, you will talk too much about your health issues no matter how persuasively I tell you that it's a bad idea. And people will ask about your health if they know there's something wrong with you. So you can't entirely avoid talking about your medical problems. Just keep your stories light, funny if possible, and short. Most importantly, recognize that it's your responsibility to change the subject as soon as you can. Other people will feel awkward changing the subject from your health problems because there's no way to do it gracefully. That's your job.

And yes, I realize this book has a lot of health-related stories in it. But I'm a professional. And if I did my job right, you're curious how my voice problem turned out.

Smile, ask questions, avoid complaining and sad topics, and have some entertaining stories ready to go. It's all you need to be in the top 10 percent of all conversationalists.

Overcoming Shyness

If you take a human from a remote tribe where no one has ever heard of a thing called swimming, and you throw him in the ocean, he'll probably panic and drown. Swimming isn't entirely natural to humans. We need to learn it. Luckily, we humans learn to swim easily with a little practice.

Shyness is analogous to swimming in the sense that we aren't born with the tools to overcome our own shyness. Some of us have more natural shyness than others. But like swimming, we can learn to overcome shyness with a little practice. And it's worth the effort. Otherwise, you'll find yourself socially drowning at every gathering or public talk.

I was so shy when I was in my twenties that I would drive to a party, park my car, break into a full sweat, then drive home without even saying hello.

I credit one of my college friends for teaching me the secret of overcoming shyness by imagining you are acting instead of interacting. And by that, I mean literally acting.

It turns out that a shy person can act like someone else more easily than he can act like himself. That makes some sense because shyness is caused by an internal feeling that you are not worthy to be in the conversation. Acting like someone else gets you out of that way of thinking.

When I fake my way past my natural shyness, I like to imagine a specific confident person I know well. I do my bad impression of that person, but it comes off much better than my default routine of breaking into a sweat, laughing too hard at my own jokes, and excusing myself to go sit in a corner and perspire.

I also like to keep a few things in mind when I feel shyness coming on. First, I remember that most people feel awkward in social situations at least some of the time. Chances are that the person you are talking to is feeling just as shy. It helps me to know I'm probably on a level playing field. The other person is only pretending to be socially talented, just as I am.

The single best tip for avoiding shyness involves harnessing the power of acting interested in other people. You don't want to cross into nosiness, but everyone appreciates it when you show interest.

You should also try to figure out which people are *thing* people and which ones are *people* people. *Thing* people enjoy hearing about new technology and other clever tools and possessions. They also enjoy discussions of processes and systems, including politics.

People people only enjoy conversations that involve humans doing interesting things. They get bored in a second when the conversation turns to things. Once you know whether you are dealing with a *thing* person or a *people* person, you can craft your conversation to their sweet spot. It makes a big difference in how people react to you, and that in turn will make you more confident and less shy.

People who appear outgoing are usually employing a learned social skill that you think is somehow natural. It probably isn't, at least not entirely. Outgoing people usually come from families with at least one outgoing parent. They observe and imitate. Being outgoing is partly genetic, but you still need to know what to say when. That part is learned. And the good news is that you can learn it, too. Observe outgoing people and steal their little tricks if you can. I've been doing that for years. It works great.

I also find it helpful to remind myself that every human is a mess on the inside. It's easy to assume the good-looking and well-spoken person in front of you has it all together and is therefore your superior. The reality is that everyone is a basket case on the inside. Some people just hide it better. Find me a normal person, and I'll show you someone you don't know that well. It helps to remind yourself that your own flaws aren't that bad compared to everyone else.

I also recommend exercising your ego the way you'd exercise any other muscle. Try putting yourself in situations that will surely embarrass you if things go wrong—or maybe even if they don't. Like any other skill, suppressing shyness takes practice. The more you put yourself in potentially embarrassing situations, the easier they all become.

In the interest of full disclosure, my own shyness dissipated when I realized I was semi-famous and had an interesting profession. Success builds confidence, and confidence suppresses shyness. If you can't control your shyness directly through the tricks I outlined, wait until you're rich and famous; the shyness might leave on its own.

Second Language

I never learned a second language despite years of trying. I can ace written tests in language classes, but when I hear another language spoken, it sounds like a clothes-dryer full of mumbling clowns. Apparently, my brain doesn't have the right wiring for learning additional languages.

A second language can qualify you for a greater range of jobs and opportunities compared to your mono-lingual peers. Where I live, in California, Spanish is the obvious choice for a second language. I've met quite a few small business owners who use Spanish to manage their employees. And if you plan to get a job that involves working with the public, Spanish is essential, at least in California. Your situation will differ, but it always makes sense to know an extra language. It's a huge competitive advantage.

If any of this chapter sounds painfully obvious, keep in mind that many different folks will read a book like this. And I remember my own galactic ignorance as a young man. It's surprising how uncommon common sense is. Also, keep in mind that California schools still teach French for some ridiculous reason, so clearly someone hasn't gotten the common sense memo.

Golf

It's an old cliché that business gets done on the golf course. I'm new to the game, but as far as I can tell, no one ever talks business on a golf course. The thing that golf does well is that it allows males, especially, to bond. Men bond with other men through common activities. And for adult men, golf is as close as you can get to a universal activity. After a certain age, it's probably the most common sport-like activity for men.

If you're resisting golf because it doesn't look fun, you're likely mistaken. Prior to learning how to golf just one year ago, I assumed that if the game was fun at all, it was a low-grade fun and certainly not worth the time and expense. I was wrong. It turns out that golf transports your brain to another dimension for the hours you are on the course. It's like a vacation for the mind. And while I wouldn't call golf relaxing, especially if you play as poorly as I do, the simple act of putting your mind in a completely new and absorbing place can help you escape your daily worries. It's like a brain vacation. It's extraordinary, really.

Women in the business world should learn golf for the same reasons as men, plus the extra reason that it opens up some tremendous dating opportunities if you're in the market. I don't know how many desirable men would prefer an average woman who golfs over a supermodel who doesn't, but I'll bet it's a substantial number. If you're a woman looking to increase your buying power in the dating pool, golf is a great competitive advantage. And you might enjoy it, too.

One more thing: If you find yourself in cocktail conversation with a male over the age of thirty, and you're looking for a topic of common interest, golf is a great go-to topic. I can't tell you how many times I've been asked "Do you golf?" It annoyed the hell out of me until I learned the game. Now I'm happy that I can so easily find common ground on a feel-good topic.

Proper Grammar

No matter how smart you are, educated people will think you're a moron if your grammar is lacking. I'm not an expert in this category, but let me tell you the few common grammar errors that make me cringe. Each of these is like leaving the restroom with toilet paper stuck to your shoe. People notice.

"If I Were . . ."

When you talk about the hypothetical future, use "were" instead of "was." Don't say, "If I was to go with you, I would enjoy myself." Say, "If I *were* to go with you, I would enjoy myself." This rule of grammar is a big one. If you get "were"/"was" grammar wrong, it's a red flag to people who know the difference.

Non-Words

It's a good idea to use words that are in the dictionary. For most of my life, I believed "brang" was a word, as in, "He brang me the ball." It was common usage in the small town where I grew up. In my late twenties, I was mortified to learn that I had been speaking a hillbilly language for most of my life. "Brang" is not in the dictionary. "Brought" is.

Supposably isn't a word either. Try "supposedly."

Fustrated isn't a word. "Frustrated" is.

Libary isn't a word. "Library" is .

Nucular isn't a word. "Nuclear" is.

"Hopefully"

Most people misuse the word "hopefully." It's bad grammar to say, "Hopefully, she will bring the dessert." Hopefully should be an adverb. Say instead, "We waited hopefully for dessert." In the latter case, hopefully is correctly modifying the verb "waited." In the first example, "hopefully" just sits there like the wrong word choice.

"I" and "Me"

The single most important grammar rule to master is when to use "I" and when to use "me". I'll bet less than 20 percent of the general public gets that right. Normally, it wouldn't matter that 20 percent of the public is judging you. That still leaves a strong majority that doesn't, and for most purposes that would be fine. The problem is that the 20 percent in this case tend to be the most well-educated and successful folks. Those are the same people you might someday want to impress if you're asking for a job, trying to get venture funding for your startup, or proposing marriage.

The simple rule for "I" versus "me" is that the sentence must make sense if you remove the other person mentioned in the sentence. For example, if you say, "Bob and I went to a movie," it would still make sense if you removed "Bob and" and said, "I went to a movie."

If the sentence is "Please give the documents to Bob and me," you can remove "Bob and" and it still makes sense as "Please give the documents to me." You'll often hear smart people get this rule wrong, so don't be fooled by how many times you hear it incorrectly.

"Less" or "Fewer"

People often say "less" when they should say "fewer." For example, it's bad grammar to say, "I have less friends than before." When the subject is plural, as in "friends," you use "fewer"—"I have fewer friends than before."

It's okay to say you have less hair than before, but if you were talking about your individual strands of hair you would say, "I have fewer strands of hair."

"Theory" Versus "Hypothesis"

Non-scientists often use the word "theory" when they mean "hypothesis." Without getting too technical, a theory is a scientific explanation of reality that is so well tested it is as good as fact.

The correct term for an unproven and untested explanation is a hypothesis. For example, I think it is possible that humans are the result of aliens seeding the earth with life that evolved over millions of years. I have no evidence for that idea, so it's merely a hypothesis. In conversations with friends, I might call it a theory. If I post about it, I'll play it safe and try to remember to call it a hypothesis. I've probably had more complaints about my inappropriate use of the word "theory" than almost every other thing I've done to anger the public, and that's a long list.

I've made most of the grammar mistakes I mentioned, and I often hear them from others. Bad grammar isn't the worst flaw you could have, but when you consider how easily you can fix it, the effort-to-reward ratio is excellent. It's well worth your effort to learn how to avoid the most common grammatical errors.

Persuasion

No matter your calling in life, you'll spend a great deal of time trying to persuade people of one thing or another. You might be a salesperson trying to close deals, a minister trying to save souls, or anyone with a boss, a family, or friends. Nearly every interaction with others involves some form of persuasion, even if it's subtle. Wouldn't it make sense to learn how to persuade more effectively?

A good starting point in learning the art of persuasion is to go to your preferred online bookstore and search for "persuasion." You'll see a number of books on the topic. Keep reading those books until they seem to be repeating the same tricks. You'll be amazed how deep the topic of persuasion is. And you'll use what you've learned in just about every business or personal interaction you have for the rest of your life. Being a good persuader is like having magical power.

There is an ethical consideration, of course. You don't want to persuade people to do things that are not in their best interest. And it might feel creepy and manipulative if you find yourself too skilled at persuasion. I've learned so much on the topic of persuasion that I intentionally dial it back when I feel like I'm in a stick fight with someone who has no stick. I'm sometimes happier not getting my way than I would be if I felt manipulative. It's a powerful skill that should be used judiciously.

I'll give you a taste of the topic just so you know what I'm talking about. For starters, some words and phrases are simply more persuasive than others, and that has been demonstrated in controlled studies. I've included a few of my own favorite persuasion words based on my own experiences.

Persuasive Words and Phrases

♦ "Because . . ."
♦ "Would you mind . . . ?"
♦ "I'm not interested."
♦ "I don't do that."
♦ "I have a rule . . ."
♦ "I just wanted to clarify . . .
♦ "Is there anything you can do for me?"
♦ "Thank you."
♦ "This is just between you and me."

Allow me to elaborate.

"Because . . ."

Studies by psychologist Robert Cialdini show that people are more cooperative when you ask for a favor using a sentence that includes the word "because," even if the reason you offer makes little or no sense.[3] Apparently, the word "because" signals reasonableness, and reasonableness allows people to let down their defenses and drop their objections.

If the science is accurate, an effective way to ask for money might look something like this: "May I borrow a hundred dollars because I don't get paid until next week?" That's not much of a justification for borrowing money; no real reason is given. The person asking for money hasn't even said why he needs it. It just feels as if a reason was offered because of "because."

I've tested this technique, and it works surprisingly well.

"Would You Mind . . . ?"

I've found that any question beginning with "Would you mind . . ." tends to be well-received. My best guess is that asking a person if he minds is signaling that you have a reasonable request that might be inconvenient. It's hard to be a jerk and say no to any request that starts with "Would you mind?" The question comes across as honest while also showing concern for the other person. It's a powerful combination.

"I'm Not Interested."

Sometimes you need to persuade someone to stop trying to persuade you. You are in that situation every time a telemarketer calls or someone tries to sell you something you don't want. The worst thing you can do in that sort of situation is give some logical-sounding reason why you don't want whatever is being sold. People who sell for a living will try to talk you out of your reason with reasons of their own. In fact, they are usually equipped with arguments against every common objection. Likewise, your friends will badger you forever if you offer nothing but good reasons for rejecting their ideas.

I've found that the most effective way to stop people from trying to persuade me is to say, "I'm not interested." You should try it. Don't offer a reason why you aren't interested. No one can say why a thing holds interest for some and not for others. There's no argument against a lack of interest. Repeat your claim of disinterest as often as it takes to end the conversation. You might be surprised how effective this method is. I've been using it for years. It's a total conversation-killer.

"I Don't Do That."

Another good persuasion sentence is "I don't do that." It's not a reason, and barely tries to be. But it sounds like a hard-and-fast rule. If someone asks you to attend the annual asparagus festival, don't say it doesn't sound fun; that's just begging the asparagus lovers in your group to endlessly describe just how joyous it could be if only you would try it. Instead, say something like, "I don't do food festivals." And if anyone asks why, say, "I'm just not interested." Some of these persuasive sentences work well in tandem.

"I Have a Rule . . ."

In a similar vein, another persuasive deterrent is to say you have a "rule." For example, let's say you have a lunch scheduled with a potential client, and your obnoxious co-worker asks if he can join you. Honesty won't work because you must coexist with your co-worker. Instead, say something along the lines of, "I have a rule of only doing one-on-one lunches with clients." It will sound convincing and somewhat polite while offering no reason whatsoever.

"I Just Wanted to Clarify . . ."

Sometimes you hear statements that are so mind-numbingly stupid, evil, or mean that you know a direct frontal assault would only start a fight. People tend to double-down when challenged, no matter how wrong they are. A more effective way to approach a dangerous social or business situation is sideways, by asking a question that starts with "I just wanted to clarify . . ."

That approach might look like this: "I just wanted to clarify. Are you saying you're okay with an eighty percent chance of going to jail, or did I hear your plan wrong?"

If you phrase your clarification question correctly, it will shine an indirect light on the problem and provide a face-saving escape path. In many cases, the clarification you receive will be an entirely new and more rational plan. No one likes to be proven wrong, but most people will be happy to "clarify," even if the clarification is a complete reversal of an earlier position. It just feels different when you call something a clarification.

"Is There Anything You Can Do for Me?"

We all find ourselves in situations where an organization or person is thwarting us from achieving whatever it is that we perceive as just and fair. Perhaps a retail store is refusing to refund you for an item you're trying to return, or you purchased the wrong model but the one you want is out of stock. You need to persuade someone to go above and beyond the rules to make you happy.

You know that if you get angry and demanding, the person you're dealing with might stick to the rules and try to brush you off. The most powerful way to approach a situation like this is to ask, "Is there anything you can do for me?" You will discover it to be an extraordinarily persuasive question.

The question frames the situation as you being the helpless victim and the person you are trying to persuade as the problem-solving hero. That's a self-image people like to reinforce when they have the chance. All you're doing is creating that opportunity. When you deputize someone to be your problem-solver, you create a situation in which they have a clear payoff: Helping nice people always feels good. All you need to do is be polite and ask a direct question. "Is there anything you can do for me?" You'll be amazed how well it works.

"Thank You."

"Thank you" can range from a casual "thanks" to an over-the-top expression of appreciation complete with details. There's a big difference in how effective each approach is likely to be.

When I took a class on how to train our dog, one of the first things we learned is that the quality of the dog treats made a big difference in how cooperative the dog would be. The trainer had the good stuff, and I believe she could make those dogs play the piano if she wanted. Our medium-quality treats were just barely good enough to keep the dogs from turning on us. The trainer admitted that the key to her superior results with dogs was partly because of snack quality.

A thank-you is like a treat for a human. When you do something generous or nice, you like to know it's appreciated. The quality of the thank you matters as much to humans as the good treats matter to dogs. If you want people to like you, pay special attention to the quality of your thanks.

Thank you notes sent by snail mail are always appreciated and still a must for the bigger occasions. But a well-written email is now socially acceptable for most common situations. No matter how you deliver a thank you, make sure it includes a little detail of what makes you thankful. Was it the surprise, the thoughtfulness, or how helpful the favor or gift was? Be specific.

For example, "Thank you so much for the ride. I was worried all day about how I would get everything done while my car is in the shop. You really saved me."

Compare that to a simple "Thank you for the ride." Any thank you is better than none, but you're missing an opportunity if you do a poor job of it. It's the sort of thing people remember when they decide who they want to work with, pick a team, or invite people to a party. Expressing gratitude seems like a small thing, but it isn't.

"This Is Just between You and Me."

Research shows that people will automatically label you a friend if you share a secret.[3] Sharing a confidence is a fast-track way to cause people to like and trust you. The trick is to reveal a secret that isn't a dangerous one.

Wrong: "I buried my boss in the backyard."

Right: "I probably shouldn't admit this, but every time Jane serves her dip, I only pretend to like it because everyone else says it's to die for."

The right approach to sharing a secret is to start small. Make sure the small secrets stay secret before you try anything riskier. One way to judge your risk is to be alert for other peoples' secrets that are being relayed to you. Someone who is bad at keeping one kind of secret is probably bad at keeping all secrets. You won't be exempt.

Decisiveness

No one is decisive all the time. The world is a complicated place, and often we're only guessing which path will be best. Anyone who is confident in the face of great complexity is insane.

However, some people *act* much more decisively than others. And that act can be both persuasive and useful. Decisiveness looks like leadership. Keep in mind that most normal people are at least a little bit uncertain when facing unfamiliar and complicated situations. What people crave in that sort of environment is anything that looks like certainty. If you can deliver an image of decisiveness, no matter how disingenuous, others will see it as leadership.

Don't confuse your artificial sense of decisiveness with a need to be right all the time. Life is messy, and you're only going to be right sometimes. You'll do everyone in your life a favor by acting decisively though, even if you have doubts on the inside.

Energy

People respond to energy in others. If you show how much you love a particular form of entertainment, it will be easier to persuade others to try it. Energy is contagious. People like how it feels. If you show enthusiasm, others will want to experience the same rush.

Insanity

In most groups, the craziest person is in control. It starts because no one wants the problems that come from pissing off a crazy person. It's just smarter and easier sometimes to let the crazy person have their way.

Crazy people also take more risks and act more confidently than the facts would warrant. That's a potent combination. Crazy-plus-confident probably kills more people than any other combination of personality traits, but when it works just right, it's a recipe for extraordinary persuasion. Cults are a good example of insanity perceived as leadership.

Suppose you're not insane. Can insanity help you? The answer is yes, but you want to use a calculated, emotional type of insanity. In any kind of negotiation, the worst thing you can do is act reasonable. Reasonable people generally cave in to irrational people because it seems like the path of least resistance.

The way fake insanity works in a negotiation is that you assign a greater value to some element of a deal than an objective observer would consider reasonable. For example, you might demand that a deal be closed before the holidays so you can announce it to your family as a holiday present. When you bring in an emotional dimension, people know they can't talk you out of it. Emotions don't bend to reason. So wrap your arguments in whatever emotional blankets you can think of to influence others. A little bit of irrationality is a powerful thing.

Is Persuasion the Same as Manipulation?

If you see persuasion as a form of manipulation and manipulation as a form of evil, that worldview will keep you from being as persuasive as you might be. I think most people hold back their full powers of persuasion because it doesn't feel good to be manipulative. It's one thing to speak your mind and voice your preferences, but you hope that other people agree with you because of the thundering rightness of your arguments. Sadly, we do not live in a world where good arguments always win. Sometimes you need to nudge people onto the right path, even if they firmly believe it to be wrong. In some cases, you have a moral obligation to be manipulative—if you know it will create a good result for all involved. For example, manipulating coworkers to do better work is usually good for everyone.

Technology (Hobby Level)

Technology once was the exclusive domain of lonely geeks. Those days are over. Every adult should have a basic understanding of how the Internet works, the steps involved in building a website, what the "cloud" is, and of course how to use personal computers, smartphones, tablets, etc. It's hard to imagine any profession or startup that wouldn't require those skills, even if you're doing nothing more than supervising vendors, outsourcing, and managing others. It's a good idea to master technology at what I would call a hobby level. You don't need to be your own tech support for the hard stuff, but you also don't want to be the only person in the room who doesn't understand the topic.

This is another case in which your personal energy can be your guide. Imagine how you feel when you find yourself in a technology discussion that you don't understand. It's not fun, and it's not energizing. You can feel your soul draining out through your socks. On the other hand, being part of the conversation is always energizing if you feel you have something to add. Technology is part of the fabric of civilization, and you need to weave yourself into it if you haven't already. Learn the basics, and you'll be a lot happier.

Proper Voice Technique

It's helpful to have different vocal strategies for different situations. Your fun voice might be higher pitched and more rapid paced whereas your serious voice might be deeper and more measured. It's important to keep a lot of distance between your fun voice and your persuasive voice. For people who know you, the serious voice will send an unambiguous signal that the topic is important and that you might be closed to negotiation.

My guess is that 20 percent or less of the general public speaks with proper voice mechanics. And by that I mean proper breath control, tone, and mouth strategies. You probably think any improvement to your voice quality would be wasted. After all, the people that you speak with understand you perfectly. But research says that voice quality is far more important to your overall health and happiness than one might imagine.[4-9] Studies say a commanding voice is highly correlated with success. Other studies suggest that both men and women with attractive voices find partners more quickly than those with less attractive voices.[6] While most of us will never be able to speak like Morgan Freeman no matter how diligently we train our voices, we're all capable of improving how we speak, and that's probably worth the effort.

One of the strangest patterns I noticed during my corporate career is that many of the higher-level managers seemed to have distinctive, interesting voices that commanded attention and gave an inexplicable weight to everything they said. I'm willing to bet that you could play voice recordings of employees to a group of volunteers and the subjects could accurately predict—at least better than chance—who will ascend to power and who will remain a worker bee. One study showed that nurse managers tended to have stronger voices, and this was correlated with a perceived higher quality of care and greater management abilities.[10]

Throughout my corporate years, I used a serious-sounding tone of voice whenever I was in "professional" mode. I was literally acting but it didn't feel disingenuous because the business world is a lot like theater. Everyone tries to get into character for the job they have. When I was a bank teller, I was obsequious to customers. When I managed people, I spoke in a way that I thought sounded authoritarian and reasonable. In meetings with higher-ups, I lowered my tone and spoke with the sort of self-assurance that only the insane come by honestly. I'm reasonably sure that my fake voice with its low notes and artificial confidence made me appear more capable than I was, and that wasn't difficult because I was largely incompetent at every corporate job I held. Despite my obvious lack of ability, nearly every boss I had—and there were many—identified me as a future corporate executive.

Keep in mind that I was poorly dressed, 5'8" tall, and prematurely balding in my twenties. I certainly didn't look like CEO material, and while I'd like to think my interior brilliance sometimes shined through, I doubt that was the case. I think my fake professional voice and fake body language was at least half the reason I was seen as management potential.

I also noticed during my corporate years that women who had never met me in person flirted like crazy on the phone whenever I used my fake professional voice. I assume the same voice qualities that indicate a potential for leadership also influences potential mates.[6] My fake confidence along with my fake low voice that screamed "TESTOSTERONE" worked like catnip on the ladies. Unfortunately, the flirting stopped as soon as anyone saw me in person. That's why I assume my fake voice was the secret sauce.

At least one voice expert believes that my fake voice with its artificially low tone was a cause of my later voice problems with spasmodic dysphonia. I don't know that to be true, but it's worth mentioning.

This book isn't designed to give you voice lessons, but I'll include a few common methods for developing your best "success voice."

For starters, breathe from the bottom of your lungs, not from the upper chest area. Proper breathing has lots of other benefits including stress reduction, increased and more efficient metabolism, and better physical stamina, so it's worth learning.[11-15] If you put your hand on your belly button and breathe correctly, that's the only part of your torso that should be rising and falling. If your upper chest is expanding when you breathe normally, you're doing it wrong. When you get your breathing right, your words will come out sounding more confident.

Next, you need to pick a tone. Some voice experts will tell you that your best and most natural tone is probably higher than the way you normally speak. Many people have a natural tendency to speak lower to other humans than they might to a pet, for example. On some level, we all understand that lower voices confer some weight to what we say.

The downside of a lower voice is that it's difficult to hear words that match background noise. In my fake voice era, no one could hear me above crowd noises. It was hard to order a drink or make conversation in any noisy situation. I've since learned to penetrate background noise by using a higher-pitched voice. It's great for communicating, but I don't expect to get any CEO offers. It's a real trade-off.

Another common speaking trick is to hum the first part of the "Happy Birthday" song and then speak in your normal voice right after. You'll notice your post-humming voice is strangely smooth and perfect. It won't last, but it gives you a target voice you can achieve with practice.

Posture is also important for good speech. If you don't sit up or stand straight, your vocal equipment will sound pinched—even if you don't notice it yourself.

When you're trying to convey a fake sense of confidence—which is often handy—you need to tell yourself you're acting. Simply speak the way you imagine a confident person would speak, and you'll nail it on the first try.

So get rid of the hemming and hawing, the "ums" and "uhs," and anything that disrupts your flow. Confident people don't speak that way. But it does take practice to get right. The quickest fix is simply to substitute silence where you once had "ums" and "uhs." It will feel uncomfortable at first, but you get used to it. I also like to form full sentences in my head before I start them, whenever that's an option. And when I know a topic is likely to come up in the near future, I practice entire conversations in my head until I can speak my thoughts fluently.

My list of combinable skills isn't meant to be comprehensive. And every person is in a unique situation. For you, maybe the right skills are photography and botany. You'll recognize them when you see them now that your mind is tuned to think in that way.

CHAPTER 22

Pattern Recognition

One of my systems involves continuously looking for patterns in life. Recently, I noticed that the high school volleyball games I attended in my role as stepdad were almost always won by the team that reached seventeen first—even though the winning score is twenty-five and you have to win by two. It's common for the lead to change often during a volleyball match, and the team that first reaches seventeen might fall behind a few more times before winning, which makes the pattern extra strange.

If the volleyball pattern is real—and that is far from settled—I would assume there is a normal explanation for it. Perhaps seventeen just feels so close to twenty-five that the team behind feels deflated and the team ahead feels extra confident. Perhaps at the high school level, the coach whose team is behind feels the need to give the bench players some time before the end of the game. Whatever the reason, the pattern seems to hold. Perhaps it will change after this book goes to print. I'll keep tracking it.

In amateur tennis, one of the oddest patterns is called the five-two curse. In tennis, the first player to win six games by at least two wins the set, so you would expect the player who first reaches five to win most of the time. What happens instead—far more often than common sense would predict—is that the weekend player who is ahead feels they can coast while the player who is behind feels they can play relaxed because the outcome seems predictable. That sort of thinking leads to a psychological advantage for the player who is behind, who often closes the gap to five-three3 without much effort. Now the player who is ahead starts to think the lead isn't so secure. Perhaps they feel the momentum has shifted. It only takes a few good shots from the opponent in the next game to reinforce that impression. The player who first gets to five games against a similarly skilled amateur will still win most of the time but not nearly as often as you would predict. If you're an amateur player with only two games compared to your opponent's five, it helps a great deal to know you have something like a 40 percent chance of prevailing. Knowing the pattern changes how you think about your chances, and that change in thinking can then improve your performance.

Successful People

Countless self-help and business books have tried to find the patterns of behavior that make people successful. If we can find out what successful people do, so the thinking goes, we can imitate them and become successful ourselves.

Stephen Covey was probably the most famous of the success-by-pattern gurus. His book *Seven Habits of Highly Effective People* sold more than 25 million copies. Covey described a good set of patterns for people to follow, but they're only a start. I'll summarize his seven habits and suggest you read his books if you want more.

1. Be Proactive
2. Begin with the End in Mind. (Imagine a good outcome.)
3. Put first things first. (Set priorities.)
4. Think win-win. (Don't be greedy.)
5. Seek first to understand then be understood.
6. Synergize. (Use teamwork.)
7. Sharpen the saw. (Keep learning.)

The holy grail of civilization is the hope that we can someday make all people successful by discovering the formula used by successful people and making it available to all. As far as I know, Stephen Covey's seven habits didn't budge the poverty rate, so there are probably deeper patterns at play.

Here's my own list of the important patterns for success that I've noticed over the years. This is purely anecdotal. I excluded the ones that are 100 percent genetic.

1. Lack of fear of embarrassment.
2. Education (the right kind).
3. Exercise.

Lacking the fear of embarrassment allows you to be proactive. It's what makes a person take on challenges that others write off as too risky. It's what makes you take the first step before you know what the second step is. I'm not a fan of physical risks, but if you can't handle the risk of embarrassment, rejection, and failure, you need to learn how, and studies suggest that is indeed a learnable skill.[1]

As far as physical bravery goes, I don't know anything about it. But I'm glad some people have it so they can shoot the other people who have it before those people shoot me. I recommend that you improve your psychological bravery but say no to anything that has a strong chance of killing you.

Then there's education. Do you know what the unemployment rate is for engineers? It's nearly zero. Do you know how many engineers like their jobs? Most of them do, despite what you read in *Dilbert* comics. And the ones who are unhappy with work can change jobs fairly easily. Generally speaking, the people who have the right kind of education have almost no risk of unemployment.

Education and psychological bravery are somewhat interchangeable. If you don't have much of one, you can compensate with a lot of the other. When you see a successful person who lacks a college education, you're usually looking at someone with an unusual lack of fear.

The next pattern I've noticed is exercise. Good health is a baseline requirement for success. But I'm not talking about the obvious fact that sick people can't get much done. I'm talking about the extra energy and vitality that good health brings. I might be getting the correlation wrong, and perhaps whatever motivates a person to succeed also motivates that person to maintain an exercise schedule. But I think it works both ways. I believe exercise makes people smarter, psychologically braver, more creative, more energetic, and more influential. In an online article about twenty habits of successful people, the second item on the list is exercise five to seven days a week.[2] Other studies back this notion—physical fitness in general and daily exercise in particular are correlated with success in business and in life.[3,4]

There's one more pattern I see in successful people: They treat success as a learnable skill. That means they figure out what they need then go get it. If you've read this far, you're one of those people. You're reading this book because it offers a non-zero chance of telling you something that might be helpful.

CHAPTER 23

Humor

If you see humor as an optional form of entertainment, you're missing some of its biggest benefits: People who enjoy humor are simply more attractive than people who don't. It's human nature to want to spend time with people who can appreciate a good laugh or, better yet, cause one.

Take it from me when I say a good sense of humor can compensate for a lot of other shortcomings in one's looks and personality. Humor makes average-looking people look cute and uninteresting people seem entertaining. Studies show that a good sense of humor even makes you look smarter.[1-3] One study showed that women seek out men with a better sense of humor because it can signal that they may be "amusing, kind, understanding, dependable . . ."[4]

Best of all and central to the theme of this book, humor raises your energy, and that can reverberate into everything you do at school, at work, or in your personal life. The boost of energy will even make you more willing to exercise, and that will raise your overall energy even more.

Humor also transports your mind away from your daily troubles. Humor puts life in perspective and sometimes helps you laugh at even the worst of your problems.

Because humor directly influences your energy, it touches every part of your life that requires concentration and willpower. And for the most part, humor is free and easily accessible. The Internet is full of humor. If you don't have funny friends, find some. If you're a reader, choose funny books. If you go to movies, choose the funny ones first and avoid anything you know will end on a sad note.

Sometimes you want to dispense a bit of your own humor. That comes naturally to some people but not most. In my experience, most people think they have a sense of humor, and to some extent that's true. But not all senses of humor are created equal. So I thought it would be useful to include some humor tips for everyday life.

You don't have to be the joke-teller in the group to demonstrate your sense of humor. You can be the one who steers the conversation to fun topics that are ripe for others to add humor. Every party needs a straight person. You'll appear fun and funny by association.

When it comes to in-person humor, effort counts a lot. When people see you trying to be funny, you free them to try it themselves. So even if your own efforts at humor fall short, you might be unleashing the pent-up humor in others. People need permission to be funny in social or business settings because there's always a risk that comes with humor. You will do people a big favor when you remove some of that risk by going first. For in-person humor, quality isn't as important as you might think. Your attitude and effort count for a lot.

Obviously you want to avoid "trying too hard" when it comes to humor. That happens if you laugh too vigorously at your own jokes or other people's jokes. So-called dry humor is the best strategy if you plan to go for quantity.

I say quality is overrated when it comes to humor, but you do need to achieve a minimum threshold. And that usually means avoiding a handful of traps. Avoid these and you're golden. So allow me to map the traps for you. I'll start with a summary, then explain.

- Over-complaining is never funny.
- Don't overdo self-deprecation.
- Don't mock people.
- Avoid puns and wordplay.

Some people—and I was one of them—believe that humorous complaints about the little aggravations of life constitute humor. Sometimes that's the case. The problem comes when you start doing too much gripe-based humor. One funny observation about a problem in your life can be funny, but five is just complaining, no matter how witty you think you are. Funny complaints wear people out.

Self-deprecating humor is usually the safest type, but here again you don't want to overshoot the target. One self-deprecating comment is a generous and even confident form of humor. You must be at least a bit self-assured to mock yourself in front of others. But if you do it too often, you can transform in the eyes of others from a confident jokester into a Chihuahua.

Don't make fun of other people too often either. If that starts to look like a pattern, people will assume you're talking behind their backs as well.

Beware of puns and other clever wordplay. The only people who appreciate puns are the people who can do them. It's like water polo; it's hard to appreciate the sport unless you've played it. If you don't know for sure that you're dealing with hardcore pun lovers, avoid puns completely. Otherwise, you're just begging for a courtesy snort or an eye roll.

Avoid the traps, and people will think you are genuinely fun. And they'll be right. But endearing yourself to others isn't the last of humor's benefits. Humor also makes you more creative, at least in the short run.[5,6] I think it has something to do with the fact that humor is a violation of straight-line thinking. Humor temporarily shuts down the common sense program in your moist robot brain and boots the random idea generator. At least it feels that way to me, figuratively speaking. Perhaps all that is happening is that humor makes you feel energized and relaxed at the same time. That is bound to help creativity.

Tailor Your Humor

One of the most reliable albeit sexist generalizations I've noticed over the years is that women tend to laugh at stories involving bad things happening to people, such as an attractive girl taking a face plant into a mud puddle on the way to the prom. Guys like that sort of humor, too, but my observation is that men are far more likely to enjoy traditional joke-like stories that are more engineered than organic.

Know your audience. Some people believe that bathroom humor and references to genitalia are the only valid forms of humor. Others look for cleverness. You won't win anyone over to your preferred brand of humor. So it's better to adapt to what others want to hear, assuming your goal is to be liked.

People generally broadcast their sense of humor from the moment you meet. You can observe what people laugh at, what sort of stories they tell, and whether they have an edgy personality. If I hear someone say, "Gosh" or "Holy mackerel," I leave out the profanity from my stories. If I say something mildly clever and get a reaction, I know I can turn the cleverness spigot on full. It's a good idea to test an approach before committing.

Jim's Colonoscopy Story

My friend Jim tells a funny story about his colonoscopy appointment. Per his doctor's instructions, he purged himself the day before the appointment by drinking a powerful laxative and spending the better part of the day in the bathroom. As Jim tells it, he was "squeaky clean" in his backdoor region by the time he visited the doctor.

By this point in his story, you can see the structure developing. As the audience, you already know something bad is going to happen to Jim somehow involving his anal area. That's the sign of a good story. Now, back to it . . .

As Jim tells the story, the cleansing process was a long and unpleasant one. But since he only needs to do it once every year or so, it's worth the unpleasantness. Jim walked into the doctor's office and proudly announced his readiness for the colonoscopy. The receptionist checked her calendar and said, "Your appointment is . . . tomorrow."

That's the punch line. It illustrates two interesting points about storytelling. First, you can probably sense that the story would be far funnier in person. You will discover that some types of humor work best in written form and others work best in person. Jim's story is an in-person type. As you read it here, you probably managed little more than a smile, if that. Told in person, it gets a huge laugh every time.

The second interesting point is that Jim's story saves the "bad part" for your imagination. His second day of cleansing will obviously be unpleasant, but the joke ends with the simple knowledge that unpleasant times are ahead. In general, you want your punch line to inspire listeners to complete the story—including the bad part—in their own minds. That allows every person to imagine the ending in the way that is most amusing to them.

Engineered Humor

An engineered joke is one that includes an unlikely or surprising solution to a problem, much like the way an engineer discovers a novel way to fix something that is broken.

For example, in 2010, the world watched the drama of the Chilean coal miners trapped underground for days. A small hole from the surface to their tiny underground space was their only source of oxygen, food, and water. The world was emotionally connected to these miners, praying for their rescue.

Meanwhile, stories started emerging that some of the miners had both wives and mistresses. My friend Laura heard the stories of the mistresses and quipped, "If I were one of those wives, I'd be shoveling dirt down that air hole."

That's an engineering solution to a problem not normally solved by engineering. You can visualize the angry wife hearing the news of her husband's mistress and shoveling dirt down the hole while cursing. It's a funny image, at least for people who have a warped sense of humor. (I laughed for about a week.)

I realize that my stereotypes about the type of humor women enjoy versus men won't hold for all people. For example, Laura created one of the best engineered jokes I've heard. But I think you'll find the gender generalization about humor to be about 80 percent true.

CHAPTER 24

Affirmations

In my book *The Dilbert Future*, I described my odd experience with something called affirmations. You'll need to know a little back story here to understand my unwavering optimism against long odds, including my voice problem.

Affirmations are simply the practice of repeating to yourself what you want to achieve while imagining the outcome you want. You can write it, speak it, or just think it in sentence form. The typical form of an affirmation would be "I, Scott Adams, will become an astronaut." The details of affirmations probably don't matter much because the process is about improving your focus, not summoning magic.

Apparently, I failed badly at my first attempt to write about affirmations in *The Dilbert Future*. I had intended to make a point about the limits of human perception and how that might be holding us back. Based on angry emails I got and the buzz on the Internet, apparently most people interpreted my point to mean I believe in magic. The skeptics of the world were apoplectic about what they perceived as my promotion of magical thinking to an irrational and gullible public.

So let me start by clearly stating that I don't believe in magic. But like most people, I have experienced several events in my life that are indistinguishable from magic in the same way a caveman might perceive that your phone is magic.* My point then and now is that you don't need to know why something works to take advantage of it. A caveman could successfully use a phone, assuming someone taught him how, while

---

*I'm paraphrasing Arthur C. Clarke's observation that any sufficiently complex technology is indistinguishable from magic.

continuing to believe its inner workings were supernatural. His faulty perception would have no impact on the usefulness of the phone, at least until it broke and he started praying to it.

Affirmations might be a bit like the caveman and the phone. You can make your own judgment about whether my story that follows is a case of coincidence, selective memory, simple luck, hard work, greater focus, mind-tuning, hidden talent, or whatever you like. My perception (which I assume for the sake of consistency is flawed) is that affirmations are useful, and I have no idea why.

Let me simply tell you what happened when I tried affirmations, and you can decide for yourself. But let's agree to rule out magic as one of the explanations.

How It Started

As I mentioned earlier, in my mid-twenties, I took classes to learn hypnosis. I got to know some of the students outside of class. One of them called me at home to say she had read a book about affirmations, tried them, and experienced some hugely unlikely results, at least according to her own estimate of the odds. She strongly recommended I try affirmations, too. It would cost me nothing but time, which I had in abundance during those years, so I said I'd give them a try. My real agenda was to debunk her claims. I assumed affirmations were complete bullshit. But it's my preference to be open-minded when I can, so I went into it with the intention of giving affirmations a fair try.

My first affirmation was "I, Scott, will become rich." The long version of the story involves two ridiculously lucky stock picks that came to me out of nowhere in separate flashes of something that felt like intuition. But I didn't trust affirmations enough to invest heavily in stocks that came to my attention through some sort of irrational process. I invested nothing in the first stock because of a paperwork snafu, and it subsequently went to the moon. I bought and quickly sold the second stock for a respectable gain and watched from the sidelines as it, too, zoomed up. Both stocks were big stories that year and among the top gainers out of a field of perhaps 10,000 possible stocks. I didn't pick any other stocks during that time.

My affirmation failed to make me rich, at least right away. But I wondered: What were the odds I could pick two of the best stocks of the year back-to-back with zero research? Obviously, it could be pure luck. A monkey could pick two winning stocks in a row at least some of the time. But it was enough of a tease to encourage me to try again with another affirmation.

My second attempt involved a girl I perceived to be far out of my league. I'll shortcut that story by saying a series of coincidences lined up to make the unlikely happen, albeit briefly. But again, that wasn't proof affirmations work. Maybe I'm just a good stock-picker and far more handsome than my lying mirror is willing to admit. Whatever the real reason for my success, I got enough of a payoff to encourage me to keep trying affirmations just in case there was something to them.

My next affirmation was more personal than I can describe here. But it happened to be the type of thing for which I could calculate the odds with some degree of certainty, like how you might know a lottery winner beat odds of ten-million-to-one. In my case, I beat odds that I calculated to be somewhere in the ten-thousand-to-one range, and none of it required hard work, skill, or connections.

I pause here to acknowledge the possibility that selective memory is behind my perceptions. Perhaps I tried lots of affirmations and only remember the ones that seemed to work. I can't rule that out. Maybe I was a good stock-picker, a total stud who didn't realize it, and lucky like a lottery winner. Or perhaps I'm terrible at estimating the odds of particular events happening. Any one of those explanations is possible.

I tried affirmations again. This time was in service of a bet. My coworker at the bank had signed up for a class to help raise her GMAT test scores. That's the test you take to qualify for a master's degree program in business, better known as an MBA. I had taken the test in my senior year of college and scored a mediocre seventy-seventh percentile, meaning 23 percent of people who took the test did better. It wasn't good enough to get into a top school, and so I had abandoned that dream. But for some reason that I don't even understand in hindsight, I bet my coworker that I could retake the test and beat her next score, whatever that might be. And I boldly (stupidly) proclaimed I would do it without a prep class. It was a dumb bet, given that she had scored in the eighty-sixth percentile her first try and expected to do better because of the class.

I took some practice tests at home and never scored much better than my original seventy-seventh percentile. I decided to put my affirmations to the test. I wanted to visualize a specific result, so I picked the ninety-fourth percentile because I thought that would be high enough to win the bet. I visualized opening the mail and seeing "94" on my test result form.

On test day, I felt I did no better than my practice tests, but I kept up my affirmations on the score of 94 and waited for the results in the mail. A few weeks later, the results arrived. I opened the letter and looked in the box with my overall score. It said 94.

Perhaps I'm just a good test-taker and my bet with a coworker inspired me. And perhaps hitting the exact score of 94 was nothing but a coincidence. All I knew for sure is that if affirmations had any kind of value, I should set my sights higher. But for the next few years, I focused on my day job and didn't use affirmations because things seemed to be going generally well without any help. I graduated from the Haas School of Business at the University of California at Berkeley and assumed I was on my way to becoming a CEO of something important someday. I didn't think I needed any help to get there.

That plan did not work out.

The next time I used affirmations was in pursuit of the rarest, most desirable job I have ever imagined. The affirmation went like this: "I, Scott Adams, will be a famous cartoonist."

That worked out better.

CHAPTER 25

Timing Is Luck, Too

When you practice affirmations and then happen to succeed in your area of focus, it feels like extraordinary luck. That's how you perceive it, anyway. The *Dilbert* success story is engorged with lucky-sounding events. I'll describe some of the luckiest parts of my story so you can get a sense for how deep luck sometimes needs to run before you find success.

The biggest component of luck is timing. When the universe and I have been on a compatible schedule—entirely by chance—things worked out swimmingly. When my timing was off, no amount of hard work or talent mattered. *Dilbert* was the best example of lucky timing you will ever see. It wasn't a complete accident that luck found me; I put myself in a position where luck was more likely to happen. I was like a hunter who picks his forest location intelligently and waits in his blind for a buck to stroll by. The hunter still must be lucky, but he manages his situation to increase his odds.

I did something similar. I tried a lot of different ventures, stayed optimistic, put in the energy, prepared myself by learning as much as I could, and stayed in the game long enough for luck to find me. I hoped a buck would eventually walk by, and with *Dilbert* it did.

Let me give you a snapshot of the luck (timing) that needed to happen for *Dilbert* to succeed.

For starters, I had to be born in a time in which newspapers existed and comics mattered. And I had to have the right genetic makeup for the work and the right upbringing. And it helped a great deal that I was born in the United States.

My first comics editor, Sarah Gillespie, immediately saw the potential in *Dilbert* when she looked over the samples I submitted to United Media. Sarah was married to an engineer who worked at IBM. When he dressed for work, he wore a white short-sleeved button-up shirt with pens in his pocket, just like Dilbert. When the other syndication companies saw *Dilbert* and didn't relate to him, they sent me polite rejection letters. When Sarah saw *Dilbert*, she related both to the content and to the writing. She championed the strip against some heavy objections within her company. Had someone else been in Sarah's job, I believe *Dilbert* would have been rejected. There was only a handful of people in the industry who were gatekeepers for new comics. What were the odds that one of them would be married to a real-life Dilbert?

For the first few years after *Dilbert*'s launch, we had trouble getting any large metropolitan newspaper to pick it up. You need the first big paper to get onboard before others see it as a worthy risk.

One day, a *Boston Globe* employee—whose job included looking at syndication submissions and recommending new comics to senior management—went on a vacation with her husband. She was driving; he was bored. The *Dilbert* sales packet happened to be in the car. The husband, who was—as luck would have it—an engineer, picked it up and started laughing. His wife didn't relate to *Dilbert* the same way, but she trusted her husband's reaction and recommended it for inclusion in *The Boston Globe*. With that sale in the bag, many of the newspapers in the Northeast followed suit.

But sales in the western United States were comatose. I soon learned why—the salesperson for that region wasn't a fan of *Dilbert*. So when he went on sales calls, he kept the *Dilbert* sales packet in his briefcase and showed other comics. Then the universe got involved. The salesman had a heart attack and died in a hotel room on the road. His replacement, John Matthews, identified *Dilbert* as the most sellable comic in United Media's stable. And sell it he did to every newspaper he visited. John is the best salesman I've ever known. Had he not been available for the job or had the original salesman lived, *Dilbert* might have been a small comic that ran in the northeast for a few years before fading to obscurity.

The good timing for *Dilbert* was relentless. In the mid-nineties, the media was focusing on the disturbing trend of corporate downsizing, and *Dilbert* got pushed to the front of the conversation as the symbol of hapless office workers everywhere. *Dilbert* was on the covers of *TIME*, *People*, *Newsweek*, *Fortune*, *Inc.*, and more. I modified *Dilbert* to be more workplace-focused than it had originally been, and it became a perfect match of a comic to an era.

At about the same time, technology itself became a celebrity. The Internet exploded, the dot-com era happened, and all-things technical were suddenly fascinating even to the general public. In the eighties, Dilbert would have been nothing but another nerd comic. In the nineties, *Dilbert* symbolized the type of technology geniuses who were transforming life on planet Earth. *Dilbert* was unexpectedly and ironically "sexy."

I had even more luck when Berke Breathed retired his popular comic strip *Bloom County*, which opened hundreds of spaces in newspapers. Later, Bill Watterson, creator of *Calvin and Hobbes*, retired and opened even more space. It was unprecedented for cartoonists at the top of their game and so young to retire. And the timing coincided with the growing spotlight on *Dilbert*, making it the most obvious replacement choice. Newspapers snapped it up like candy.

I mentioned my hand problem—the focal dystonia—in an earlier chapter. My career would have been over if not for the simultaneous development of Wacom's Cintiq product, which allowed me to draw directly to the computer with no worries. What were the odds that the problem and the solution existed at the same time? If my hand problem had happened five years earlier, I might have retired from cartooning.

To sum it up, the success of *Dilbert* is mostly a story of luck. But I did make it easier for luck to find me, and I was thoroughly prepared when it did. Luck won't give you a strategy or a system—you have to get that yourself.

I find it helpful to see the world as a slot machine that doesn't ask you to put money in. All it asks is for your time, focus, and energy—to pull the handle over and over. A normal slot machine that requires money will bankrupt any player in the long run. But the machine that has rare yet certain payoffs and asks for no money up front is a guaranteed winner if you have what it takes to keep yanking until you get lucky. In that environment, you can fail 99 percent of the time while knowing success is guaranteed. All you need to do is stay in the game long enough.

CHAPTER 26

A Few Times Affirmations Worked

A few years into my cartooning career, *The Wall Street Journal* asked me to write a guest editorial about the workplace. That article was titled "The Dilbert Principle," and it got a great response from readers. An editor for Harper Business contacted me and asked if I would be willing to write a book around the same topic. I agreed and started writing. During that time, and usually while running on the treadmill at the gym, I repeated my new affirmation in my head: "I, Scott Adams, will be a number-one bestselling author."

The Dilbert Principle started strong and within a few weeks hit number one on *The New York Times* nonfiction bestseller list. In a matter of months, my follow-up book, *Dogbert's Big Book of Business*, joined it in the number two slot. The success of the two books brought me a lot of attention and put a turbo boost on sales of *Dilbert* to newspapers. The *Dilbert* website was getting huge traffic by the standards of the day, and I had a booming speaking career on the side. The licensing business for *Dilbert* took off, too. Suddenly, it seemed as if everything I touched was working.

With so many good things happening, I convinced myself that I could do just about anything that I set my mind to. I discounted the affirmations as being nothing more than a way to focus, and I figured I no longer needed that crutch.

So I didn't use affirmations when I worked as co-executive producer of the animated *Dilbert* TV show that ran for two half-seasons on the now-defunct UPN network. The first half-season did well, but we lost our time slot the following season because of a simple communication problem that resulted in the show getting moved to a new time slot. Viewers had trouble finding the show, and the ratings tanked. At the same time, the network decided to remake itself as a channel focusing on African-American viewers. Dilbert was cancelled after the second half-season. I had mixed feelings about the show's premature death because it was a lot of work, and not the fun kind.

I also didn't use affirmations when I invested in my first or second restaurant, and in the long run, neither of those worked out.

I didn't use affirmations when I started my vegetarian burrito company, which never took off.

I can't tell you I believe affirmations *caused* my few successes or that not using affirmations doomed other projects to failure. I can only tell you what I did and when. As I've explained, there are several perfectly reasonable explanations for the pattern. The one that stands out in my mind is that I really had no love for the work involved in the TV show, the Dilberito, or the restaurants. And I felt relief when each ended. The pattern I noticed is that the affirmations only worked when I had a 100 percent unambiguous desire for success. If I could have snapped my fingers and made the TV show, the Dilberito, and the restaurants successful, I would have done it. But I knew I wouldn't have enjoyed ongoing management of any one of them. Did my mixed feelings matter? I'll never know.

I only used affirmations one more time. And in that case, I had no mixed feelings. I wanted something as much as a person can want.

"I, Scott, will speak perfectly."

CHAPTER 27

Voice Update I

Months had passed since my last Botox shot to my vocal cords. My voice was so weak and unpredictable that it was a struggle to accomplish the simplest human interactions. I'm a natural optimist, but the reality was that spasmodic dysphonia had no cure, and I was likely to spend the rest of my life without ever again experiencing a conversation.

I couldn't speak on the phone except to people who knew my situation and were willing to keep conversations to short yes or no answers. I couldn't order my own food at restaurants, couldn't talk to people at social gatherings, couldn't continue my speaking tour, and generally couldn't enjoy life. I was often depressed, which I understand happens to most people with this condition. The loneliness was debilitating.

Blogging kept me alive. When I wrote a blog post, I was communicating. People understood me, mostly, and left fascinating comments and responses. Blogging made me feel less lonely. It kept me sane but only barely.

I wasn't looking forward to the next several decades of life as a non-talker. It felt like my personal hell. But I hadn't given up. I didn't know how to give up.

Incurable health problems often attract quack cures. I tried most of the ones that weren't dangerous. Drinking a certain brand of cough syrup didn't work. Acupuncture didn't work. Mineral supplements didn't work. Stutter cures didn't work. Three different approaches to voice therapy didn't work. The Alexander Technique* didn't work. Iron supplements didn't work. Changing my diet didn't work.

I hadn't spoken normally for over a year. It was slowly killing me.

But what I *did* have was a two-part system. To identify the pattern that caused my voice to be its worst, I created a spreadsheet and recorded every factor I guessed might be at work, including diet, hours of sleep, exercise, practice talking, and even the number of Diet Cokes consumed. If I could find the pattern behind my worst voice days, I would know what I needed to change. But no pattern emerged.

The second part of my system involved scouring the planet for any mention of the words "spasmodic dysphonia" in a medical context. Luckily, I was born in the right era, so the scouring was done by Google using their Google Alerts function. I just plugged in the keywords. Any mention of my condition anywhere on the Internet generated an email message that went to my phone that lives in my left-front pants pocket. I got several alerts per week, but none looked promising. Usually, the articles on the Internet discussed the incurability of the condition—no surprise given that the medical consensus was that my condition was caused by a brain abnormality. Those are hard to fix.

No one wants to feel lonely and depressed. But on the plus side, misery alters your appetite for risk. If someone had suggested a plan for fixing my voice that had a 50 percent chance of killing me, I would have taken it in a heartbeat.

I checked my phone often to see if any Google alert emails had come in. And I waited. *Homo sapiens* have been around for 150,000 years. My best hope was that one of us, somewhere on Earth, would figure out a cure for this problem within my lifetime, before the condition devoured what was left of my optimism. My odds were not good. But I was far from giving up. In fact, I was mad as hell, and for me, anger is sometimes enough. My attitude was always the same: Escape from my cell, free the other inmates, shoot the warden, and burn down the prison.

In my car, every day, I repeated over and over, "I, Scott Adams, will speak perfectly." I believed it would happen because I *needed* to believe it.

---

*The Alexander Technique is a method for moving in a conscious way with the goal of removing tension from your body.

CHAPTER 28

Experts

Many years ago, in my late twenties, I asked a doctor to look at a strange lump that formed on my neck, about half the size of a Ping-Pong ball. I asked what it might be, and he said, "Well, two possibilities. It's either cancer or . . . I don't know what else it could be. I'll schedule you for X-rays."

I have a vivid memory of sitting in the doctor's waiting room with the other patients who were there for the same reason: *maybe* cancer. The doctor would enter the room with some X-rays in hand, call out a name, and if the news was good, he would announce it before the patient even rose from his chair. "Mr. Gonzales? Good news. Your X-rays are clean." A few minutes later, "Mrs. Johnson, the X-rays look great. It's all good."

Then it was my turn. "Mr. Adams? Please step into my office."

Yikes.

The doctor showed me the X-rays and said that from the looks of it, it was probably some sort of neck cancer. I slumped in my chair.

The doctor explained that it *might* be something harmless. He explained that sometimes a lump looks just like cancer on an X-ray, but it turns out to be just "one of those things" and no big deal. He scheduled me for a biopsy to settle it once and for all.

The appointment was set for the following week. For seven days, I was like Schrőedinger's Cat, maybe dead and maybe not. I lived alone in San Francisco and didn't have much of a social support structure. It was just me and my one room apartment. My bed was also my couch. It was a long week.

At the appointment, the nurse technician described the biopsy procedure. Time slowed to a crawl, and I could hear my own heartbeat. The technician explained that he would put a needle into the lump and draw out some fluid. If it was blood, I probably had cancer. If the fluid was clear, it was just "one of those things," and no big deal.

The needle went in, and time slowed again as the technician sucked out the liquid just beyond my peripheral vision. *Say something, you bastard!* He knew the result in the first second. He made me wait until he was done.

The needle was full of clear fluid. "I guess it was just one of those things," he said. "Let me get the rest of it."

I left the hospital a few minutes later with a tiny bandage and a new outlook on life. Food tasted better for weeks. Annoying people were no longer annoying. Trees were fuzzy balls of wonder. Cold air was refreshing instead of annoying. And I learned that sometimes experts get it wrong on the first try.

Dealing with experts is always tricky. Are they honest? Are they competent? How often are they right? My observation and best guess is that experts are right about 98 percent of the time on the easy stuff but only right 50 percent of the time on anything that is unusually complicated, mysterious, or even new.

Years later, when a psychologist offered me Valium to fix my voice problem, I recognized the situation as the type in which experts are wrong half of the time. That made it easy for me to say no to the Valium and keep searching for a less-druggy solution. When I made the decision, it felt like intuition, whatever that is. But I think it would be more accurate to say it was the result of pattern recognition plus optimism.

If your gut feeling (intuition) disagrees with the experts, take that seriously. You might be experiencing some pattern recognition that you can't yet verbalize.

CHAPTER 29

Association Programming

When I worked for Crocker National Bank, my coworkers and I had a good laugh at a summer intern who espoused a whacky theory about success being a function of the neighborhood you choose to live in. His plan was to get into the best apartment he could afford in an upscale neighborhood no matter how many roommates that might require him to have. He'd let some sort of vague magic do the rest. He was willing to work hard, go to school, obey the law, and take all the other normal steps to success. But he figured that could only take him so far. The real kicker was his brilliant plan to live among rich people until he could become one by association.

I recall cleverly mocking him to the delight of all who were within earshot. He seemed like such a rational guy in every other way. But this rich-by-association scheme was just plain stupid. Upon interrogation, I learned he wasn't suggesting he would network and make important contacts with his well-to-do neighbors. There was no defined mechanism to explain how proximity to rich people would make him successful. The best he could offer was his observation that life had patterns, and this was one of them: You become like the people around you.

A few years later, I learned more than I wanted to know about the workings of Alcoholics Anonymous. My ex-girlfriend had a need for their services, and I learned that it works better than most alternatives for people with drinking problems.[1,2] One of Alcoholics Anonymous' rules involves keeping away from people who are bad influences. That seems obvious when you think about it, given the power of peer pressure and that sort of thing. In this situation, who you associate with makes a big difference. But this is a special case and quite different from the rich-by-association hypothesis. Still, there was enough similarity between the two cases that it began to register with me as a potential pattern.

More recently, I saw a study that said hanging around with overweight people can cause you to gain weight.[3-9] I would not have imagined that to be true. But I can imagine several mechanisms that would explain it. If each of your friends are fifty pounds overweight and you're only sporting an extra ten, you probably don't feel much pressure to change. And if your corpulent friends keep steering you toward fast-food joints when you're together, that can hurt, too. So it seems entirely plausible that hanging around with overweight people can influence your own waistline. Still, that's very different from the rich-by-association theory that has no obvious mechanism.

After *Dilbert* launched, I continued working my day job at Pacific Bell for several years. Since then, my old boss, Mike Goodwin (who was also the guy who named *Dilbert*), wrote and published a book about his father's experience in a Japanese prisoner-of-war camp. (Spoiler alert: It didn't go well.) The book, *Shobun*, was his first attempt as a writer. It didn't strike me as a huge coincidence that two cubicle rats from Pacific Bell both became published writers. The world is full of such ordinary coincidences.

After I left Pacific Bell, I learned that another fellow who sat across the cubicle wall from me subsequently wrote a book about his stint in prison for murder. He's out of jail now, and because I have a policy of being kind to people who strangle acquaintances with belts, I'd like to say he's a fine fellow and his book is excellent. It's called *You Got Nothing Coming: Notes from a Prison Fish*, by Jimmy Lerner. What are the odds that three people in one little corner of Pacific Bell could all become published authors? I understand that coincidences are normally just that, but they seem special because we don't get to see all the things that *don't* happen. Still, my pattern detector perked up. Here were two guys who shared my proximity and ended up following a similar model. Did their proximity to me matter in some way, perhaps by example or inspiration? Or would they have written books anyway? There's no way to know.

But there's more to the story. Back up several years to my time as a supervisor in the technology wing of Crocker National Bank, before *Dilbert* was even an idea. One of the employees I managed came to me one day and announced his plan to write an article about a spreadsheet trick he discovered. His plan was to submit it to a trade magazine and see if they would pay. He had no experience as a writer, but his idea was clever and worthy of sharing. I encouraged him to submit his work, and to my surprise, the magazine accepted it and paid him a hefty (at the time) fee of $1,500. They even rewrote most of the article, which they called "editing" and he called "butchering." Still, he proved that a guy in a cubicle can become a published writer and make money at it. He went on to write several more articles that also got published. Did my association with him make it more likely I would later pursue a career in cartooning? I think it did. It made success outside my field seem accessible. It made it real.

Humans are social animals. There are probably dozens of ways we absorb energy, inspiration, skills, and character traits from those around us. Sometimes we learn by example. Sometimes success appears more approachable and ordinary because we see normal people achieve it, and perhaps that encourages us to pursue schemes with higher payoffs. Sometimes the people around us give us information we need, or encouragement, or contacts, or even useful criticism. We can't always know the mechanism by which others change our future actions, but it's clear it happens, and it's important.

Years ago, I mocked an intern for thinking his choice of neighbors would influence his career. If he's reading this, I'd like to offer my apology. I can easily see that where you live might influence the energy you put into your career. Living near optimistic winners is sure to rub off to some extent. And I advise you to consider this fact a primary tool for programming your moist robot self. The programming interface is your location. To change yourself, part of the solution might involve spending more time with the people who represent the change you seek.

For example, you'll find it much easier to exercise in an environment where others are exercising. When you watch others exercise, you activate the exercise subroutine in your own brain. Likewise, it's often easier to work when others are working in the same room, so long as they don't bug you too much.

Given our human impulse to pick up the habits and energy of others, you can use that knowledge to literally program your brain the way you want. Simply find the people who most represent what you would like to become and spend as much time with them as you can without trespassing, kidnapping, or stalking. Their good habits and good energy will rub off on you.

CHAPTER 30

Happiness

The only reasonable goal in life is to maximize your total lifetime experience of something called happiness. That might sound selfish, but it's not. Only a sociopath or a hermit can find happiness through extreme selfishness. A normal person needs to treat others well to enjoy life. For the sake of argument, let's assume you're normal(ish).

If you want to boost your happiness, understand what happiness is and how it works. You might think the science of happiness is obvious, but it's not. Pursuing happiness without understanding the mechanisms behind it is like planting a garden without knowing the basics of fertilization, pest control, watering, and frost. It's easy to pop a seed in the ground, but it takes a deeper understanding of the gardening arts to grow something wonderful. Happiness, like gardening, only *seems* simple. If you don't believe me, look at the tomato plant in my garden. I gave it water and sunlight. What more could it need?

Let's start by defining happiness and agreeing on what causes it. My definition of happiness is that it's a feeling you get when your body chemistry is producing pleasant sensations in your mind. That definition is compatible with the science of happiness.[1-6]

It's tempting to imagine happiness as a state of mind caused by whatever is happening in your life. By that way of thinking, we're largely victims to the cold, cold world that sometimes rewards our good work and sometimes punishes us for no reason. That's a helpless worldview that can blind you to a simple system for being happier.

Science has done a good job in recent years of demonstrating that happiness isn't as dependent on your circumstances as one might think. For example, amputees often return to whatever level of happiness they enjoyed before losing a limb.[7-9] And you know from your own experience that some people seem to be happy no matter what is going on in their lives while others can't find happiness no matter how many things are going right. We're all born with a limited range of happiness, and the circumstances of life can only jiggle us around within the range.

The good news is that anyone who has experienced happiness probably has the capacity to spend more time at the top of their personal range and less time near the bottom. In my case, my baseline is on the fence between happy and unhappy, so staying near the top of my narrow range makes all the difference. To do that, I treat myself like the moist robot I am and manipulate my body chemistry as needed. I also try to improve my situation and circumstances wherever I can, but I see that as 20 percent of the solution. The big part—the 80 percent of happiness—is nothing but a chemistry experiment. And it's hugely helpful to think of it that way. You can't always quickly fix whatever is wrong in your environment, and you can't prevent negative thoughts from drifting into your head. But you can easily control your body chemistry through lifestyle, and that in turn will cause your thoughts to turn positive while making the bumps in your path feel less disruptive.

Let's get to the mechanics of manipulating your body chemistry. Obviously, your doctor can give you a pill to change your mood. Antidepressants are big business. And you can change your chemistry by drinking alcohol or using recreational drugs. The problem with each of those methods is that they come with risks and side effects you'd rather avoid. I advocate a more natural approach.

For starters, the single biggest trick for manipulating your happiness chemistry is being able to do what you want *when* you want. Contrast that with the more common situation in which you might be able to do all the things you want, but you can't often do them *when* you want.

For example, you might enjoy eating a delicious meal. But if the only time you were allowed to eat delicious food was right after you already filled your stomach with junk food, the delicious meal would not make you happy. A mediocre meal when you're starving will contribute more to your happiness than an extraordinary meal when you're not hungry. The timing of things can be more important than the intrinsic value of the things.

Napping is another perfect example of the importance of timing. A good nap can be a wonderful thing, but if the only available time to nap is an hour before bedtime, a nap would do you little good. You need to control the order and timing of things to be happy. It's important to look at happiness in terms of timing because timing is easier to control than resources. It's hard to become rich enough to buy your own private island, but, relatively speaking, it's easier to find a job with flexible hours. A person with a flexible schedule and average resources will be happier than a rich person who has everything except a flexible schedule. Step one in your search for happiness is to continually work toward having control of your schedule.

Parents understand what I'm talking about. Most parents love their kids and are glad they had them. At the same time, kids remove almost all flexibility from your schedule, especially if you're the stay-at-home parent. It's no wonder that parents who seem to have everything—nice house, great kids, good friends—still find themselves in misery during the years their kids are young. Those parents might have all the "stuff" they could ask for, but they have no flexibility to enjoy what they want when they want.

As I write this chapter, I'm sitting in a comfortable chair with my trusty dog, Snickers, while enjoying a warm cup of coffee. I just came from a good workout, so I'm feeling relaxed and in the mood to write. By any definition, what I'm doing is work, but because I can control the timing of it on this particular day, it doesn't feel like work. I transformed work into pleasure simply by having control over *when* I do it.

In your personal life and your career, consider schedule flexibility when making any big decision. Realistically, sometimes you do need to suck it up, work long hours, watch the kids, and do your duty. Just remember to keep your eye out for ways to maximize your schedule freedom in the long term. It's something you want to work toward. Not everyone reading this book will become work-from-home cartoonists, but you can certainly find a boss who values your productivity over your attendance.

That brings me to the next important mechanism for happiness. Happiness has more to do with where you're heading than where you are. A person who is worth $2 billion will feel sad if he suddenly loses $1 billion because he's moving in the wrong direction, even if the change has no impact on his ability to buy what he wants. But a street person will celebrate discovering a new dumpster behind an upscale restaurant because it means good eating ahead. We tend to feel happy when things are moving in the right direction and unhappy when things are trending bad.

The directional nature of happiness is one reason it's a good idea to have a sport or hobby that leaves you plenty of room to improve every year. Tennis and golf are two perfect examples. With either sport, an average player can continue improving well past the age of sixty. Slow and steady improvement at anything makes you feel as if you are on the right track. The feeling of progress stimulates your body to create the chemicals that make you feel happy.

When you choose a career, consider whether it will lead to a lifetime of ever-improved performance, a plateau, or a steady decline in your skills. As a cartoonist, my drawing skills have slowly improved over most of my career, and that is a source of happiness for me. If you are lucky enough to have career options but only one of them affords a path of continuous improvement, choose that one, all else being equal.

The next element of happiness you need to master is imagination. I wrote about this in the context of raising your energy, which is closely related to happiness, but it bears repeating in this chapter. Pessimism is often a failure of imagination. If you can imagine the future being brighter, those thoughts lift your energy and goose the chemistry in your body to produce a sensation of happiness. If you can't even *imagine* an improved future, you won't be happy—no matter how well your life is going right now.

I find it useful to daydream that the future will be better than today and by far. I like to imagine a future that is spectacular and breathtaking. The daydreams need not be accurate in terms of predicting the future. Simply imagining a better future hacks your brain chemistry and provides you with the sensation of happiness today. Being happy raises your energy level and makes it easier to take steps toward real-world happiness. This is another case in which your imagination can influence the real world. Don't let reality control your imagination. Let your imagination be the user interface to choose your own reality.

The next important thing to remember about happiness is that it's not a mystery of the mind, nor is it magic. Happiness is the natural state for most people whenever they feel healthy, have flexible schedules, and expect the future to be good.

As I write this next paragraph, a few days have passed, and now I'm sitting at a table in my health club. I exercised, I had my healthy reward snack, and now I'm thoroughly happy even though I'm working at rewriting and tweaking this chapter. Taking care of my body always influences my happiness more than whatever task I'm involved in. That's an important point because normally when you feel unhappy, you blame your mood on whatever your environment is serving up to you. It's easy to blame your environment because you know you can interpret almost anything as bad news or potential bad news. Just add pessimism and cynicism to any observation, and you can manufacture bad news out of thin air. If you know anyone who routinely interprets good news as bad, you know how easily it can be done. I'm here to tell you that the primary culprit in your bad moods is a deficit in one of the big five: flexible schedule, imagination, sleep, diet, or exercise.

I've explained to a number of people my observation that exercise, diet, and sleep influence mood. The usual reaction is a blank expression followed by a change of topic. No one wants to believe that the formula for happiness is as simple as daydreaming, controlling your schedule, napping, eating right, and being active every day. You'd feel like an idiot for suffering so many unhappy days while not knowing the cure was so accessible. I know from experience that you might accept the idea that daily lifestyle choices are perhaps a small part of what causes your bad moods. But you probably think most of your crabbiness is caused by the idiots and sociopaths in your life, plus your inexplicable bad luck on any given day. Based on a lifetime of observation, my best estimate is that 80 percent of your mood is based on how your body feels, and only 20 percent is based on your genes and your circumstances, particularly your health.

Ask yourself this question: At times when you've exercised earlier in the day, eaten well, hydrated, and had enough sleep, what percentage of those times would you find yourself in a good mood? I'll bet you don't know the answer to that question because it's not the sort of thing anyone pays attention to. But now that I've put the idea in your head, you'll automatically find yourself noticing the link between daily body maintenance and your not-so-mysterious happiness. I predict you'll observe that your good moods are highly correlated with exercise, diet, and sleep.

Exercise has two very different benefits that are hard to untangle. The exercise itself releases natural pain-relieving substances, endorphins, and that gives you a direct feeling of well-being.[10-15] But exercise is also a mental escape from whatever was stressing you before you laced your athletic shoes. That's why I recommend forms of exercises that occupy your mind at the same time as your muscles.

Exercise also helps you sleep better, so that's a double benefit.[16] Of the big five factors in happiness—flexible schedule, imagination, diet, exercise, and sleep—my pick for the most important is exercise. If exercise sounds like a lot of work, wait for my chapter on the easiest way to become active.

If the five elements for happiness seem incomplete, that's intentional. I know you might also want sex, a soul mate, fame, recognition, a feeling of importance, career success, and lots more. My contention is that your five-pronged pursuit of happiness will act as a magnet for the other components of happiness you need. When you're fit, happy, and full of energy, people are far more likely to have sex with you, be your friend, and hire you, sometimes all in the same day.

If you're chubby, tired, horny, and unhappy, then your best long-term solution probably isn't Match.com. I'm a proponent of online dating services because the evidence shows they work. But a smarter approach is to take care of yourself first and use that success as leverage to get everything else you need.

I'll cap this discussion by telling you the story of how I felt when my cartooning career reached its high point. It was the late nineties, and I had just deposited the biggest check of my life, thanks largely to a multi-book publishing deal. I had the precise job I had wanted since childhood. I was officially rich. I was as famous as I wanted to be. And I was suddenly and profoundly sad. What the hell was going on?

After some self-reflection, I realized that I was feeling adrift. I no longer had a primary purpose in life because I already achieved it. It was an eerie feeling, unreal and unsettling. I had no kids at the time, so I had no reason to achieve anything more. I dipped well below my baseline happiness, and I wasn't rebounding.

The way I climbed out of my funk was by realizing that my newly acquired resources could help me change the world in some small but positive ways. That was the motivation for creating the Dilberito, which I hoped would make nutrition convenient and perhaps contribute to a trend. In the long run, the Dilberito didn't work out. But it was 100 percent successful in giving me a meaningful purpose, which allowed my optimism and energy to return.

Unhappiness caused by too much success is a high-class problem. That's the sort of unhappiness people work all their lives to get. If you find yourself there—and I hope you do—you'll find your attentions naturally turning outward. You'll seek happiness through service to others. I promise it will feel wonderful.

Routine

Barry Schwartz, author of *The Paradox of Happiness*, tells us that people become unhappy if they have too many options in life. The problem with options is that choosing any path can plague you with self-doubt. You quite rationally think that one of the paths not chosen might have worked out better. That can eat at you.

Choosing among attractive alternatives can also be exhausting. You want to feel as if you researched and considered all your options. That's why I find great comfort in routine. If you ask me today where I will be at 6:20 AM on Saturday morning in the year 2033, I'll tell you I will be at my desk preparing for my daily live stream. That's what I was doing last Saturday at that time and what I plan to do this Saturday as well. I can't recall the last time I woke up and looked at my options for what to do first. It's always the same, at least for the first few hours of my day.

Likewise, I always have my first sip of coffee at about 5:10 AM, and a protein bar to keep me from getting hungry again until late afternoon. I never waste a brain cell in the morning trying to figure out what to do when. Compare that to some people you know who spend two hours planning and deciding for every task that takes one hour to complete. I'm happier than those people.

Recapping the happiness formula:

Eat right.
Exercise.
Get enough sleep.
Imagine an incredible future (even if you don't believe it).
Work toward a flexible schedule.
Do things you can steadily improve at.
Help others (if you've already helped yourself).
Reduce daily decisions to routine.

If you do those eight things, the rest of what you need to stimulate the chemistry of happiness in your brain will be a lot easier to find. In fact, the other components of happiness that you seek—such as career opportunities, love, and friends—might find their way to you if you make yourself an attractive target.

CHAPTER 31

Health

This is a good time to remind you that nothing in this book should be seen as advice. It's never a good idea to take advice from cartoonists, and that's a hundred times more important if the topic is health-related. I don't know how many people have died from following the health advice of cartoonists, but the number probably isn't zero.

So don't view this chapter or anything else I write as advice. In the coming pages, I'll make reference to some interesting and useful studies about diet. And I'll describe my own experiences. That will address two dimensions of your bullshit filter—scientific studies and the experience of a smart friend—but just to be on the safe side, talk to your doctor before embracing any ideas in this book.

My value on the topic of diet, if any, is in simplification. The simple diet plan that works for me is this: *I eat as much as I want, of anything I want, whenever I want.* I weigh a trim 155 pounds and have never felt better. My healthy weight is not a genetic gift. In years past, I have weighed as much as 168 pounds, which looks portly on my 5'8" frame.

Obviously, there are some tricks involved with my too-easy-to-be-true diet plan. The tricks are simple, but they will take some explaining. Let's start with the part about eating "anything I want." The trick there is to change what you *want*. Yes, that's possible, and it's probably easier than you imagine. Once you *want* to eat the right kinds of food for enjoyment, and you don't crave the wrong kind of food, everything else comes somewhat easily.

You probably need some convincing that people can reprogram their food preferences. But consider how differently food tastes when you are famished versus when you have a full stomach. It's the same food, but your enjoyment level is radically different. The best meal I've ever tasted was a week after dental surgery because I hadn't had solid food for days. An ordinary dish of angel hair pasta tasted as if it had been delivered by a deity and carefully paired to my DNA. A month later, the same meal was boring.

I'm sure you've had similar experiences in which bland or even bad food tastes great when you're hungry. Your taste preferences are more like a suggestion from your brain than a result of hard-wiring.

You have also observed that your tastes in food evolve as you age. A kid who can tolerate nothing but mac and cheese matures into an adult who can't get enough sushi. And I imagine you've had the experience of getting sick soon after eating a specific type of food and finding that the coincidental association completely alters your preference for the food later.

You also might have discovered that some foods you thought were awful-tasting can be delightful if prepared and seasoned to your liking. Technique must be factored into your taste preferences as well.

Your food preferences change continuously throughout your life, but you probably never put much effort into *deliberately* changing your preferences. I'll describe some tricks for doing just that. If the tricks work, you, too, can eat "whatever you want" because eventually you'll only want food that is good for you.

I used to crave ice cream in a big way. At one point in my life, I consumed up to two heaping bowls of vanilla bean ice cream per day. During those years, broccoli seemed like the sort of thing that jailers forced prisoners to eat as punishment. Over time, I trained myself to reverse my cravings. Now ice cream is easy to resist, but I'm not comfortable going two days without a hit of broccoli. This transformation in cravings was the result of a deliberate effort to change my preferences. I set out to hack my brain like a computer and rewire the cravings circuitry.

If the thought of no longer craving your favorite food sounds like a sacrifice, it isn't. That's an illusion caused by the fact that it's nearly impossible to imagine losing a craving of any kind. Cravings feel like they grow directly from our core. They feel a part of us. My experience is that cravings can be manipulated. I've successfully erased cravings for a wide variety of less-healthy foods. I do them one at a time, and it's a lot easier than you might think.

It also works the other way; I can instill cravings for healthy foods where I previously had no such desires. There's a limit to this trick in the sense that you probably can't get past a truly nasty taste. But most healthy food is closer to bland than obnoxious.

Healthy food has a bad reputation with most normal eaters because we associate healthy food with the worst tastes and textures in the category. If healthy food makes you think of tofu, rice cakes, or anything that tastes like soap, you're probably not too keen on developing a craving for healthy eating. Think instead of delicious, salted nuts, a buttery ear of corn, or a banana, and you're closer to the mark. (I'll talk later about the tradeoffs of consuming salt and butter.)

Changing your food preferences is a straightforward process, and it starts the way all change starts: by looking at things differently. It's my job to do the hard part and show you a different way to look at the familiar topic of diet. Your part will happen naturally as your own thought process gently nudges your behavior along a predictable and controlled pathway of cause and effect.

My experience, as odd as it sounds, is that I can change my food preferences by thinking of my body as a programmable robot as opposed to a fleshy bag full of magic. This minor change in perspective is more powerful than it seems. Most people believe there is no strong connection between what they eat and how they feel. I call that perception the Fleshy Bag of Magic worldview. When you think of yourself as a fleshy bag of magic, you assume there is either no direct connection between what you eat and how you feel, or you think your diet has some impact, but it's unpredictable because life is complicated and there are too many factors in play.

Most adults understand the basic cause-and-effect of their diet choices. They know that overeating makes them feel bloated, beans make them gassy, and spicy food might make their noses run. Those causes and effects are so obvious that they're hard to miss. But have you ever tracked your mood, problem-solving ability, and energy level in relation to what you recently ate? For most people, the answer is no. You probably think your mood is caused by what's happening in your life, not the starchy food you ate for lunch.

If you look at your life from some distance, you can see that today is a lot like yesterday Tomorrow won't be that different either. Our lives stay roughly the same while our moods can swing wildly. My proposition, which I invite you to be skeptical about, is that one of the primary factors in determining your energy level and therefore your mood is what you've eaten recently.*

Look for the Pattern

Don't take my word for it. The *food is mood* hypothesis probably doesn't pass your common sense filter. It's the sort of thing you need to experience for yourself. You're wired to believe that your mood is determined by whatever good or bad events have happened in your life recently plus your genetic makeup. My observation, backed by the science, is that the person who eats right won't be bothered as much by the little bumps in life's road. They will have greater optimism, too.

When bad luck comes around, your reaction to it is a combination of how bad the luck is plus how prepared your body is for the stress. You can't prevent all bad luck from finding you, but you can fortify yourself to the point where the smaller stuff bounces off. Your mood is a function of chemistry in your body, and food may be a far more dominant contribution to your chemistry than what is happening around you, at least during a normal day.

Remember the first time someone told you it would be hard to rub your stomach and pat your head at the same time? You probably didn't believe it until you tried it yourself. Some types of knowledge can only be acquired by experience. The diet connection to mood is one of those categories of knowledge that must be experienced. Nothing I can tell you

---

*In the fitness chapter that follows, I'll talk about how exercise influences mood. Diet affects mood by influencing your energy levels and your brain's chemistry. Exercise influences mood by keeping your stress under control. Get both of those right.[1-11]

in a book will convince you that food is the dominant determinant of mood if you've lived your entire life without noticing that some types of food make you sleepy and probably cranky as a result. The only way you'll believe that food drives your mood is by testing it in your daily life. By that I mean simply asking yourself how you feel at any given moment and then making a mental note of what you ate recently. Look for the pattern.

You might wonder why, if food controls mood, you haven't noticed it already. The biggest reason is that you probably eat meals that are a combination of lots of different ingredients. You rarely isolate one kind of food just to see how it feels. You probably believe the reason you're sleepy after a big meal is simply because you ate a lot and so your body is diverting its energy from your brain and muscles to your digestive system. You think you're sleepy in the afternoon because someone told you that's what lunch does to people. You're not a scientist who isolates one kind of food and does rigorous analysis. You eat when you're hungry and try to sleep when you're tired. The deeper truths about diet do a good job of hiding.

The best way to test the food-is-mood hypothesis is to enjoy a hearty lunch at a Mexican restaurant—a virtual paradise of carbs—and monitor how you feel in a few hours. Check your energy level at about 2:00 PM. Do you feel as if you would prefer exercising or napping? I'll tell you the answer in advance: You'll want the nap.

Do you think your sleepiness in the afternoon might be a simple function of the time of day? That's easy to test. Wait a few days and try the same experiment with breakfast instead of lunch. Order pancakes and hashbrown potatoes. See if you can stay awake until lunchtime. It won't be easy. That experiment will tell you whether the time of day is more important than what you eat.

If you're thinking the "heaviness" of the meal or the quantity is the cause of your sleepiness, try your Mexican food experiment again another day but only eat half as much. You'll discover that quantity doesn't matter as much as you thought.

For the sake of comparison, experiment for a few days by skipping bread, potatoes, white rice, and other simple carbs. Eat veggies, nuts, salad, fish, or chicken. Now see how you feel a few hours after eating. I'll bet the idea of exercising sounds more appealing after eating those types of foods compared to the day of your Mexican food experiment.

Don't take my word for anything on the topic of diet. People are different, and it seems we learn something new about nutrition every week. You should also have a healthy skepticism about diet studies because they're notoriously bad at sorting out correlation from causation. People who eat caviar probably live longer, but it's not the caviar keeping them alive; there's a known correlation between income and life expectancy. Diet studies are hard to trust because there are so many contradictory ones, and often they look at specific populations, not the average person.

Whenever it's practical and safe, consider your body a laboratory in which you can test different approaches to health. Eat something specific, such as a bowl of white rice, and see how you feel later. Or eat lots of carbs and weigh yourself at the end of the week. Look for the patterns. Which foods make you energetic, and which make you sleepy? Which ones can you eat without gaining weight, and which ones make you expand like a Macy's parade balloon? When you get a handle on your own diet cause-and-effect patterns, you might discover they differ from my experience. For example, you might have wheat or gluten sensitivity or a lactose intolerance, or maybe you never get tired in the afternoon no matter what you eat. It's important to figure out what works for you. And that will require experimenting.

In my case, eating simple carbs depletes my energy so thoroughly that a few hours after consuming them I can fall asleep within thirty seconds of closing my eyes. I literally use white rice like a sleeping pill on evenings I've had too much coffee. But your body might respond differently or less dramatically to both coffee and white rice. You need to experiment to know for sure. Just remember that it is chemistry, not magic, controlling your energy.

I haven't mentioned pasta in my list of simple carbs to avoid, and that's intentional. In my experience, pasta doesn't make me sleepy and cranky like other simple carbs. I first discovered that pasta was mood-neutral by eating a lot of it over the years and paying attention to how I felt later. While potatoes send me straight to my napping chair, pasta is a perfect pre-workout snack. When studies later confirmed that pasta isn't especially high on the glycemic index, it matched my own experience and passed my personal bullshit filter. When it comes to diet, you want to stay consistent with science but also look for confirmation in your personal experience.

Peanuts are another example in which science and my own experience lined up. The science says that because peanuts have a high concentration of fat, they satisfy your appetite efficiently and provide fuel.[12-18] The unpredicted outcome of adding fat-laden peanuts to your diet is that they improve your ability to lose weight. My experience matches the science exactly. Peanuts do satisfy my appetite, and the pattern I notice is that I eat smaller meals on days I eat peanuts.

Likewise, I find I can eat as much cheese as I want—I eat a lot of it on most days—and it does a great job of satisfying my hunger without making me tired. And if I do a good job with the rest of my diet, I don't gain weight. I don't believe science backs me up on the benefits of cheese, and if my cholesterol were high, I would steer clear. I have some doubts about cheese, but for now I enjoy the taste and appreciate the hunger-squashing utility of it. I'll keep looking at the science as it evolves. Ask your doctor before you follow my lead on cheese. I only mention cheese because it illustrates my approach to choosing foods, not because I necessarily choose right. I'm trying to provide a rational template for diet choices, not a specific prescription for everyone.

Prior to reading this book, the way you probably looked at food was in terms of good versus bad, fattening versus low-calorie, carbs versus protein, or some combination of those. All those ways of looking at food have power to help you steer away from bad diet choices. The problem with the common view of food is that it will always make you feel as if you're in a battle with yourself. You *crave* bad foods because they are so darned tasty. You struggle to resist.

Science has demonstrated that humans have a limited supply of willpower.[19-21] If you use up your supply resisting one temptation, you limit your ability to resist others. Struggling to do *anything* has a steep price because you don't want to use up your willpower and energy on something as unimportant as staying away from the candy drawer. You might need your willpower later for something more substantial. So what you need is a diet system that doesn't rely on willpower. And that means reprogramming your food preferences so willpower is less necessary. I'll explain how to do that in a minute.

Some people reading will compare the idea of reprogramming your brain to self-hypnosis, and that might feel creepy or unlikely to work. A better approach, as I mentioned, is to think of your body as a moist, programmable robot whose outputs depend on its inputs, not magic. Imagine you're an engineer who is trying to find the user interface for your moist robot body so you can make some useful adjustments. It's as if you have one menu choice labeled "Make Sleepy" and another labeled "Energize." You can choose "Make Sleepy" simply by eating simple carbs.

If the idea of reprogramming your mind sounds like L. Ron Hubbard's *Dianetics* and the process of "auditing," which is at the core of Scientology, that's about half right. The part that's right is that *Dianetics* also attempts to change behavior by changing the way you look at yourself and what makes you do what you do. Interestingly, as I pointed out earlier in this book, you can get good results by doing the right thing for the wrong reasons. For example, if you believe alcohol is the Devil's urine, that might eliminate your risk of drinking and driving. You can often get good results from inaccurate worldviews. Some famous philosophers, some scientists, and at least one cartoonist would speculate that inaccurate worldviews are the only kind there are.

Does *Dianetics* work in terms of creating good outcomes for its followers? I have no data to answer that question. But I wouldn't be surprised if auditing does work for some people. Based on my experience, I think you could replace the auditing process in Scientology with an Ouija board and still have good outcomes for some people.

The Food-Exercise Connection

The traditional view of weight maintenance is that you need to exercise and watch your diet to get good results. That's mostly true, but a more useful way to look at the connection between food and exercise is not as equal partners. A more practical view is that food is the fuel that makes exercise possible. When you eat simple carbs for lunch, you find yourself wanting a nap more than you want to spend an hour on the treadmill. If you stuff yourself for dinner, you might cancel your plans to go for a run. If you manage your diet right, you'll want to exercise more, and that will translate into doing so. The starting point for good health is diet. Once you get your diet right, your energy level will increase, and you'll find yourself more in the mood for exercise.

It can be doubly hard to change your diet and start an exercise program at the same time, at least in the usual way people do these things because both objectives require willpower. A smarter approach is to use a system to remove willpower from your diet choices—as I'll explain in a bit—and let your increased energy guide you toward a natural preference for being more active. I'll have more to say about exercise later as well. The main point for both diet and exercise is that you want to reduce the amount of willpower required. Any other approach is unsustainable.

Breaking the Simple-Carb Addiction

The willpower you need to resist simple carbs such as white potatoes, white bread, and white rice must come from somewhere, and as I mentioned earlier, studies show that using willpower for anything reduces how much you have in reserve for other temptations. The approach that works for me involves stealing willpower from the part of my brain that tries to avoid overeating. You might want to give my method a try. For a few months, eat as much as you want of anything that is not a simple carb. That frees up your willpower so you can use it to avoid those delicious and convenient simple carbs.

If you were hungry and I said you couldn't eat the delicious bread in the breadbasket in front of you, that would take great willpower to resist. But if I said you couldn't have the delicious bread but could have anything else you wanted right now, suddenly the bread would be easy to resist. An attractive alternative makes willpower less necessary. It frees up your stockpile of willpower for other uses. In my system, all you need to do is eat as much as you want of anything that isn't a simple carb and keep to that for a few months.

Would this plan make you gain weight for a few months? For some people, it might. But the short term doesn't matter; you're in this for the long haul. It's a system, not a diet with a specific weight goal. Remember, goals are a trap. You want systems, not goals. The first part of the system is to break your addiction to simple carbs.

My experience is that after you break the addiction, it isn't hard to recover from the occasional french fry binge. Food isn't like alcohol, where one drink can send an alcoholic back to the bottom. Eating a piece of bread is only a pebble in the road for someone who has broken the carb addiction.

If for several months you give yourself permission to eat as much as you want of the foods that don't include addictive simple carbs, you'll discover several things. For starters, you'll have more energy without the simple carbs. And that will translate into keeping you more active, which in turn burns calories.

Another change you'll notice after a few months without simple carbs is that your cravings will start to diminish. The sensation you feel as a preference for certain foods can be in reality more of an addiction than a true preference. For example, there was a long period in my life in which I couldn't go a whole day without eating a giant Snickers candy bar. The first bite gave me a feeling of euphoria I enjoyed in every particle of my being. But after a few months of eating as much as I wanted of healthier food, I lost the craving for Snickers bars. What I thought was some sort of deep genetic disposition to chocolate was actually more of an addiction. After a few months of staying off the chocolate, I lost the craving. Later, when I ate a Snickers bar just to test what would happen, I barely enjoyed it. It felt like nothing but unnecessary calories.

Just to be clear, I don't include Snickers in the category of simple carbs that sap your energy. My experience was that the combination of chocolate and peanuts generally pepped me up, exactly as their commercials suggest. My only problem with Snickers is that I binged on them.

I've had less success losing my desire for white rice and potatoes. Apparently I have a genuine preference for those tastes. But the desires aren't so strong that I would pass up an apple to eat poorly. Today, when I look at a pile of mashed potatoes, I automatically associate them with feeling crappy in an hour. And if that isn't enough to keep them off my plate, I give myself permission to eat as much as I want of good food instead. The diversion usually works.

Diet Coke

In the interest of full disclosure, I have over the course of my life consumed far too much Diet Coke. I have routinely consumed as many as twelve Diet Cokes per day. This was in the context of nearly every medical and nutritional expert warning against it. My problem was that I truly enjoyed each Diet Coke I drank, and when I looked for the science about the health risks, I saw a lot of correlation but no clear causation. But I kept an eye on it just in case the science became settled on one side or the other.

A few months ago, as part of my process for writing this book, I put my concept of cravings management to the ultimate test: I quit Diet Coke, cold turkey, after forty-plus years of extraordinarily regular consumption. The first week was hard, I admit. But I substituted coffee, which I also love, whenever I craved Diet Coke, and that greatly reduced my need to use willpower. Week one was a challenge. By week four, it was easy to resist Diet Coke. Eight weeks later, I see Diet Coke as a weird little colored water full of chemicals I don't need. My cravings are completely gone. Giving up Diet Coke didn't require much willpower beyond the first several days. I'm even enjoying my greater coffee consumption because I feel more alert all day. And coffee in moderation gets high marks from science for promoting good health.[27-32]

The reason I picked Diet Coke for my cravings elimination test is that while I'm not convinced that diet soda is especially unhealthy for the occasional consumer, I wasn't so sure that drinking twelve cans a day was contributing to a healthy life. And while the studies on the dangers of diet sodas stop short of being convincing—at least to me—at some point, the sheer tonnage of negative health correlations reached a tipping point for my personal risk profile. So just to be clear, I am not personally aware of any *proven* health problems from an occasional diet soda. I just don't like the odds.[33-35]

How to Know What to Eat

One of the biggest barriers to healthy eating is the inconvenience factor. Life is so busy for most of us that convenience trumps most other considerations. We do what's easiest even if we know it shortens our lives. What you want is for healthy food to be more convenient than unhealthy food. I'll give you a few tips that can help. But first let me describe just how hard it is to even *know* what is healthy, much less find it.

My observation is that most people think they already know which foods are healthy. People know vegetables are good for you and cheeseburgers are not. But you don't have to drill far down into the details of diet options before even well-informed people become unsure. Are eggs healthy this week? How about rye bread? What about butter? Turkey? You quickly get into grey areas in which even experts disagree.

Suppose you are so well-informed that you could accurately sort food into categories of good and bad and get the right answer every time. That's only a fraction of what you need to know. Within the category of healthy foods, can you further rank them? If you can, it would make sense to stick with the best of the best and avoid the lower quadrant of the so-called healthy foods. Is an apple better than broccoli? Is an avocado worse than a banana? How much healthier would you be if you ate the best of the healthy foods and avoided the less-good-but-still-okay foods? Is it a big difference or a small one?

How hard is it to get variety in your diet? It might be easy to eat a variety of foods that have different names and appearances, but are they that different nutritionally? Would you be better off eating an apple and an orange or an apple and a tomato? Which one gives you a more complete nutritional boost?

Any doctor or nutrition expert will tell you that eating a balanced diet will get you all the vitamins and minerals you need. That opinion is nearly 100 percent accepted by all smart people. The problem is that it's mathematically impossible. You can prove that to yourself by googling the nutritional information for everything you eat on any given day in which you're sure you did a good job with both your food variety and healthy choices. I've done this experiment and found that you can't get anywhere near the US government's Daily Recommended Intake of vitamins and minerals. You would have to eat a wheelbarrow full of food to come close.

The nutritional shortfall of normal food is what prompted me to bring the Dilberito to market. I thought it would do some good for the world that had rewarded me so handsomely for *Dilbert*. The fortified burrito business failed like most of the things I've tried. But during the process, I learned a lot about vitamins and minerals. The main takeaway is that nutrition presents itself as science but is perhaps 60 percent bullshit, guesswork, and bad assumptions. The rest is marketing.

> In the process of failing at the fortified burrito business, I learned most of what you'll read in this chapter. That's what I call failing forward. Any time you learn something useful, you come out ahead. In this case, my focus on a healthy diet has probably lengthened my lifespan.

In some narrow areas, nutrition science is reasonably solid. Researchers know that pregnant women need vitamin E. We know that vitamin C is needed to avoid scurvy. And the data suggests good things about vitamin D. There are other clearly beneficial vitamins as well. But if you look at any store shelf of vitamins and minerals, most of them haven't been researched to the extent you would want for health-related products.

Further complicating nutrition science is the inconvenient fact that no two humans are alike. Does a 120-pound vegetarian woman who is trying to get pregnant need the same vitamins and minerals as an obese coal miner with gout? No two people have the same lifestyle, health, and genetics.

While my fortified burrito company failed for ordinary business reasons, I would have bowed out eventually as I lost my faith in the Daily Recommended Intake levels of vitamins and minerals as sufficiently credible. During the Dilberito years, it seemed as if every week a new study would come out that challenged what I thought I knew. It was deeply unsettling.

It's impossible to know with any precision what you should be eating and how often you should eat it. Nutrition science is shockingly incomplete. At best, you can avoid the obvious diet mistakes. But where science gives us uncertainty, sometimes you can creep up on the truth through personal observation and pattern recognition. If you know anyone who maintains an ideal adult weight without the services of a personal chef or a personal trainer, wouldn't you like to know how? Ask anyone who has a healthy weight what they eat, then be on the lookout for the pattern.

Know Why You're Eating

We eat for more than one reason. I find it useful to understand what is making me eat so I can adjust my food choices accordingly.

For example, scientists know that your brain triggers the hunger sensation and hunger hormones like leptin and ghrelin when you don't get enough sleep.[22-26] The next time you have one of those days when you can't eat enough to satisfy your hunger, ask yourself how much sleep you got the night before. You'll surprise yourself at how often a bad night of sleep leads to non-stop eating.

When tiredness sparks your hunger and you've had all the calories you need for a while, try eating peanuts or mixed nuts to suppress your appetite. Cheese also works, at least for that specific purpose. The fat in those foods acts as an appetite satisfier. Nuts and cheese have lots of calories, but you'll find that suppressing your appetite at the expense of some extra calories is still a net gain if the alternative is to eat until everything in your kitchen is gone.

I often find myself doing social eating just because someone else in the family happens to be snacking in the kitchen. I wander in, start a conversation, and the next thing I know something unnecessary is heading for my stomach. It's almost automatic and mindless. I have just enough awareness to steer myself toward the lowest-calorie items. I don't need nuts or cheese because I'm not actually hungry. I just need something to do while I hang out. So I go for the celery or carrots or cucumbers in my fridge that are prepped and waiting. When you eat for social reasons, aim for the lowest-calorie options. You don't need to suppress your appetite if the reason you're eating isn't hunger.

How to Make Healthy Food Taste Good

Perhaps the biggest obstacle to healthy eating is flavor. You might love the taste of everything that's bad for you while being less enthusiastic about so-called healthy foods. As your friend who eats a vegetarian diet plus an occasional fish, I'll tell you how to get the flavor you need from otherwise boring food.

The first rule of eating right is avoiding foods that feel like punishment. No one gives out medals for choking down a big bowl of boredom. If eating a healthy diet feels unpleasant, you're doing it wrong. And you're wasting your limited stockpile of willpower. You might have your own list of awful-yet-healthy foods. Feel free to avoid them so long as that leaves you plenty of other options.

I find that most people who have poor diets believe healthy food has bland or unpleasant flavor. That impression is double-true if the first thing you think of in a vegetarian diet is tofu, and I find that is often the case. As a public service, I've listed below the condiments, seasonings, and ingredients that can add flavor to most foods that would be otherwise bland. These are the taste sensations I live on while never feeling the slightest twinge of flavor deprivation. Your tastes will differ, so this is just a template to make the point about how many flavors you can enjoy in a healthy diet.

Vegetarian flavors:

- ◆ Soy sauce
- ◆ Cilantro
- ◆ Lemon
- ◆ Salt
- ◆ Pepper
- ◆ Butter (or butter substitute)
- ◆ Garlic
- ◆ Onion
- ◆ Curry
- ◆ Cheese
- ◆ Tomato sauce
- ◆ Salsa
- ◆ Vegetable broth
- ◆ Honey
- ◆ Salad dressings
- ◆ Balsamic vinegar
- ◆ Black bean sauce
- ◆ Hot sauce

You'll notice that salt and butter are on my list, and you probably associate both of those with a bad diet. I'd like to make an argument in favor of including copious amounts of both salt and butter in your diet, *so long as you're adding them to otherwise healthy food.*

Here I'll remind you again—because I can't say it too often—be wary of health ideas from cartoonists. Check with your doctor before you install a salt lick in your living room or start eating butter by the stick.

Let's start with salt. For years, science has produced conflicting reports about the health risks of salt for people who have no special risk for heart disease. Given the number of studies undertaken to uncover the hidden risks of salt, I would expect a clear answer by now. Science has not provided it.

Everything in life is a calculated risk, and I've decided that using salt as much as I want allows me to thoroughly enjoy some healthy foods that I wouldn't otherwise eat. For example, a salted carrot is delicious, but an unsalted carrot is like chewing on a stick. Steamed and salted brussels sprouts are one of my favorite foods, but plain brussels sprouts hold no appeal.

The key to enjoying salt without worrying about a heart attack is that you need to have a healthy diet in general, exercise regularly, and keep a healthy body fat composition. It also helps if you don't have high blood pressure. If you're built like a barrel, eat pork for breakfast, and have lost all your uncles to heart disease, your doctor will probably advise you to take salt out of your diet just to be on the safe side. Keep in mind that your doctor probably isn't a salt expert, so caution will always be a doctor's first instinct. You can find plenty of information on salt studies on the Internet. Make up your own mind but keep your eyes open because new salt studies come out on a regular basis.

My argument in favor of butter is similar to salt. Butter is a good appetite suppressant. As with salt, it helps me enjoy healthy foods. Steamed broccoli with some butter and pepper is delicious. Plain broccoli is boring. If butter helps you eat more vegetables and your weight is under control, butter is probably an acceptable risk. Check with your doctor to be sure.

You can do your own test on the appetite-suppressing quality of cheese and butter. Try steamed vegetables with butter and parmesan cheese one day and remember how you felt after. The next day, try steamed vegetables with just soy sauce. The soy sauce is a great flavor, but you'll find yourself hungry before you swallow the last bite. Soy sauce works best when you're doing social eating or you are eating healthy fat in some other form to keep you feeling satisfied.

Think of healthy eating as a system in which you continually experiment with different seasonings and sauces until you know exactly what works for you. You want to be able to look at a vegetable and instantly know five ways to make it delicious, at least two of which don't require much effort. When you change what you know about adding flavor to food, that alone will change your behavior. You'll no longer need much willpower to resist bad food because you will be just as attracted to the healthy stuff.

Adjusting Your Lifestyle for Healthy Eating

As I mentioned earlier, studies show that having overweight friends can make you overweight yourself.[36-39] I don't automatically trust studies that uncover correlations without knowing the mechanism behind them, but I have noticed that my weight does fluctuate depending on the company I keep. At the moment, my business partner in a side venture is an Ironman athlete. And as I write this paragraph, I am sitting next to a friend who looks like he stepped off the cover of a fitness magazine. For the past year or so, I've spent more time with unusually fit people than at any other time in my life. That's mostly a coincidence. But just as the studies suggest, I've somehow managed to drift into the best physical shape of my adult life. And I don't feel that I used any extra willpower to get there. It feels as if the social influence makes it easier. I don't know if the reason is that I feel competitive or that people naturally imitate the people around them in the same way we adopt accents when we move to other parts of the country. Whatever the reason, science, common sense, and my personal experience are in agreement: Hanging out with fit people can cause you to become more like them. And that passes my bullshit filter.

I'm not suggesting you should stop accepting invitations from your overweight friends. But in the upcoming fitness chapter, I'll suggest joining some organized sport teams if you can. That will expand your social circle to include people who enjoy exercise. In time, your sport friends will play a bigger role in your social life. That can only be good.

Coffee

If you don't drink coffee, you should think about two to four cups a day. Coffee can make you more alert, happier, and more productive. It might even make you live longer. Coffee can also make you more likely to exercise, and it contains beneficial antioxidants and other substances associated with decreased risk of stroke (especially in women), Parkinson's disease, and dementia. Coffee is also associated with decreased risk of abnormal heart rhythms, Type 2 diabetes, and certain cancers.[27-32,62-67] Any one of these benefits of coffee would be persuasive, but cumulatively, they make it a no-brainer.

An hour ago, I considered doing some writing for this book, but I didn't have the necessary energy or focus to sit down and start working. I did, however, have enough energy to fix myself a cup of coffee. A few sips in, I was happier to be working than I would have been doing whatever lazy thing was my alternative. Coffee literally makes me *enjoy* work. No willpower needed.

Coffee also allows you to manage your energy so you have the most when you need it. My experience is that coffee drinkers have higher highs and lower lows energy-wise than non-coffee-drinkers, but that tradeoff works. I can guarantee that my best thinking goes into my job. Meanwhile, I save my dull-brain hours for household chores and other simple tasks.

The biggest downside of coffee is that once you get addicted to caffeine, you can get a "coffee headache" if you go too long without a cup. Luckily, coffee is one of the most abundant beverages on earth, so you rarely need to worry about being without.

Coffee costs money, takes time, gives you coffee breath, and makes you pee too often. It can also make you jittery and nervous if you have too much. But if success is your dream, and you want to operate at peak mental performance, coffee is a good bet. I highly recommend it. In fact, I recommend it so strongly that I feel sorry for anyone who hasn't developed the habit.

Pleasure Unit Hypothesis

I don't think it's a coincidence that celebrities do a good job of staying thin. Obviously, they have the free time and resources to do it right. And for them, fitness has an enormous financial upside. But I think celebrities have another ace in the hole, too, because their lives are fabulous in general. The happier you are in one area of your life, the less effort you'll put into searching for happiness elsewhere. And that can translate into caring less about the taste quality of your meal.

For example, if I gave you a choice of eating your favorite food or watching a boring television show, you'd probably choose the tasty food. But if I gave you a choice of your favorite food or a trip to your dream destination that has everything you want except great food, you'd choose the dream destination. Eating right depends a great deal on your non-food alternatives. If you get your entire life in order, it will be much easier to have an ideal weight.

This is a circular problem, of course, because reaching a healthy weight can improve the quality of your career, health, and social life. You need to eat well to enjoy the rest of your life, and you need the rest of your life to be in good shape to more easily resist bad food choices. Everything is connected. That's why I include diet and fitness in a book about success. If you get your health in order, success will come more easily. But if you get success without good health, you won't be able to enjoy it.

The Healthy Eating Summary

The Simple, No-Willpower Diet System

1. Pay attention to your energy level after eating certain foods. Find your pattern.
2. Remove unhealthy, energy-draining food from your home.
3. Stock up on *convenient* healthy food (e.g., apples, nuts, bananas, etc.) and let laziness be your copilot in eating right.
4. Stop eating foods that create feelings of addiction: white rice, white potatoes, desserts, white bread, fried foods.
5. Eat as much healthy food as you want, whenever you want.
6. Get enough sleep because tiredness creates the illusion of hunger.

7. If your hunger is caused by tiredness, try healthy foods with fat such as nuts, avocados, protein bars, and cheese to suppress the hungry feeling.
8. If you're eating for social reasons only, choose the healthiest options with with the fewest calories.
9. Learn how to season healthy-yet-bland foods.
10. In time, you will lose your cravings for bad food without feeling like you're making a sacrifice.

That's a system for eating right over the long term. The surest way to identify someone who won't succeed at weight loss is that they tend to say things like, "My goal is to lose ten pounds." Weight targets often work in the short run. But if you need willpower to keep the weight off, you're doomed in the long run. The only way to succeed long term is by using a system that bypasses your need for willpower.

CHAPTER 32

Fitness

As a boy growing up in a small town, I played four or five sports in a day, rode my bike for miles, went for a swim, and finished the evening doing gymnastics on the furniture. Active play, sports, and other exercise were a huge part of my life. It was hard to imagine a day without them. Fitness as a kid was fun, so it seemed easy.

When I became an adult, life kept getting in the way of exercise. I found it hard to carve out the time for fitness and even harder to find a way to enjoy it. If I played a pickup soccer game in the park on a Sunday, I would be so bruised and sore that I wouldn't feel good enough to exercise again until Thursday. When I tried to turn myself into a recreational runner, the rest of my brain and body had other plans. It turns out that running only works for me if I'm chasing some sort of ball or if something with fangs is chasing me.

I tried tennis with some success, but finding a partner of equal ability, matching our schedules, and finding available public courts was all a chore. I was lucky to play once a week. I certainly understand why so many adults let their fitness slide. Exercise is hard work in every imaginable sense. When you add marriage and kids into the mix, exercise can become completely impractical for many people. I get that. So considering all of life's natural barriers to remaining fit, is there any system that can work?

I think so. After a lifetime of trying nearly every exercise tip, trick, fad, and sometimes scientifically proven techniques, I have condensed the entire field of fitness advice into one sentence:

Be Active Every Day

Allow me to acknowledge how spectacularly useless that sounds. I'm sure you already knew that being active is a good thing. You're probably thinking that a cartoonist has nothing to offer on the topic of fitness. I'll be the first to admit that you might be right. But stick with me for a page or two and I might surprise you. I'm not a health and fitness expert by any stretch of the imagination, but I do have a cartoonist's knack for simplification. And simplification might be just what you need.

Simplification is often the difference between doing something you know you should do and putting it off. You don't mind brushing your teeth because it's simple. But you probably put off finding out why there's a strange smell coming from the attic. That could get complicated.

Simplification done right also helps connect the important parts of exercise, diet, career, finance, and your social life. If any of those becomes too complicated, you're forced to borrow time, willpower, and resources from something else you also care about. I won't try too hard to sell you on the benefits of simplicity because you see them in your own life every day.

If you are young and don't have crushing responsibilities, you probably have everything you need to exercise regularly. But after a certain age, life transforms exercise from one of your highest priorities to the thing you give up first when things get busy. That can literally be a death trap.

My challenge in this chapter is to convince you that if you get one simple thing right—being active every day—all other elements of fitness will come together naturally *without the need to use up your limited supply of willpower.*

That last part is the key. In my experience, any form of exercise that requires willpower is unsustainable. To stay fit in the long run, you need to limit your exercise to whatever level doesn't feel like work, just as kids do. When you take willpower out of the equation and achieve a solid baseline of daily physical activity, your natural inclination will be to gradually increase your workout. You'll do it because you want to and because it feels easy—and because it feels good. No willpower needed.

If you walk two miles every day for a month and enjoy the leisurely pace, your brain will automatically start to think that walking an extra mile might be even more fun—or that running half the way and walking the rest might be interesting. That's how you turn boredom into a tool. When you are active every day and your body feels good about it, you'll find it easier to exercise more rather than less. Ask any dedicated runner, biker, or swimmer how they feel on the occasional off day. They don't like it. That's where you want to be. And the only way that happens is if you make fitness—of any kind—a daily habit. Once exercise becomes routine, you won't need willpower to keep going because your body and brain will simply prefer physical activity to being a couch spud. And your natural inclination for variety will drive you to do more stuff over time.

You probably know someone who is a long-distance runner, putting in five to ten miles every day. If you're not that fit yourself, you might think those runners have extraordinary willpower. That's probably more of an illusion than reality. Long-distance runners are born with a certain genetic gift that allows them to feel good when running. No one needs willpower to do the things they enjoy.

Most normal adults, including me, find running to be little more than the most cost-effective way to be bored and uncomfortable. A dozen times over the course of my life, I have tried to force myself to enjoy running, or at least to do it anyway for the health benefits. Each time, my willpower crapped out a few weeks into it.

You wouldn't flap your arms and try to fly just because you saw how well it worked for a bird. Likewise, I don't recommend adopting an exercise plan just because people who have completely different bodies and brains seem to enjoy it. No matter how charismatic that exercise guru on YouTube sounds, don't believe that someone else's specific fitness plan will work for you. No one is like you.

What you need is a natural and easy way to evolve a fitness routine that works for your specific brain and body. And you want to do that without relying on willpower. The starting point for that journey is nothing more than physically activity every day regardless of the specifics.

I did an Amazon.com search on the keyword "exercise" and got 125,508 book suggestions. I'm not trying to be the 125,509th variation on largely familiar material. I haven't read many of those books, but I assume most of them require you to use a degree of willpower. That's a losing strategy no matter how you dress it up or how inspirational the author might be. In the long run, any system that depends on your willpower will fail. Or worse, some other part of your life will suffer as you deplete your limited stockpile of willpower on fitness.

The fitness approach I prefer differs from the norm both in its simplicity and because it doesn't require willpower at any stage. In fact, if you follow the system of being active every day, you'll feel more energetic, and that can replenish your willpower.

I use the word "active" in an intentionally ambiguous way. That's what makes the rule a system and not a goal. As you know, goals are for losers. If the rule were "Run ten miles every day," that would be a goal. And it would probably set you up for failure since most people can't do something specific every day. But almost everyone can be active in *some* way every day. That could mean anything from playing basketball to cleaning the garage to taking a walk. Under my system, any physical exertion counts, and none is better than the other. I'll explain in this chapter how all paths can lead to optimal fitness if you follow a few simple rules for manipulating your willpower.

The most important and powerful part of the "Be active every day" system is the "every day" part. Everything springs naturally from that. And if you have trouble fitting exercise into your busy schedule as most adults do, I'll give you some suggested fixes for that, too.

Fitness is a simple experience made absurdly complicated by market forces. If you want to make money as a fitness expert, you must make a novel claim about the value of your product or service. Each new idea is layered on top of old ideas until the entire field is so complicated it becomes intimidating.

How often should you work out? What should you eat before and after working out? Should you have a different diet for cardio workouts versus weightlifting? How much should you customize your workouts for your age, gender, and situation? Will an abdominal exercise hurt your back or help it? How much rest should you get between days of weightlifting? Is long-distance running beneficial enough to your overall health to justify the wear and tear on your knees? The questions and complexity are endless. Here are a few of the exercise "musts" you hear all the time.

1. Thirty minutes of aerobic exercise daily.
2. Stretch.
3. Hydrate.
4. Eat protein within thirty minutes of strength training.
5. Carb-load the night before a big exercise day.
6. Do resistance and weight training every other day.
7. Do three sets of ten to fifteen reps.
8. Get lots of rest.
9. Vary your workout to create "muscle confusion."
10. Use proper form for lifting.

That's just a partial list. The only people who can do all that right are serious athletes, personal trainers, the unemployed, and the socially unpopular. For everyone else, it's simply not practical.

For married people, an excellent way to fail at exercise starts like this:

YOU: "Hey, honey, would you like to take a walk with me in an hour?"
SPOUSE: "It depends. Maybe."

(And then life gets in the way.)
Here's another way to fail.

YOU: "I'm going to the gym at two o'clock."
SPOUSE: "But that's exactly when Timmy needs to be taken to his birthday party."

And another . . .

YOU: "Chris asked me to play tennis at seven tonight."
SPOUSE: "I was hoping to see a movie with you then, but if you like Chris more than you like me, fine."

By the way, if you assumed "spouse" means "wife" in those examples, you might be a sexist jerk. It works both ways. As soon as you try to satisfy two schedules instead of one, all your seemingly optional activities such as exercise get pushed to "later." So what's the fix?

There are three practical ways to schedule exercise in a marriage or marriage-like situation:

1.   Join an organized team.
2.   Always exercise at the same time every day.
3.   Exercise together (if you both really mean it).

When my wife, Shelly, tells me she has a tennis league match scheduled on a Thursday night, her absence never makes me feel abandoned. For starters, I always have advance notice and can make my own plans, which is great. But even more important, I know Shelly didn't pick the specific date and time of the match. The fact that the game is scheduled by some unknown third party makes it okay with me because I know that Shelly didn't make a conscious choice to be away at that specific time. Sure, sure, on some level, it's the same thing because Shelly knew in advance that matches would be on Thursday nights, and she chose to join the team. But it *feels* different. And that's what matters. Whenever you can, join a team sport that has a set schedule. Your spouse will still be inconvenienced, but it won't feel personal.

If team sports aren't your thing, the next best solution is to schedule your exercise for the same time every day. Shelly can tell you where I will be on any given Tuesday at 12:40 PM. I will be at the gym, just finishing my resistance training and heading for some stretching before cardio. Shelly finds my regular exercise schedule inconvenient at times, but it doesn't feel personal because it's my system. I don't *decide* to be unavailable for a romantic lunch with my wife; I simply have an exercise *system*. On some level it's the same, but it sure feels different. And that's the beauty.

I exercise at lunchtime because mornings are better for my creative work and afternoons are unpredictable in terms of work and family time. Other successful exercisers get up long before the sun to do their workouts. Still others go straight from work to the gym. In each case, the key is to have a predictable system. The method that *never* succeeds is exercising whenever you have some spare time. If you're like most adults, you haven't seen spare time in years.

Motivation to Exercise

My system for staying in the mood to be active every day has several parts. I already explained the importance of diet in keeping your energy up. After that, the most important rule is that you should never exercise so much in one day that you won't feel like being active the next day. To put that another way, the right amount of exercise today is whatever amount makes me look forward to being active tomorrow.

My old exercise system involved working out so hard I could barely move the next day. No pain, no gain, I thought. I figured the harder I pushed myself, the better. But pushing takes willpower, and if I use up my willpower at the gym, I can barely drive past the donut shop without being sucked in there.

And the soreness is like a penalty for exercising. Humans aren't that different from dogs: If you give me a penalty every time I do something, eventually I'll find a reason to stop doing it. And that reason will be something along the lines of "too busy."

What you want is for your daily exercise to give you a reward every time. Light exercise does just that; it reduces your stress and boosts your energy. Over time, as you become fitter, you will naturally increase your exercise level, but by then your body will be equipped to handle it.

If you want to make a habit of something, the worst thing you can do is pick and choose which days of the week you do it and which you don't. Exercise becomes a habit when you do it every day without fail. Taking rest days between exercise days breaks up the pattern that creates habits. It also makes it too easy to say today is one of your non-exercise days—and maybe tomorrow, too.

Reward

I find it important to reward myself after exercise with a healthy snack I enjoy, some downtime that involves reading interesting articles on my phone, or a nice cup of coffee. By putting those pleasures at the immediate end of my exercise, I develop a strong association between the exercise and the good feelings. That's habit-forming.

As I've mentioned—and it's worth repeating—a big part of my exercise motivation is coffee. Coffee boosts athletic performance but more importantly makes you willing to put in the effort. [68-70] If you're not exercising every day and don't drink coffee, maybe you should give it a try. I can't tell you how many times I ruled out exercise because I was too tired, only to completely change my mind after a cup of coffee.

I also find that ibuprofen (as found in Advil and other brands) helps reduce my soreness on those days I overdo it. If I take the ibuprofen on days I'm stiff, there's a good chance I'll feel up to exercising the next day. Without the ibuprofen, I feel like the Tin Man on *The Wizard of Oz*—all I want is my oil can. I can't recommend ibuprofen for you because I'm not a doctor and because there are risks if you overdo it. Ask your doctor.

So how do you exercise on those days when all you want to do is sit on the couch, eat ice cream, and feel bad? Can you jump-start your body when one part of your brain knows that exercise is a good idea but another part of your brain is using its veto power?

The trick I've found that works best takes advantage of certain cues in your life, or "keys," as hypnotists like to call them. For example, if you were bitten by a German Shepherd dog as a child, every time you see that type of dog you might get a little burst of fear. That's a cue—a key. Your life is full of these little cues and keys that can control your attitude. The trick is manipulating your own cues in a way that programs your mind.

Here's what I do when I know I should exercise but I feel too tired and droopy to imagine doing a vigorous workout. Instead of doing what I feel I can't do, I do what I *can* do—which is put on my exercise clothes and lace my sneakers. (You might call them tennis shoes or running shoes where you live.) Central to my method is that I grant myself 100 percent permission to NOT exercise, even after getting suited up for it.

This is important because I know I won't take the first step of donning my exercise clothes if I feel committed to something that just seems impossible in my current frame of mind.

But once the sneakers and shorts are on, a funny thing happens, and it happens quickly. The physical feeling I get from my exercise clothes triggers my going-to-the-gym subroutine in my brain, and my energy kicks up a notch. It's like Pavlov's salivating dogs. The exercise clothes cause me to think positive thoughts about exercising, and that boosts my energy.

Suddenly, the idea of exercising seems possible if not desirable. There's one more step, and this, too, requires granting yourself permission to back out at any time. I drive to my local gym, walk in, look around, and see how I feel. About 95 percent of the time, this set of cues puts me in a sufficient mood to go ahead and exercise, and that in turn boosts my mood. But sometimes—and this happened perhaps five times this year, which is typical—I get to the gym, look around, turn, and leave. As I drive home, I'm not thinking I failed. In fact, I feel exactly the opposite. Failure is for people who have goals. If my goal is to exercise, leaving the gym without breaking a sweat looks and feels like failure. But what I have is not a goal; it is a system. And the system allows leakage. It's designed that way. As I drive home from the gym—a seemingly wasted trip—I never feel defeated. Instead, I feel I'm using a system that I know works overall. I win if I exercise, and I win (albeit less) if I use my system and decide not to work out. Either way, my attitude improves. And at least I get out of the house and clear my head. It's all good.

Don't be concerned about how much or how little you exercise. All that matters in the long run is that you make exercise a daily habit. Studies indicate that moderate levels of exercise are optimal for longevity.[71-75]

Over time, you'll naturally gravitate toward adding the variety and challenge that your body can handle.

Hair-Care Death-Spiral

In 2011,United States surgeon general Dr. Regina M. Benjamin made headlines by saying that too many women were skipping exercise because of hair-related issues. In her view, this qualified as an important health issue. *The New York Times* quoted Benjamin as saying, "'Often times you get women saying, 'I can't exercise today because I don't want to sweat my hair back or get my hair wet.' When you're starting to exercise, you look for reasons not to, and sometimes the hair is one of those reasons."[76]

Dr. Benjamin's observations match my own—and yours, too, most likely, I don't think I need to explain why putting your hair above your health is a loser strategy in the long run.

If you're a woman caught in the hair-care death-spiral, nothing I've said in this book will be much help unless you escape. Allow me to offer a possible solution.

I'm going to start with the assumption that there are three main reasons a woman wants great-looking hair: 1) attract sexual partners, 2) improve career potential, and 3) feel good about herself. Everyone is different, but those three causes probably cover 85 percent of the reasons.

The first two reasons (sexual partners and career options) are about influencing how others view you. And I would argue that feeling good about yourself only has meaning because you know you are influencing others to feel the same way. So really, hair-care is about influencing how other people feel about you. We're all social animals, so there's nothing wrong with that. The world only works when we care how other people think.

On the topic of women's hair, I can only speak from a heterosexual man's perspective. I encourage you to check with the men in your life for confirmation. My best guess is that what I say next is as near a universal opinion as men can have:

We Prefer You Healthy.

I've never known a man who would prefer an unhealthy-looking woman with movie star hair over a fit woman with a ponytail. And if I ever do meet that guy, I'll try to avoid him because he sounds like a creep.

A hiring manager will always have a subconscious bias for the healthier-looking applicant, male or female. Humans evolved to have favorable opinions about anyone who looks healthy because it's a marker for good reproductive odds. That's why society needs laws that limit discrimination against the differently abled. If your main reason for spending time on your hair is to feel good about yourself, a healthy body will always trump a good hairdo.

I won't pretend to understand the minds of women when it comes to hair. And every woman is different. Some women are three different people before lunchtime. But I can tell you with certainty that men prefer you to be in good health, even if it means we miss the best of your hair potential.

I would imagine it's very hard to break a hair-care routine that has been part of your life for years. But it might help to think of this in a different way. If you skip exercise because of your hair, remind yourself during those many hours of brushing, curling, straightening, and drying that the long-term payoff for your efforts is to become less attractive, less employable, and less healthy. When you change how you think, you eventually change how you behave.

Having great hair is a short-term goal. Fitness is a system. Systems are for winners.

CHAPTER 33

Voice Update II

Three years had passed since I lost my voice. It was getting hard to imagine it could ever be fixed. Outwardly, my life looked to be on track. *Dilbert* was running in over 2,000 newspapers in sixty-five countries. I married Shelly, and we started building a home. Externally, things were great, but on the inside, I was badly damaged. My optimism was getting its ass kicked twenty-four hours a day, but somehow it still had a pulse.

The simple things in life had become terrors. Every time the phone rang, my heart sank. Every time someone asked a question, I died a little on the inside. Emotionally, it was confusing. Half my life was great while half was darkly broken. I continued doing my affirmation—"I, Scott, will speak perfectly."— but I was running out of potential remedies to try. My future looked bleak.

One day, another Google Alert showed up in my email inbox. Unlike the numerous false leads, this one looked promising. A doctor in Japan was reporting success treating spasmodic dysphonia with a surgical procedure on the neck. I was willing to fly to Japan if needed. I would have swum there if I had to. By then,I had experienced so many disappointments in my search for a cure that Shelly couldn't muster much enthusiasm for my new longshot hope. I know she didn't enjoy seeing me get my hopes up and hers as well just to be thrown against the rocks time and time again.

Following protocol, I took the news of this new operation to my regular doctor, Dr. Smith, who referred me to my Ear-Nose-Throat doctor, Dr. Cornelius Jansen III. Dr. Jansen hadn't yet heard of this new surgery, and he was concerned that the reports of success might be exaggerated.

He explained that some proclaimed medical breakthroughs are more credible than others, so I shouldn't assume this report was accurate. I wasn't surprised. Realistically, how likely is it that you can fix a brain abnormality by rigging up some sort of workaround in the neck? It sounded iffy even to me.

But in the interest of exploring every option, Dr. Jansen recommended I speak to one of the top professionals in the field, Dr. Edward Damrose of the otolaryngology department at the Stanford School of Medicine. Dr .Damrose was familiar with the reports coming from Japan, but he suggested I contact a doctor closer to home who was pioneering a different type of surgery for spasmodic dysphonia. He referred me to Dr. Gerald Berke at the UCLA Medical Center.

I got off the phone with Dr. Damrose feeling puzzled. How could there be a surgical fix for this condition that I hadn't heard about until now? How could this be true if there was no mention of it on websites dedicated specifically to this disorder? The only explanation I could imagine was that this would be another false lead to another dead end. But my system was to follow all leads, no matter how ridiculous or unlikely.

I made an appointment with Dr. Berke for an initial visit and flew from my home near San Francisco to Los Angeles to meet with him. Dr. Berke is an interesting character: brilliant, confident, and a little bit mysterious. A small herd of doctors from other practices followed him from room to room to learn his ways. Dr. Berke and his tag-along doctors examined me and confirmed the diagnosis of spasmodic dysphonia. Then he explained that he had been perfecting a surgery for this condition over the past several years, with about an 85 percent success rate, which in this context means the patient had a better voice after surgery than before—not a perfect voice, but substantially improved. Unfortunately, some people got worse after surgery, losing what little was left of their voices. But Dr. Berke had a good idea why some patients were less successful, and he was refining his technique to account for it.

But here's the interesting part. Dr. Berke's surgery involved opening the front of the neck, cutting the nerves that lead from the brain to the vocal cords, then building a new path using nerves borrowed from elsewhere in your neck. Once the rewiring was done, the patient waited three-and-a-half months until the new nerve pathways regenerated and the voice came back. Until then, the patient's brain and vocal cords wouldn't be connected. There were no follow-up visits to the doctor. It either worked or it didn't.

Does that sound like the way you fix a brain abnormality? It didn't sound like a logical solution to me. So I asked for a list of past patients as references. I was hopeful but skeptical. The operation didn't make sense to me, and I was still scratching my head as to why none of this had appeared on the Internet yet.

I emailed some of Dr. Berke's patients and set up a time to speak with them—if you can call it that—by phone. This was the one group of folks I could speak to confidently on the phone because they were skilled at deciphering my broken, raspy attempts at words. They also understood that the call was mostly about them doing the talking.

And talk they did. Perfectly. Not one of them had a hitch or a hesitation in their words. There was no hoarseness or clipped syllables. Each described the recovery from the operation as unpleasant because you choke nearly every time you try to eat or drink for quite some time, but they were unanimous in saying it was worth it.

Obviously, I was only talking to the lucky people who had the best results, but I was feeling good about the possibility. Still, I needed to satisfy my curiosity about one thing: I asked Dr. Berke how he figured out that nerve surgery in the neck could fix a brain abnormality. What evidence did he see that others did not?

His answer fascinated me. I suppose it explains why doctors follow him around. I'm paraphrasing, but Dr. Berke explained that it was an inspiration that somehow emerged from the sum of his knowledge about necks and throats and voices and nerves and all the rest. He didn't call it genius, but if this surgery worked, no other description would fit quite as well.

If I decided to do the surgery, there was something on the order of a 15 percent chance my voice would not improve. In that scenario, the surgery itself might eliminate any chance I could benefit from some future treatment. It was a one-way trip to a destination unknown.

I scheduled the surgery.

CHAPTER 34

Luck

L et's talk about the elephant in the room when it comes to any discussion of success: luck.

My worldview is that *all* success is luck if you track it back to its source. Steve Jobs needed to be born with Steve Jobs' DNA, and he needed to meet a fellow named Steve Wozniak. If Bill Gates had been born where I was born, he would have been shooting woodchucks on weekends to help the local dairy farmers instead of learning to program computers. Warren Buffett makes a similar observation about his own skills, saying, in effect, that if he had been born in an earlier time, his natural talents wouldn't have matched the opportunities.

My worldview is that every element of your personality—from your perseverance to your risk tolerance to your ambition to your intelligence—is a product of pure chance. You needed the genes you were born with and the exact experiences of your life to create the person you are with the opportunities you have. Every decision you make is a simple math product of those variables.

What good is a book that discusses success if success is entirely luck? That's a perfectly reasonable thing to wonder. And it matters because if you believe all success is based on luck, you're not likely to try as hard as if you believe success comes from hard work. No matter what genes and circumstances you have, history tells us you still need to work hard to pull it off. Does a belief in pure luck work against you?

It can, but it doesn't need to.

This book has just become part of your experience. If I did my job right, some parts of it will repeat in your head and be reinforced by your own observations. Like any experience, you can't help but be changed by a book, if only a trivial amount. But everyone is different. One book can have a profound effect on one person and a tiny impact on another.

In the coming year, assuming you made it through this entire book, notice how many times you are reminded of something I wrote. Is there a time you don't feel like exercising but you remember my trick of putting on your exercise clothes anyway? Do you steer clear of the simple carbs for lunch because you noticed they make you sleepy during the day? Are you looking for ways to turn your failures into something good?

You wouldn't buy a book if it didn't have the potential to change you in some way, even if that change is just entertainment or an increase in your knowledge. Books change us automatically, just as any experience does. And if a book helps you see the world in a more useful way or amps up your energy, it becomes part of the fabric of your personal luck.

You're a different person now than you were when you started this book—literally. Some of your cells have died and been replaced. Your body has matured, even if only a few hours. And your brain has modified its internal structure based on its chemistry and all your outside influences, including what you read. If anything in this book sticks in your mind, it will probably get reinforced over time. You're a new person now.

You don't need to *do* anything as a result of reading this book. You've already changed.

CHAPTER 35

Voice Update III

The nurses rolled me into the operating room on a gurney. I was already drugged up with stress-reducing medicines that were working wonders. I couldn't have been happier as the anesthesiologist asked me to count backwards from a hundred. I made it to ninety-eight. It felt like dying happy.

The recovery period was wretched. I choked on nearly everything I tried to swallow, and that situation lasted months. I could whisper because that doesn't involve the vocal cords. But my vocal cords might have been on the moon as far as my brain was concerned. They weren't talking to each other.

Luckily, cartooning doesn't require speaking. I was back to work in a few days once the brain-fog of surgery lifted. And I waited. Dr. Berke told me that nerves regenerate at a very predictable rate. In three-and-a-half months, if the surgery worked, the nerves would make their first full connection between my brain and my vocal cords. And after that, it might take a year to speak in a truly normal way. And that is only if the surgery worked.

I often tried to speak during those months, just to see what would happen. But indeed, my brain was no longer communicating with my vocal cords. It was an odd feeling. So I whispered when I was at home, wrote notes when I was in noisy environments, choked on everything that went down my throat, and waited. I also repeated my affirmations in my head, if for no other reason than to prop up my optimism.

I, Scott Adams, will speak perfectly.

Three-and-a-half months after the surgery, almost to the day, Shelly stood in our living room and stared at me with disbelief. She said, "You just . . . *talked*." And indeed, I had. It wasn't much of a voice. It was weak and breathy, and I couldn't sustain it beyond a few words at a time. But right on schedule, my brain and my vocal cords were becoming reacquainted. It wasn't success. It was just a start. I had months to go before knowing if the surgery had worked in any meaningful way. And I was worlds away from my affirmation of speaking "perfectly." But it was something. It was a lot. I cried.

In the months that followed, my voice steadily improved. The dropping of syllables that defines spasmodic dysphonia was 100 percent gone, but my voice was weak, uneven, and sometimes hoarse. Luckily, these were fixable problems given time and practice. And by that point, I was quite knowledgeable about proper voice technique, thanks to my many hours of voice therapy while I was searching for a cure.

Interestingly, my brain was no longer practiced in vocal fluency. Long after my vocal cords were functioning normally, I had trouble forming coherent sentences. Speaking fluently in full sentences was something I hadn't done for nearly four years. But over time, my fluency returned, too.

Several years after the surgery, I couldn't say I had necessarily achieved my affirmation of speaking "perfectly," if such a thing even exists. I had a weak and nasally voice before I ever got spasmodic dysphonia, so that seemed like the realistic upper limit for my recovery. And for most of my life, people couldn't hear me over crowd noise because my tone seemed to blend exactly with the background. For me, getting back to normal meant getting back to a crappy voice. That would have felt like success.

To my surprise, that's not exactly what happened. Thanks largely to all my voice training before the operation and to what Dr. Berke hypothesized might have been a "latent spasmodic dysphonia" all my life, I ended up with a far more functional voice than ever before. I have no problem projecting in noisy environments, and since much of life is noisy, that is a big, *big* improvement.

I still get a bit hoarse after exercise. And I'll never have a radio-quality voice. So aesthetically, my voice remains less than ideal. But functionally, my voice is indeed perfect. I have escaped from my prison cell of silence. And life has never been more enjoyable or more satisfying.

But there's one more thing I need to do, if you recall, or perhaps a few more things. I wasn't planning a simple escape from my voice prison. I had promised myself that if I escaped, I would free the other inmates, kill the warden, and burn down the prison. That was one of my big motivations for this book. I wrote it, in part, for some poor soul in the middle of nowhere who has lost his voice to spasmodic dysphonia, and with it, all enjoyment of life. It's also for anyone who has an unsolvable problem, health-wise or otherwise. If you think your odds of solving your problem are bad, don't rule out the possibility that what is really happening is that you are bad at estimating odds.

Update: Since the original publication of this book, my voice has steadily improved with use. These days, I do nearly two hours of livestreaming daily, and one of the most common compliments I receive is that people like my voice.

CHAPTER 36

A Final Note about Affirmations

I know from experience that readers of this book will be dispropor-tionally interested in my stories about affirmations. I'm sure I will be proclaimed a witch, a moron, or both. So let me answer those inevitable objections in advance.

When I speak of affirmations these days, I try to say as clearly as possible that they *appear* to have a beneficial value. The reality is if affirmations somehow steered the universe like magic, science probably would have discovered that force by now. I don't foresee the day when affirmations get scientific backing, at least not in the sense of testing for the existence of magic or psychic powers.

I think you and I can agree that affirmations are a phenomenon of the mind and belong in the domain of psychology. Viewed in that light, we can imagine that doing affirmations might have a predictable impact on the brain, perhaps in terms of focus, motivation, or any number of other chemical reactions. Those reactions would, we can assume, either be beneficial or harmful to the pursuit of success. So in one sense, affirmations are no more special than any form of positive thinking, prayers, visualization, chanting, or the like.

That said, I can tell you that in my case affirmations *appear* to have more power than you might expect from positive thinking. The illusion is that the world itself is changing to satisfy the affirmations. Allow me to offer some explanations of why affirmations *appear* to be influencing more than just the person using them.

The most obvious explanation for the apparent power of affirmations is **selective memory**. There is plenty of science to support the idea what we humans tend to remember what we want to remember and forget what we'd rather forget. With affirmations, we might expect to remember the coincidental good luck and forget the bad luck. The result of that selective remembering gives us the incorrect impression that affirmations work more often than you might reasonably expect from chance alone.

Another perfectly good explanation of the apparent power of affirmations is that people who report success with it are liars, with no more credibility than the people who report being abducted by aliens. In my case, I know I didn't lie about my experiences, but you have no way to be sure I'm telling the truth.

False memory is another possible explanation for why affirmations appear to work. Perhaps we remember victories that weren't so amazing in reality, or we remember normal events as being huge coincidences. False memories are so common that you've certainly experienced them. For example, you might remember a childhood event in some detail and learn later that it happened to your sibling, not you. Humans form false memories quite easily, so that must be one potential explanation of why affirmations appear to work.

Another reason affirmations appear to work is that **optimists tend to notice opportunities** that pessimists miss.[1,2] A person who diligently writes affirmations day after day is the very definition of an optimist, even if only by actions. Any form of positive thinking—prayer or the like— would presumably put a person in a more optimistic mindset. And because optimists have been shown in studies to notice more opportunities than pessimists, the result can look like luck.

Studies also show that a person need not be a natural-born optimist to get the benefits of better perception.[3,4] You can train yourself to act like an optimist—and writing affirmations is probably good training—so you get the same benefits as natural optimists when it comes to noticing opportunities.

Whether you are a born optimist or you become one through affirmations, prayer, or positive thinking, you end up with several advantages that make it easier for luck to find you. Optimists notice more opportunities, have more energy because of their imagined future successes, and take more risks. Optimists make themselves an easy target for luck to find them.

Another explanation for the apparent power of affirmations is that we have the causation wrong. Perhaps only the people who know deep down that they have the right stuff to succeed will even bother with affirmations. In my case, that would mean that somewhere in my mind, before I had written my first book, my subconscious somehow knew I had the talent to write a proper book—despite having no relevant writing experience or training. That explanation sounds reasonable to me, but it still means affirmations are useful, just in a different way than you might imagine. Under this explanation of the power of affirmations, they act as a sort of message from your subconscious to your rational mind telling you that you have the right stuff even if your common sense argues otherwise. This would be useful for people who have real talent but don't believe in it; surely there are a lot of people in that camp.

Another explanation for the apparent power of affirmations is that our tiny human brains have not evolved to the point where they can give us an accurate impression of our reality. Instead, our little brains create illusions that have survival benefits and some sort of internal consistency, nothing more.

We know the brain creates illusions because there are so many competing religions in the world. Assuming *you* picked the right religion, all those other poor souls are living in lies. Your neighbor might think he remembers his previous life while you think you saw God during your heart surgery. You can't both be right. But you could both be wrong, and both of you might be experiencing delusions of reality that somehow don't kill you.

The point is that affirmations *might* have a perfectly sensible scientific explanation that involves anything from multiple universes to quantum strangeness, or anything else that baffles our tiny brains and causes us to invent delusions to compensate for our feelings of uncertainty. To put it in simpler terms, affirmations might work for perfectly logical reasons our brains aren't equipped to understand.

If you follow me on X, you know I'm fascinated by the possibility that we humans are nothing but holograms living in a computer simulation. It sounds ludicrous when you first hear the idea, but the math is oddly compelling. Consider what we humans would do 1,000 years from now if we knew an asteroid was heading our way and there were no escape. I think we'd upload our personalities to computers, perhaps with our DNA as part of the code, and launch the computers into space so our culture, memories, and minds could live forever. Now for the math: If you pick any point in time, there will be infinitely more time transpiring *after* any given time than before, assuming the Big Bang marks the start of time. So if you believe humans will someday be on the brink of extinction for any reason, there is a vastly greater chance we are already the simulations left behind.

Some have argued that the universe is too young for the hologram scenario to have played out. But if we are holograms, the age of the universe as we perceive it is nothing but a variable from the programmer. The real age could be trillions of years.

It's a fun thought experiment, but you probably don't buy into it. So I only include it for completeness. If we are indeed nothing but computer-generated entities, affirmations could be nothing more than an unremarkable bit of programming code.

I'll reiterate that I have no objective information to suggest affirmations have worked for me or that they might work for you. And please don't direct-message me to ask for the detailed instructions on affirmations so you can do it "right." I've gotten hundreds of those requests already, and I always say some version of "I dunno." But for what it's worth, I don't think affirmations are sensitive to exactly how many times you write them, whether you use a keyboard or pen, whether you throw away the paper you wrote on, how many weeks you do it, or any other detail. I can't imagine the process of affirmations—if it works at all—is sensitive to the little details. I think a deep and consistent focus on what you want is all that is required. But that's just my gut feeling.

You might see an inconsistency between affirmations and the theme of this book, specifically the parts where I say goals are for losers and systems are for winners. Affirmations look a lot like focusing on goals.

But I would argue that doing affirmations is a system that helps you focus, boosts your optimism and energy, and perhaps validates the talent and drive that your subconscious always knew you had. If you plan to try affirmations, I recommend keeping your objectives broad enough to allow some luck. It's probably better to affirm future wealth than to try to win a specific lottery.

Humans will always think in terms of goals. Our brains are wired that way. But goals only make sense if you also have a system that moves you in the right direction.

So what do *I* believe about affirmations?

I believe I tried affirmations on several occasions and the results I remember—or think I remember—appear to be borderline miraculous. So to me, affirmations are an ongoing mystery. All I know for sure is that I've never heard of anyone being harmed, emotionally or otherwise, by affirmations. I tried affirmations out of curiosity and because it was free. I didn't need a better reason.

Now you know what I know.

CHAPTER 37

Summary

I covered a lot of topics in this book, so I thought it would be helpful to provide a summary to wrap it all up. Keep in mind that if you skipped to the end of the book to read this section, it will seem extraordinarily unpersuasive out of context.

The model for success I described herein looks roughly like this: Focus on your diet first and get that right so you have enough energy to *want* to exercise. Exercise will further improve your energy, and that in turn will make you more productive, more creative, more positive, more socially desirable, and more able to handle life's little bumps.

Once you optimize your personal energy, all you need for success is luck. You can't directly control luck, but you can move from strategies with bad odds to strategies with good odds. For example, learning multiple skills—talent-stacking—raises your odds of success dramatically compared to learning just one or two skills. If you learn to control your ego, you can pick strategies that scare off the people who fear embarrassment, thus competing against a smaller field. And if you stay in the game long enough, luck has a better chance of finding you. Avoid career traps such as pursuing jobs that require you to sell your limited supply of time while preparing you for nothing better.

Happiness is the only useful goal in life. Unless you are a sociopath, your own happiness will depend on being good to others. And happiness tends to happen naturally whenever you have good health, resources, and a flexible schedule. Get your health right first, acquire resources and new skills through hard work, and look for opportunities that will give you a flexible schedule.

Some skills are more important than others, and you should acquire as many of those key skills as possible, including public speaking, business writing, a working understanding of the psychology of persuasion, basic technology concepts, social skills, proper voice technique, good grammar, and the fundamentals of accounting. Develop a habit of simplifying. Learn how to make small talk with strangers and avoid being an asshole. If you get that stuff right—and almost anyone can—you will be hard to stop.

It might help you to think of yourself as a moist robot, not a skin-bag full of magic and mystery. If you control the inputs, you can determine the outcomes, give or take some luck. Eat right, exercise, think positively, learn as much as possible, stay out of jail, and good things can happen.

Look for patterns in every part of life, from diet to exercise. Try to find scientific backing for your observed patterns and use yourself as a laboratory to see if the patterns hold for you.

Most important, understand that goals are for losers and systems are for winners. People who seem to have good luck are often the people who have a system that allows luck to find them. I've laid out some systems in this book that seem to work for me. Your experience will differ, but it always helps to be thinking in terms of systems and not goals.

And always remember that failure is your friend. It's the raw material of success. Invite it in. Learn from it. And don't let it leave until you pick its pocket. That's a system.

The End

Acknowledgments

I'd like to thank my science and medical researcher, Zora DeGrandpre, for keeping me within shouting distance of rational thought.

A big thank you to Adrian Zackheim for somehow knowing I had this book in me before I did. Someday you have to explain to me how you do that.

Thank you to my brother, Dave, who I use as my writing muse. When I'm trying to find the perfect way to word a funny thought, I just imagine how I would say it to my brother. When editors say my writing is "voicey," that's why.

Thank you to Maria Gagliano for your masterful edits to the first version of this book.

Thank you to Emily Libresco, my Princeton-bound writing assistant who did a terrific job critiquing the first draft. If any of you are worried about the next generation, don't be. They make us look like chimps.

And thank you to Joshua Lisec for the *Second Edition* edit and revamp of this book as well as for the independent publishing assist.

Notes

Chapter 1
The Time I was Crazy

1. Cyranowski JM, Zill N, Bode R, et al. Assessing social support, companionship, and distress: National Institute of Health (NIH) Toolbox Adult Social Relationship Scales. Health Psychology 2013;32:293-301.
2. Shiovitz-Ezra S, Leitsch SA. The role of social relationships in predicting loneliness: the National Social Life, Health, and Aging Project. Social Work Research 2010;34:157-67.

Chapter 11
The Energy Metric

1. Wierzbicki MRD. Journal of General Psychology 1978;99:25.
2. Khoury RM. Social Behavior & Personality: An International Journal 1977;5:377.
3. Greengross G, Martin RA, Miller G. Personality traits, intelligence, humor styles, and humor production ability of professional stand-up comedians compared to college students. Psychology of Aesthetics, Creativity, and the Arts 2012;6:74-82.
4. Weisfeld G, Nowak N, Lucas T, et al. Do women seek humorousness in men because it signals intelligence? A cross-cultural test. Humor: International Journal of Humor Research 2011;24:435-62.

5. Hauck W, Thomas J. The relationship of humor to intelligence, creativity, and intentional and incidental learning. J Experimental Education 1972;40.
6. Avner Z. Facilitating Effects of Humor on Creativity. Journal of Educational Psychology 1976;68:318-22.
7. Paavonen EJ, Pennonen M, Roine M, Valkonen S, Lahikainen AR. TV exposure associated with sleep disturbances in 5- to 6-year-old children. Journal Of Sleep Research 2006;15:154-61.
8. Brunborg GS, Mentzoni RA, Molde H, et al. The relationship between media use in the bedroom, sleep habits and symptoms of insomnia. Journal Of Sleep Research 2011;20:569-75.

Chapter 12
Managing Your Attitude

1. Iwase M, Ouchi Y, Okada H, Yokoyama C. Neural substrates of human facial expression of pleasant emotion induced by comic films: a PET Study. Neuroimage 2002;17:758-68.
2. Addicted to Smiling. Can the simple act of smiling bring pleasure? . 2011. (Accessed 4/16, 2013, at http://www.psychologytoday.com/ blog/your-brain-food/201112/addicted-smiling.)
3. Wood RI, Stanton SJ. Testosterone and sport: Current perspectives. Hormones And Behavior 2012;61:147-55.
4. Jarrett C. Faster, higher, stronger! Psychologist 2012;25:504-7.
5. Edwards DA, Kurlander LS. Women's intercollegiate volleyball and tennis: Effects of warm-up, competition, and practice on saliva levels of cortisol and testosterone. Hormones And Behavior 2010;58:606-13.
6. Carré JM, Putnam SK. Watching a previous victory produces an increase in testosterone among elite hockey players. Psychoneuroendocrinology 2010;35:475-9.
7. Suay F, Salvador A, González-Bono E, et al. Effects of competition and its outcome on serum testosterone, cortisol and prolactin. Psychoneuroendocrinology 1999;24:551–66.

8. Schabel BJ, Franchi L, Baccetti T, McNamara JA, Jr. Subjective vs objective evaluations of smile esthetics. American Journal Of Orthodontics And Dentofacial Orthopedics: Official Publication Of The American Association Of Orthodontists, Its Constituent Societies, And The American Board Of Orthodontics 2009;135:S72-S9.
9. Rodrigues CdDT, Magnani R, Machado MSC, Oliveira OB. The perception of smile attractiveness. The Angle Orthodontist 2009;79:634-9.
10. Bohrn I, Carbon C-C, Hutzler F. Mona Lisa's smile—Perception or deception? Psychological Science 2010;21:378-80.

Chapter 13
Its Already Working

1. George JM. Personality, affect, and behavior in groups. Journal of Applied Psychology 1990;75:107-16.
2. Masini BE. Socialization and selection processes of adolescent peer groups. US: ProQuest Information & Learning; 1998.

Chapter 18
Recognizing Your Talents and Knowing When to Quit

1. Ericsson KA, Charness N. Expert performance: Its structure and acquisition. In: Ceci SJ, Williams WM, eds. The nature—nurture debate: The essential readings. Malden: Blackwell Publishing; 1999:199-255.
2. Manes S, Andrews P. Gates: How Microsoft's Mogul Reinvented an Industry and Made Himself The Richest Man in America: Touchstone, Simon and Schuster; 1994.

Chapter 21
The Math of Success

1. Wikipedia. (Accessed 4/16/2013, at http://en.wikipedia.org/wiki/List_of_cognitive_biases.)
2. The Hidden Traps in Decision Making. 2006. (Accessed 4/20, 2013, at http://graduateinstitute.ch/webdav/site/mia/users/Rachelle_Cloutier/public/Hashemi%20Decision%20Making%20and%20Leadership%20in%20Crisis%20Situations/Hammond%20Hidden%20Traps%20in%20Decision%20Making.pdf.)
3. Cialdini R. Influence: The Psychology of Persuasion (Collins Business Essentials) pg.13-14, NY, NY: HarperBusiness; 2006.
4. De Sciolo, P.,Kurzban, R., The Alliance Hypothesis for Human Friendship, PLoS One, http://www.plosone.org/article/info%3Adoi%2F10.1371%2Fjournal.pone.0005802 (Accessed 4/24/2013)
5. Vukovic J, Feinberg DR, DeBruine L, Smith FG, Jones BC. Women's voice pitch is negatively correlated with health risk factors. Journal of Evolutionary Psychology 2010;8:217-25.
6. Kleemola L, Helminen M, Rorarius E, Isotalo E, Sihvo M. Voice Activity and Participation Profile in assessing the effects of voice disorders on quality of life: Estimation of the validity, reliability and responsiveness of the Finnish version. Folia Phoniatrica et Logopaedica 2011;63:113-21.
7. Gallup GG, Jr., Frederick DA. The science of sex appeal: An evolutionary perspective. Review of General Psychology 2010;14:240-50.
8. Meulenbroek LFP, de Jong FICRS. Voice quality in relation to voice complaints and vocal fold condition during the screening of female student teachers. Journal of Voice 2011;25:462-6.
9. Golub J, Chen P, Otto K, Hapner E, Johns M. Prevalence of Perceived Dysphonia in a Geriatric Population. Journal of the American Geriatrics Society 2006;54:1736-9.

10. Farrand PF. Generic health-related quality of life amongst patients employing different voice restoration methods following total laryngectomy. Psychology, Health & Medicine 2007;12:255-65.

11. Wong CA, Laschinger HKS, Cummings GG. Authentic leadership and nurses' voice behaviour and perceptions of care quality. Journal of Nursing Management 2010;18:889-900.

12. Zope SA, Zope RA. Sudarshan kriya yoga: Breathing for health. International Journal Of Yoga 2013;6:4-10.

13. Liu X, Miller YD, Burton NW, Brown WJ. A preliminary study of the effects of Tai Chi and Qigong medical exercise on indicators of metabolic syndrome, glycaemic control, health-related quality of life, and psychological health in adults with elevated blood glucose. British Journal Of Sports Medicine 2010;44:704-9.

14. Kuan S-C, Chen K-M, Wang C. Effectiveness of Qigong in promoting the health of wheelchair-bound older adults in long-term care facilities. Biological Research For Nursing 2012;14:139-46.

15. Jefferson Y. Mouth breathing: adverse effects on facial growth, health, academics, and behavior. General Dentistry 2010;58:18.

16. Breathe away stress in 8 steps. Try this simple technique to enjoy a variety of health benefits. Harvard Men's Health Watch 2012;17:5.

Chapter 22
Pattern Recognition

1. Foust J. Wave Rider. Yoga Journal 2005:69-70.

2. 20 Habits of Successful People. 2013. (Accessed 4/21, 2013, at http://www.guruhabits.com/successful-people/.)

3. Goldsby MG, Kuratko DF, Bishop JW. Entrepreneurship and Fitness: An Examination of Rigorous Exercise and Goal Attainment among Small Business Owners. Journal of Small Business Management 2005;43:78-92.

4. McDowell-Larsen S, Kearney L, Campbell D. Fitness and leadership: is there a relationship?: Regular exercise correlates with higher

leadership ratings in senior-level executives. Journal of Managerial Psychology 2002;17:316 - 24.

Chapter 23
Humor

1. Wierzbicki MRD. Journal of General Psychology 1978;99:25.
2. Khoury RM. Social Behavior & Personality: An International Journal 1977;5:377.
3. Greengross G, Martin RA, Miller G. Personality traits, intelligence, humor styles, and humor production ability of professional stand-up comedians compared to college students. Psychology of Aesthetics, Creativity, and the Arts 2012;6:74-82.
4. Weisfeld, G.,Nowak, NT.,Lucas, T.,Weisfeld, CC.,Imamoğlu, E.,Olcay,M.,Shen, J.Parkhill, MR.. Do women seek humorousness in men because it signals intelligence? A cross-cultural test. Humor: International Journal of Humor Research 2011;24:435-62.
5. Hauck W, Thomas J. The relationship of humor to intelligence, creativity, and intentional and incidental learning. J Experimental Education 1972;40.
6. Avner Z. Facilitating Effects of Humor on Creativity. Journal of Educational Psychology 1976;68:318-22.
7. Paavonen EJ, Pennonen M, Roine M, Valkonen S, Lahikainen AR. TV exposure associated with sleep disturbances in 5- to 6-year-old children. Journal Of Sleep Research 2006;15:154-61.
8. Brunborg GS, Mentzoni RA, Molde H, et al. The relationship between media use in the bedroom, sleep habits and symptoms of insomnia. Journal Of Sleep Research 2011;20:569-75.

Chapter 29
Association Programming

1. Trice H, Roman P. Sociopsychological Predictors of Affiliation with Alcoholics Anonymous. A Longitudinal Study of Treatment Success. Social Psychiatry 1970;5:51-2.
2. Arkowitz H, Lilienfeld S. Does Alcoholics Anonymous Work? Scientific American 2011.
3. Tamburlini G, Cattaneo A, Knecht S, et al. The spread of obesity in a social network... Christakis NA, Fowler JH. The spread of obesity in a large social network over 32 years. N Engl J Med 2007;357:370-9. New England Journal of Medicine 2007;357:1866-8.
4. Christakis NA, Fowler JH. The spread of obesity in a large social network over 32 years. New England Journal of Medicine 2007;357:370-9.
5. Boothe A, Brouwer R. Unmet Social Support for Healthy Behaviors Among Overweight and Obese Postpartum Women: Results from the Active Mothers Postpartum Study. Journal of Women's Health (15409996) 2011;20:1677-85.
6. Sallis JF, Grossman RM, Pinski RB, et al. Environmental Support For Eating And Exercise Change Scales. Ten-year outcomes of behavioral family-based treatment for childhood obesity 1994;13:373-83.
7. Kulik N. Social support and weight loss among adolescent females. US: ProQuest Information & Learning; 2012.
8. Jelalian E, Sato A, Hart C. The Effect of Group-Based Weight-Control Intervention on Adolescent Psychosocial Outcomes: Perceived Peer Rejection, Social Anxiety, and Self-Concept. Children's Health Care 2011;40:197-211.
9. Chan NK-C, Gillick AC. Fatness as a disability: Questions of personal and group identity. Disability & Society 2009;24:231-43.

Chapter 30
Happiness

1. Wright R. Dancing to evolution's tune. The good news: we're born for fun. The bad news: it's not built to last. Time 2005;165:A11-A.
2. Pert C. Molecules & Choice. Shift: At the Frontiers of Consciousness 2004:20-4.
3. Pelletier M, Bouthillier A, Lévesque J, et al. Separate neural circuits for primary emotions? Brain activity during self-induced sadness and happiness in professional actors. NeuroReport: For Rapid Communication of Neuroscience Research 2003;14:1111-6.
4. Park A. Molecules of emotion: why you feel the way you feel. Visions: The Journal of Rogerian Nursing Science 2008;15:56-7.
5. Foss L. The necessary subjectivity of bodymind medicine: Candace Pert's Molecules of Emotions. Advances in Mind-Body Medicine 1999;15:122-34.
6. Conboy L, Bisaz R, Markram K, Sandi C. Role of NCAM in emotion and learning. Advances In Experimental Medicine And Biology 2010;663:271-96.
7. Price EM, Fisher K. Additional Studies of the Emotional Needs of Amputees. Journal of Prosthetics and Orthotics, 2005;17:52.
8. Giummarra MJ, Georgiou-Karistianis N, Nicholls MER, Gibson SJ, Chou M, Bradshaw JL. The menacing phantom: What pulls the trigger? European Journal of Pain 2011;15:e1-e8.
9. Akarsu S, Tekin L, Safaz I, Göktepe AS, Yazicioğlu K. Quality of life and functionality after lower limb amputations: comparison between uni- vs. bilateral amputee patients. Prosthetics And Orthotics International 2013;37:9-13.
10. Steinberg H, Sykes EA. Introduction to symposium on endorphins and behavioural processes: Review of literature on endorphins and exercise. Pharmacology, Biochemistry and Behavior 1985;23:857-62.
11. Sokumbi O, Moore A, Watt P. Plasma levels of beta-endorphin and serotonin in response to specific spinal based exercises. South African Journal of Physiotherapy, 2008;64:31.

12. Harbach H, Hell K, Gramsch C, Katz N, Hempelmann G, Teschemacher H. β-Endorphin (1-31) in the plasma of male volunteers undergoing physical exercise. Psychoneuroendocrinology 2000;25:551-62.
13. Francis KT. The role of endorphins in exercise: a review of current knowledge. Journal of Orthopaedic & Sports Physical Therapy 1983;4:169-73.
14. Dishman RK, O'Connor PJ. Lessons in exercise neurobiology: The case of endorphins. Mental Health and Physical Activity 2009;2:4-9.
15. aan het Rot M, Collins KA, Fitterling HL. Physical exercise and depression. The Mount Sinai Journal Of Medicine, New York 2009;76:204-14.
16. Flausino, N.H.,Da Silva,P., Martuscelli,J.,Queiroz, S.,Souza,T.,Mello,S. Túlio, M. Physical exercise performed before bedtime improves the sleep pattern of healthy young good sleepers. Psychophysiology 2012;49:186-92.

Chapter 31
Health

1. Jacka FN, Kremer PJ, Leslie ER, et al. Associations between diet quality and depressed mood in adolescents: results from the Australian Healthy Neighbourhoods Study. Australian & New Zealand Journal of Psychiatry 2010;44:435-42.
2. Dunne A. Food and mood: evidence for diet-related changes in mental health. British Journal of Community Nursing 2012:S20-4.
3. Davison KM, Kaplan BJ. Vitamin and mineral intakes in adults with mood disorders: comparisons to nutrition standards and associations with sociodemographic and clinical variables. Journal of the American College of Nutrition 2011;30:547-58.
4. Annesi JJ. Predictors of exercise-induced mood change during a 6-month exercise and nutrition education program with obese women. Perceptual & Motor Skills 2009;109:931-40.

5. Centre for R, Dissemination. Scientific evidence of interventions using the Mediterranean diet: a systematic review (Structured abstract). In: Serra-Majem L, Roman B, Estruch R, eds.; 2006:S27-S47.

6. Soh NL, Walter G, Baur L, Collins C. Nutrition, mood and behaviour: A review. Acta Neuropsychiatrica 2009;21:214-27.

7. Parker G, Gibson NA, Brotchie H, Heruc G, Rees AM, Hadzi-Pavlovic D. Omega-3 fatty acids and mood disorders. American Journal of Psychiatry 2006;163:969-78.

8. Crisp AH. Sleep, activity, nutrition and mood. The British Journal of Psychiatry 1980;137:1-7.

9. Bhat RS. You are what you eat: Of fish, fat and folate in late-life psychiatric disorders. Current Opinion in Psychiatry 2009;22:541-5.

10. Appleton KM, Rogers PJ, Ness AR. Updated systematic review and meta-analysis of the effects of n-3 long-chain polyunsaturated fatty acids on depressed mood. American Journal of Clinical Nutrition 2010;91:757-70.

11. Appleton KM, Hayward RC, Gunnell D, et al. Effects of n-3 long-chain polyunsaturated fatty acids on depressed mood: systematic review of published trials. American Journal of Clinical Nutrition 2006;84:1308-16.

12. Traoret CJ, Lokko P, Cruz ACRF, et al. Peanut digestion and energy balance. International Journal Of Obesity (2005) 2008;32:322-8.

13. Reis CEG, Bordalo LA, Rocha ALC, et al. Ground roasted peanuts leads to a lower post-prandial glycemic response than raw peanuts. Nutrición Hospitalaria: Organo Oficial De La Sociedad Española De Nutrición Parenteral Y Enteral 2011;26:745-51.

14. O'Byrne DJ, Knauft DA, Shireman RB. Low fat-monounsaturated rich diets containing high-oleic peanuts improve serum lipoprotein profiles. Lipids 1997;32:687-95.

15. Mattes RD, Kris-Etherton PM, Foster GD. Impact of peanuts and tree nuts on body weight and healthy weight loss in adults. The Journal of nutrition 2008;138:1741S-5S.

16. Devitt AA, Kuevi A, Coelho SB, et al. Appetitive and Dietary Effects of Consuming an Energy-Dense Food (Peanuts) with or between

Meals by Snackers and Nonsnackers. Journal Of Nutrition And Metabolism 2011;2011:928352-.

17. Claesson AL, Holm G, Ernersson A, Lindström T, Nystrom FH. Two weeks of overfeeding with candy, but not peanuts, increases insulin levels and body weight. Scandinavian journal of clinical and laboratory investigation 2009;69:598-605.

18. Nuts for You. Tufts University Health & Nutrition Letter 2012;30:1-4.

19. Kohlstadt I. More than willpower: Curbing food cravings during weight reduction. Townsend Letter 2009:50.

20. Jeffery RW, Wing RR, Mayer RR, Jeffery RW, Wing RR, Mayer RR. Perceived Barriers to Adherence. Are smaller weight losses or more achievable weight loss goals better in the long term for obese patients? 1998;66:641-5.

21. Dulloo AG. Explaining the failures of obesity therapy: willpower attenuation, target miscalculation or metabolic compensation? International Journal of Obesity 2012;36:1418-20.

22. Spiegel K, Tasali E, Penev P, Van Cauter E. Brief communication: Sleep curtailment in healthy young men is associated with decreased leptin levels, elevated ghrelin levels, and increased hunger and appetite. Annals Of Internal Medicine 2004;141:846-50.

23. Schmid SM, Hallschmid M, Jauch-Chara K, Born J, Schultes B. A single night of sleep deprivation increases ghrelin levels and feelings of hunger in normal-weight healthy men. Journal Of Sleep Research 2008;17:331-4.

24. Pejovic S, Vgontzas AN, Basta M, et al. Leptin and hunger levels in young healthy adults after one night of sleep loss. Journal Of Sleep Research 2010;19:552-8.

25. Landis AM, Parker KP, Dunbar SB. Sleep, hunger, satiety, food cravings, and caloric intake in adolescents. Journal of Nursing Scholarship 2009;41:115-23.

26. Brondel L, Romer MA, Nougues PM, Touyarou P, Davenne D. Acute partial sleep deprivation increases food intake in healthy men. The American Journal Of Clinical Nutrition 2010;91:1550-9.

27. Lopez-Garcia E, Rodriguez-Artalejo F, Rexrode KM, Logroscino G, Hu FB, van Dam RM. Coffee consumption and risk of stroke in women. Circulation 2009;119:1116-23.

28. Freedman ND, Park Y, Abnet CC, Hollenbeck AR, Sinha R. Association of coffee drinking with total and cause-specific mortality. The New England journal of medicine 2012;366:1891-904.

29. Arab L, Biggs ML, O'Meara ES, Longstreth WT, Crane PK, Fitzpatrick AL. Gender differences in tea, coffee, and cognitive decline in the elderly: the cardiovascular health study. Journal of Alzheimer's Disease 2011;27:553-66.

30. Coffee drinking lowers mortality risk in women. Harvard Women's Health Watch 2008;16:6-7.

31. Coffee does not increase risk of developing CAD. Journal of Family Practice 2006;55:757-8.

32. Campos HA. Coffee Consumption and Risk of Type 2 Diabetes and Heart Disease. Nutrition Reviews 2007;65:173-9.

33. Yantis MA, Hunter K. Is diet soda a healthy choice? Nursing 2010;40:67-.

34. Nettleton JA, Lutsey PL, Wang Y, Lima JA, Michos ED, Jacobs DR, Jr. Diet soda intake and risk of incident metabolic syndrome and type 2 diabetes in the Multi-Ethnic Study of Atherosclerosis (MESA). Diabetes Care 2009;32:688-94.

35. Do you really need that diet soda? Research connects the drinks to higher heart risks. Harvard Health Letter / From Harvard Medical School 2012;37:4-.

36. Tamburlini G, Cattaneo A, Knecht S, et al. The spread of obesity in a social network... Christakis NA, Fowler JH. The spread of obesity in a large social network over 32 years. N Engl J Med 2007;357:370-9. New England Journal of Medicine 2007;357:1866-8.

37. Christakis NA, Fowler JH. The spread of obesity in a large social network over 32 years. New England Journal of Medicine 2007;357:370-9.

38. Boothe A, Brouwer R. Unmet Social Support for Healthy Behaviors Among Overweight and Obese Postpartum Women: Results from

the Active Mothers Postpartum Study. Journal of Women's Health (15409996) 2011;20:1677-85.

39. Sallis JF, Grossman RM, Pinski RB, et al. Environmental Support For Eating And Exercise Change Scales. Ten-year outcomes of behavioral family-based treatment for childhood obesity 1994;13:373-83.

40. Rajaram S, Sabaté J. Health benefits of a vegetarian diet. Nutrition (Burbank, Los Angeles County, Calif) 2000;16:531-3.

41. Liu RH. Health benefits of fruit and vegetables are from additive and synergistic combinations of phytochemicals... Fourth International Congress on Vegetarian Nutrition: proceedings of a symposium held in Loma Linda, CA, April 8-11, 2002. American Journal of Clinical Nutrition 2003;78:517S-20.

42. Key TJ, Davey GK, Appleby PN. Health benefits of a vegetarian diet. The Proceedings Of The Nutrition Society 1999;58:271-5.

43. Benzie IFF, Wachtel-Galor S. Vegetarian diets and public health: biomarker and redox connections. Antioxidants & Redox Signaling 2010;13:1575-91.

44. Vegetarianism: addition by subtraction. An increasing number of studies are finding health benefits from a low- or no-meat diet. Harvard Health Letter / From Harvard Medical School 2004;29:6-.

45. McEvoy CT, Temple N, Woodside JV. Vegetarian diets, low-meat diets and health: a review. Public Health Nutrition 2012;15:2287-94.

46. Hart J. The health benefits of a vegetarian diet. Alternative Complementary Ther. 2009;15:64.

47. Deriemaeker P, Aerenhouts D, De Ridder D, Hebbelinck M, Clarys P. Health aspects, nutrition and physical characteristics in matched samples of institutionalized vegetarian and non-vegetarian elderly (> 65yrs). Nutrition & Metabolism 2011;8:37-.

48. Wright J, Wang C-Y. Trends in Intake of Energy and Macronutrients in Adults From 1999–2000 Through 2007–2008. NCHS Data Brief 2010;49.

49. Layman D. Dietary Guidelines should reflect new understandings about adult protein needs. Nutrition & Metabolism 2009;6.

50. WHO., FAO., UNU. Protein and amino acid requirements in human nutrition: Report of a joint FAO/WHO/UNU expert consultation WHO Technical Report 2007;Series 935.

51. Woolf PJ, Fu LL, Basu A. vProtein: identifying optimal amino acid complements from plant-based foods. Plos One 2011;6:e18836-e.

52. Willcox DC, Willcox BJ, Todoriki H, Suzuki M. The Okinawan diet: health implications of a low-calorie, nutrient-dense, antioxidant-rich dietary pattern low in glycemic load. Journal of the American College of Nutrition 2009;28:500S-16s.

53. Schechter S. Nutrients-dense green foods: Mining the motherlode. Better Nutrition 1998;60:16.

54. Phillips F. Vegetarian nutrition. Nutrition Bulletin 2005;30:132-67.

55. Beyond Brown Rice: 10 Whole Grains to Discover for Your Diet. Tufts University Health & Nutrition Letter 2006;24:4-5.

56. Practice points: translating research into practice. Protein sources in a healthful vegetarian diet. Journal of the American Dietetic Association.,1999;99:820-.

57. Mangels R. SCIENTIFIC UPDATE. Vegetarian Journal 2011;30:26-7.

58. Majchrzak D, Singer I, Männer M, et al. B-vitamin status and concentrations of homocysteine in Austrian omnivores, vegetarians and vegans. Annals Of Nutrition & Metabolism 2006;50:485-91.

59. Lightowler HJ, Davies GJ. Micronutrient intakes in a group of UK vegans and the contribution of self-selected dietary supplements. The Journal Of The Royal Society For The Promotion Of Health 2000;120:117-24.

60. Haddad EH. Meeting the RDAs with a vegetarian diet. Topics in Clinical Nutrition 1995;10:7-16.

61. Some vegans may need food supplements. Better Nutrition for Today's Living 1993;55:18.

62. George SE, Ramalakshmi K, Mohan Rao LJ. A perception on health benefits of coffee. Critical Reviews In Food Science And Nutrition 2008;48:464-86.

63. Butt MS, Sultan MT. Coffee and its consumption: benefits and risks. Critical Reviews in Food Science & Nutrition 2011;51:363-73.

64. Arendash GW, Cao C. Caffeine and coffee as therapeutics against Alzheimer's disease. Journal Of Alzheimer's Disease: JAD 2010;20 Suppl 1:S117-S26.

65. Acreman S. The benefits and drawbacks of drinking coffee. Cancer Nursing Practice 2009;8:8.

66. What is it about coffee? Research is showing benefits for everything from depression to liver disease. Is it just the caffeine? Harvard Health Letter / From Harvard Medical School 2012;37:4-5.

67. Brewing up health benefits for coffee. Tufts University Health & Nutrition Letter 2008;25:4-5.

68. Wiles JD, Bird SR, Hopkins J, Riley M. Effect of caffeinated coffee on running speed, respiratory factors, blood lactate and perceived exertion during 1500-m treadmill running. British Journal Of Sports Medicine 1992;26:116-20.

69. Graham TE. Caffeine and exercise: metabolism, endurance and performance. Sports Medicine 2001;31:785-807.

70. Astorino TA, Roberson DW. Efficacy of acute caffeine ingestion for short-term high-intensity exercise performance: a systematic review. Journal Of Strength And Conditioning Research / National Strength & Conditioning Association 2010;24:257-65.(Accessed at http://well.blogs.nytimes.com/2012/06/06/moderation-as-the-sweet-spot-for-exercise/.)

71. Rollins G. Moderate exercise reduces the risk of heart disease and death in men with type 2 diabetes. Report On Medical Guidelines & Outcomes Research 2003;14:10.

72. Gleeson M, Walsh NP. The BASES Expert Statement on Exercise, Immunity, and Infection. Journal of Sports Sciences 2012;30:321-4.

73. Moderate exercise: no pain, big gains. Harvard Men's Health Watch 2007;11:1-5.

74. No sweat: new guidelines for moderate exercise. Harvard Men's Health Watch 2001;6:1-4.

75. O'Connor, A. Surgeon General Sees Hair Care as Exercise Barrier for Women, http://query.nytimes.com/gst/fullpage.html?res=980D-E7DF1E38F935A1575BC0A9679D8B63&ref=reginambenjamin (Accessed 5/29/2013).

Chapter 36
A Final Note About Affirmations

1. Wiseman R. The Luck Factor. Skeptical Inquirer, 2003;27.Tempt Luck Your Way. 2009. (Accessed 4/22, 2013, at http://www.psychologytoday.com/blog/creativityrulz/200912/tempt-luck-your-way.)
2. Smith MD, Wiseman R, Harris P, Joiner R. On being lucky: The psychology and parapsychology of luck. European Journal of Parapsychology 1996;12:35-43.Smith MD, Wiseman R, Harris P. The relationship between 'luck' and psi. Journal of the American Society for Psychical Research 2000;94:25-36.

23296931R00171